Royal Economics Society Prize Monograph

Libertarian conflicts in social choice

To Rose and Mark

Libertarian conflicts in social choice

JOHN L. WRIGLESWORTH
Queen Mary College, London

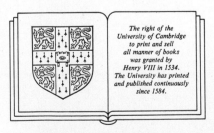

The right of the
University of Cambridge
to print and sell
all manner of books
was granted by
Henry VIII in 1534.
The University has printed
and published continuously
since 1584.

CAMBRIDGE UNIVERSITY PRESS

Cambridge
London   New York   New Rochelle
Melbourne   Sydney

Published by the Press Syndicate of the University of Cambridge
The Pitt Building, Trumpington Street, Cambridge CB2 1RP
32 East 57th Street, New York, NY 10022, USA
10 Stamford Road, Oakleigh, Melbourne 3166, Australia

First published 1985

Printed in Great Britain at the University Press, Cambridge

Library of Congress catalogue card number: 84–28587

British Library cataloguing in publication data

Wriglesworth, John
Libertarian conflicts in social choice. –
(Royal Economic Society prize monograph)
1. Social choice
I. Title II. Series
302.1'3   HB846.8

ISBN 0 521 30503 9

AN

Contents

Preface

The field of social choice has enlarged enormously since its formal beginning in 1950 when Kenneth Arrow first published his celebrated general impossibility theorem. There now exists a multitude of social choice theorems all illustrating the difficulties of formulating a desirable choice procedure based on individual values. One such notable theorem is Amartya Sen's 'The Impossibility of a Paretian Liberal'. This shows that the Pareto principle (asserting the priority of unanimous preference rankings) can conflict with a mild requirement of individual liberty (in the form of a person being 'decisive' over certain personal matters). First published in 1970, this result has itself been instrumental in starting a line of inquiry that has led to a rather voluminous amount of comment and extension. This book is an attempt systematically to evaluate, criticise and extend the most important parts of this very varied literature.

It begins, in Chapter 1, by defending the presence of libertarian requirements in social choice. It has been argued that individual rights should be considered outside the realm of the subject: rights should be exercised *prior* to, and *independently* of, the social choice process. Several arguments are put forward to justify why consideration of individual liberty (along with other social criteria) must be explicitly incorporated into social choice analysis. Chapter 2 then formally establishes a framework for incorporating individual rights into social choice. It is immediately seen that a natural assignment of rights can lead to social conflict in that, for certain sets of individual preferences, not all individuals can have their rights respected if choice is to be made. The Chapter then proceeds to formulate libertarian conditions which can be satisfied for all conceivable sets of individual preferences. In Chapter 3 it is shown how such libertarian conditions can conflict with other well-known social conditions in social choice. The most apparently disturbing such conflict is that with the Pareto principle. The nature of this conflict is examined in some depth and it is shown how it relates to a broader class of Arrovian type impossibility theorems. The next two chapters evaluate two broad classes of resolution approaches to this conflict. Chapter 4 considers resolutions which are achieved through modifying (weakening) the libertarian requirement such that the implementation of rights will always be consistent with the Pareto principle. In contrast, Chapter 5 considers resolutions which are achieved by modifying the Pareto principle in order that it may be made consistent with rights implementation. In the light of the preceding analysis, Chapter 6 considers the properties that a resolution procedure should satisfy. It is argued that neither of the approaches of the two previous chapters can be deemed appropriate for all types of Pareto–libertarian conflict. A more pragmatic approach is called for based on more information regarding the environment from which choice is to be made. Chapter 7 extends the analysis to permit groups, rather than only individuals, to have rights. Attention is focused on types of group structure which are both necessary and sufficient to assure that group rights (as determined by some specific types of group voting rules) and the Pareto principle will be consistent with each other in social choice. Finally, Chapter 8 summarises the main results and conclusions of the previous chapters and consolidates the author's view of the present state of research, as presented and developed in this book.

An unfortunate (though necessary) drawback to much of the social choice literature is that the formal logical analysis employed can be very difficult to follow for the uninitiated; much may seem to be written in an esoteric language all of its own. I am afraid the present book, in parts, is no exception. The reader who is not acquainted with the mathematical logic used is urged to read very carefully both parts of the first chapter of Amartya Sen's *Collective Choice and Social Welfare*. This presents very clearly the basic principles of logic, set theory and binary relations which are extensively used in much of the analysis of the following chapters.

I must now express my indebtedness to those who have helped me in the preparation of this book. Most prominent among these is Amartya Sen. My interest in the subject began when I attended his brilliant series of social choice lectures given at the University of Oxford for the M. Phil. degree. Later, as supervisor for my doctorate (on which this book is based) he was a continued source of inspiration and encouragement. Thanks are also due to Wulf Gaertner and Batra Pattanaik who, as my examiners, made many useful comments on various aspects of the work. Also, I would like to thank the Royal Economic Society for the honour of being awarded their first monograph prize for this work. For financial support I am grateful to the Economic and Social Research Council, Lincoln College (Oxford) and to Queen Mary College (London). Finally, I would like to thank Francis Brooke of the Cambridge University Press who has been extremely helpful in the last stages of preparing the typescript.

4th August 1984   JOHN L. WRIGLESWORTH

Notation and abbreviations commonly used

Symbolic logic

∃	the existential quantifier (there exists)
∀	the universal quantifier (for all)
→	implication (if . . . , then . . .)
↔	equivalence (if and only if)
=	identity (the same as)
∈	element of (belongs to)
∉	is not an element of (does not belong to)
⊆	subset of (is contained in)
⊄	not a subset of (is not contained in)
∩	intersection of (elements belonging to both sets)
∪	union of (elements belonging to either set)

Other symbols and abbreviations

$. . . x, y, z, w, . . .$	social states of the world
x_i (or x_j)	a feature alternative for issue i (or j) within a social state
X	the set of all technologically conceivable states of the world
S	a subset of X, often the 'available' set of social states
M_i (or M_j)	a set of feature alternatives for issue i (or j)
n	the number of issues in a social state
$. . . a, b, c, d, . . .$	individuals
m	the number of individuals
R_b	the preference ordering of individual b over the set of social states (reflexive, complete and transitive)
$xR_b y$	interpreted as: individual b finds x at least as good as y
P_b	the asymmetric factor of R_b ('is better than')
I_b	the symmetric factor of R_b ('is indifferent to')
$\{R_b\}$	a preference profile for the set of individuals, one preference ordering for each individual in the given society
$C(S, \{R_b\})$	social choice function

$\mathscr{R}$	rights system
SRS	standard rights system
SRI	standard rights implementation rule
T	group structure
$\{\emptyset\}$	empty set (the set of no elements)
$N(G)$	number of elements in set G

Conditions variously imposed on the choice function

CHAPTER 1

Introduction

1.1   The role of rights in social choice

This book is concerned with the direct implications of incorporating a *mild* libertarian requirement on social choice. The general problem of social choice can be viewed as how society can best choose amongst a set of alternative social states and it is the strong belief that libertarian rights should be properly incorporated into the social choice framework that has motivated the research undertaken for this book. In this context a basic and a weak libertarian premise is that if two states of the world, x and y, differ only with respect to a person b's business alone, then if person b prefers x to y, y should not be chosen if x is available.

Before formally incorporating rights into a framework of social choice (which will be dealt with in Chapter 2) I wish to consider a major objection to the above libertarian premise. Briefly it is that rights should be treated as some 'control' an individual has over certain states of affairs and such alternatives as he dismisses by this personal control should not be considered as available options in social choice. Rights exercising determines the set of options open for social choice. One of the leading proponents of this view is Nozick (1974):

The exercise of these rights fixes some features of the world. Within the constraints of these fixed features, a choice can be made by a social choice mechanism based upon a social ordering, if there are any choices left to make! (p. 166)

Given that an individual has a right to a choice over a pair of alternatives, what is socially important, it is argued, is that the choice is *his*. The outcome of his choice may well be socially undesirable but this is irrelevant, the value in society of individual rights comes from the allowed *freedom* to choose. Social choice must therefore be constrained by the personal exercising (through personal control) of rights rather than having rights explicitly incorporated into the social choice procedure itself.

I wish to separate two aspects of this argument for independent criticism (though the two aspects are *not* independent from each other).

(1) Social choice should not concern itself with alternatives which are dismissed by rights exercising (through direct control of an individual or by some procedure implementing the right in accordance with the

1

individual's desires). Given that x and y differ only with respect to a person b's business alone and person b prefers x to y, y should never be considered in any social choice problem from an available set of options.

(2) Social choice should not implement a right by a procedure based on the individual's desires but allow that individual to implement his right through his own personal control over that decision. Given that x and y differ only with respect to a person b's business alone then person b must be allowed full control, through his own personal action, to dismiss one of these alternatives from the choice set.

The main difference between these aspects may be made clearer by noting that in (1) the implementation of a right may not be directly controlled by the individual himself though this implementation will be carried out independently of a social evaluation of the alternatives; and in (2), the alternative which is dismissed through the personal control of the individual can still be in the initial set of options evaluated by the social choice procedure. This allows a social judgement of the form: it is better that x is chosen over y when this is the result of person b's personal control over alternatives which differ solely with respect to his own business.

Let us consider (1) first.

Nozick, illustrating the point, has provided the following example:

If I have a right to choose to live in New York or Massachusetts, and I choose Massachusetts, then alternatives involving my living in New York are not appropriate objects to be entered in a social ordering. (Nozick, 1973, p. 62).

Sen has argued against this illustration of the argument in (1):

If I believe that it is a better society which – given other things – lets Nozick decide where he wishes to live, then I must *assert* that it is socially *better* that Nozick should be permitted to live in Massachusetts as desired by him. If Nozick is forced out of Massachusetts, then one would wish to say not only that Nozick's rights have been violated, but that society is worse off – given other things – by stopping Nozick from living where he wishes. (Sen, 1976, p. 230)

It is important that by saying society is better off one does not mean that the alternative dismissed by the implementation of a right is, in itself, socially undesirable. Society is better off because this alternative is dismissed as a result of the *implementation of an individual's right*. The existence of this right is of social value in itself, independent of the nature of the outcome of the implementation of this right. It is better for Nozick to live in Massachusetts precisely because *he* desires this. Such a social comparison between Nozick living in Massachusetts or in New York cannot be made if Nozick living in New York is not admitted into the set of alternatives available for such social comparison.

Rights are hardly ever 'absolute' in the sense that one can never universally say that under all logically possible circumstances a right must be implemented (either through direct control of the individual himself, or otherwise), for example the right to free expression through peaceful marches in public streets. In most circumstances this right should be implemented. However, if it is the British fascist organisation 'the National Front' planning such a march this right may well be justifiably withheld, since the consequential social disruption in terms of physical violence and disorder is so costly that it outweighs the social value of free expression. If all states which involve the National Front not marching are excluded from the set of states available for social comparison then any possibility of a social judgement that the march should be banned becomes impossible — under *any* circumstances.

An island which has a population of 1800 people has enjoyed self-determination for 150 years. They should have a right to continue to self-determine their lives. However, if the cost of defending this 'self-determination' involves over three million lives being lost, then there is a strong case for violating their rights. This is not to say that the islanders' self-determination is not of value and not worth some cost to secure it. My only point is that there exist circumstances (albeit extreme in this example) where the value of the right is outweighed by other *social* considerations. If all states of the world where the islanders do not have self-determination were excluded from the set of social options available for choice, then choice must involve only states which give the islanders the right to self-determination and this should be sought at all costs.

Now let us consider the argument presented in (2) above. Should rights be specified as some personal control over certain states of affairs? Consider the following example taken from Sen (1983a, Section VII).

There is a person, Ed, who is unconscious after a car accident. His companion who is unhurt knows about Ed's moral beliefs and strengths of conviction. The doctors tells the companion that she can treat Ed in one of two ways, A and B, and while she is certain that both would be effective, she is also certain that A would be very much better for Ed in terms of side-effects. However, Ed's companion knows that though Ed would agree that treatment A is better for his health, he would have very strong objections to it since its development involved cruelty to animals. Thus Ed's companion knows, without doubt, that Ed would prefer treatment B. It seems reasonable to argue that Ed's liberty would be served better if the doctor gave treatment B even though Ed himself is not exercising any direct control over the particular choice. Sen states that this choice would better serve Ed's 'indirect liberty'. Examples of 'indirect liberty' are not uncommon to find, and to not characterise liberty as taking account of this would yield a very limited notion of liberty indeed.

The social choice characterisation of liberty compares what emerges with what a person *would have chosen*, whether or not he actually does the choosing. (Sen, 1983*a*, Section VII)

Thus the social choice framework permits analysis of indirect liberty while the interpretation of rights as 'control' of an individual over his personal affairs does not.

1.2   Some clarifying matters

Before embarking on the more formal analysis of rights in social choice, it is necessary to make clear some assumptions which will be kept, without question, throughout the book.

Firstly, individuals' preferences will be assumed to be honest reflections of their respective 'desires'. The problem of extracting such honest preferences will not be discussed. Thus individuals trying to manipulate social choice by deliberate misspecification of their preferences will never arise. This problem, though important, could not possibly be dealt with in an adequate way without taking up a disproportionate amount of space within the present book, the object of which is to examine the implications of rights *given* the honest preferences in social choice.

Secondly, none of the libertarian conditions presented here are intended to summarise, in totality, the concept of liberty in society. The argument in Section 1.1 is that the libertarian premise reflects an aspect of liberty which should be accepted by all libertarians, and indeed some non-libertarians as well.

Finally, the assignment of rights in this monograph, in terms of allocating each individual's pairs of alternatives which differ with respect to each individual's business alone, is assumed to be decided on the basis of non-utility information, in particular the nature of the alternatives concerned. It is not assumed that the rights assignments are determined according to the nature of individual preferences.

CHAPTER 2

The Gibbard paradox

2.1   Introduction

This chapter formalises a framework for rights in social choice. It is seen that under some circumstances rights of individuals can conflict with each other in the sense that whatever is chosen from a set of alternatives, somebody's rights will be seen to be violated. The chapter proceeds to analyse different ways of resolving this problem.

2.2.   A framework for rights in social choice

If two states of the world x and y differ only with respect to a person b's business alone, then, if person b prefers x to y, y should not be chosen if x is available. This, as has been argued in Chapter 1, constitutes an acceptance of a mild form of personal liberty in social choice. How can this best be formalised into a framework of social choice?

Gibbard (1974) formalised rights in terms of *issues*. He argued that since a person b is granted rights over a pair of social alternatives because they differ with respect to his business alone, we can thus isolate, and explicitly define, this personal issue (and other peoples' personal issues) by defining a social alternative in terms of component 'feature alternatives', one for each issue in the state of the world. Following Gibbard, a formal framework for analysis will now be stated.

Social alternatives   Each alternative will be represented by a number of distinct features. Assuming there are n of them we can represent a typical alternative as $x = (x_1, x_2, \ldots, x_n)$. For each issue $i = 1, 2, \ldots, n$ let there be a finite set M_i of feature alternatives for issue i, each with at least two elements. Assuming the features are technologically separable from each other, the set X of *all technologically possible* alternatives is the cartesian product $M_1 \times M_2 \times \ldots \times M_n$; it consists of every n-tuple $(x_1, x_2, \ldots x_n)$, with $x_1 \in M_1, x_2 \in M_2, \ldots, x_n \in M_n$. The issues may be 'personal' to some individual, e.g. a person's wall colour, or may be 'public' like the issue of nuclear disarmament. Within this issue framework it is assumed that the number of issues exceeds the number of individuals.

Individual preferences Assume there are $m \geqslant 2$ individuals b, each having a preference ordering R_b (reflexive, complete and transitive) over X. Let P_b and I_b be the asymmetric and symmetric factors of R_b respectively. Let $\{R_b\}$ represent a profile for society, one ordering R_b for each individual b.

The social choice function Assume there exists a choice function $C(S, \{R_b\})$ defined over X which is a functional relation such that the choice set C is non-empty for *every* non-empty subset S of X, and for *every* logically possible set of preference profiles $\{R_b\}$. A condition of 'unrestricted domain' is incorporated into the definition of $C(S, \{R_b\})$. This does not mean that choice need be based on preferences of individuals.

We must now incorporate rights into this framework by formalising a libertarian condition. This can be done in two steps. The first is to define a rights assignment or 'rights system'. The second is to define a 'rights implementation rule'. Consider, first, two general definitions.[1]

Rights system A rights system $\mathscr{R}$ is an assignment of ordered pairs of alternatives to individuals. A rights system will be a set of ordered triples of the form $\langle x, y;b \rangle$; if $\langle x, y;b \rangle \in \mathscr{R}$ it will be said that $\mathscr{R}$ assigns $\{x, y\}$ to b.

Rights implementation format A right to x over y for $\langle x, y; b \rangle \in \mathscr{R}$ is implemented if $y \notin C(S:x \in S, \{R_b\})$ whenever some condition, to be defined, relating b, x and y is fulfilled.

We now choose a specific rights system and specific rights implementation rule, and define a libertarian condition as the combination of the two. The following two definitions collectively define Gibbard's libertarian condition L, the one he postulates 'most naturally' follows from the issue framework developed.

Standard rights system (SRS) For every individual b there is at least one private issue j such that, for every pair of alternatives x and y,

$$\text{if } \forall i \, (i \neq j): x_i = y_i, \text{ then } \langle x, y;b \rangle \in \mathscr{R}$$

Pairs of alternatives $\{x, y\}$ such that $\forall i(i \neq j): x_i = y_i$, will be termed '$j$-variants'. Note that we have assumed the number of issues exceeds the number of individuals.

Standard rights implementation rule (SRI) If $\langle x, y;b \rangle \in \mathscr{R}$ and xP_by then $y \notin C(S:x \in S, \{R_b\})$.

---

[1] This distinction is similar to, but not the same as, the distinction Gibbard (1974) makes between the assignment of rights and the exercising of rights.

Condition L (Gibbard's 'inconsistent' libertarian, Gibbard (1974), p. 291). SRS and SRI respectively exist and operate in society.

Note that, given this condition, choice must now take account of certain preferences of individuals.

This condition is *not* meant to summarise all that a libertarian thinks should hold in society, but only one aspect of what he believes should hold. Indeed, many non-libertarians might agree on such a condition.

Let us consider an example that will clarify the above definitions and that will illustrate the apparent attractiveness of this formulation of rights. Let there be a two person society. Let person 1 be called Wales and person 2 be called Scotland. Let there be four alternatives, each with two feature alternatives.

D_1D_2 (Wales devolved from the United Kingdom, Scotland devolved from the United Kingdom)

D_1N_2 (Wales devolved from the United Kingdom, Scotland not devolved from the United Kingdom)

N_1N_2 (Wales not devolved from the United Kingdom, Scotland not devolved from the United Kingdom)

N_1D_2 (Wales not devolved from the United Kingdom, Scotland devolved from the United Kingdom)

This example fits well into the issue framework. Wales is assigned the issue of Welsh devolution (issue 1) and Scotland is assigned the issue of Scottish devolution (issue 2). For each issue, $j = 1, 2$, there are two feature alternatives, devolution and staying in the United Kingdom. Rights are assigned according to SRS on the basis that if two alternatives differ only with respect to one party's issue j, then that party should be assigned this pair (i.e. over j-variants). Thus the rights system is:

$\langle D_1D_2, N_1D_2 ; \text{Wales} \rangle$ $\quad$ $\langle D_1D_2, D_1N_2 ; \text{Scotland} \rangle$

$\langle N_1D_2, D_1D_2 ; \text{Wales} \rangle$ $\quad$ $\langle D_1N_2, D_1D_2 ; \text{Scotland} \rangle$

$\langle D_1N_2, N_1N_2 ; \text{Wales} \rangle$ $\quad$ $\langle N_1D_2, N_1N_2 ; \text{Scotland} \rangle$

$\langle N_1N_2, D_1N_2 ; \text{Wales} \rangle$ $\quad$ $\langle N_1N_2, N_1D_2 ; \text{Scotland} \rangle$

The standard rights implementation rule implies that if Wales prefers x to y, where x is a 1-variant of y then y should not be chosen when x is available. Similarly, if Scotland prefers x to y where x is a 2-variant of y, then y should not be chosen when x is available.

However, Gibbard has shown that this apparently appealing rights system and the 'natural' rights implementation rule results in an empty choice set for some logically possible preferences of society.

Theorem 2.2.1 (see Gibbard (1974), Theorem 1) *No choice function* $C(S, \{R_b\})$, *satisfies condition L.*

The proof may be illustrated with reference to the above example. Let the preferences of the two parties (Wales and Scotland) be:

Wales	Scotland	
N_1D_2	D_1D_2	
D_1N_2	D_1N_2	descending order of strict preference
N_1N_2	N_1N_2	
D_1D_2	N_1D_2	

According to SRS and SRI, and thus condition L:
(1) Wales should dictate that N_1N_2 and D_1D_2 should not be chosen.
(2) Scotland should dictate that D_1N_2 and N_1D_2 should not be chosen.
Thus no alternative in the set $\{N_1N_2, N_1D_2, D_1D_2, D_1N_2\}$ should be chosen.
   This impossibility result is often called the 'Gibbard paradox' after Farrell (1976).

2.3   Respecting rights consistently

Condition L is the combination of SRS and SRI. These two aspects of condition L help us to classify two broad approaches to solving the Gibbard paradox. The first, which will be classified under the heading 'rights system modification', solves the paradox by weakening the specification of SRS. The second, classified under the heading 'rights implementation modification', solves the paradox by weakening the specification of SRI.

2.3.1   *Rights system modification*

The standard rights system, which Gibbard uses, is very strong. Consider the following three aspects:
(1) Rights are assigned with respect to issues.
(2) All individuals are allocated at least one personal issue.
(3) Each individual, given an issue j, is assigned *all* pairs that differ with respect to their jth feature, i.e. an individual b allocated an issue j is assigned *all* j-variants.
   The paradox is robust to a significant weakening of aspects (2) and (3). It may be the case that in some specific examples not *all* individuals should be allocated an issue. However, there need be only two individuals that are allocated issues for the impossibility result to go through, as should be clear from

the preceding section. It may also be the case that an individual, given an issue j, should not have rights over all j-variants. For example, a person b's issue j may be 'volume of his record player' and $M_j = \{$very noisy, noisy, quiet, very quiet$\}$. Though, everything else equal, the choice between 'quiet' and 'very quiet' should be up to the individual, there might be some concern (e.g. from a next-door neighbour) if he is given rights to choose, everything else equal, between 'very noisy' and 'noisy'. However, two individuals who are allocated rights with respect to just two feature alternatives in their respective M_j is sufficient for the impossibility result to go through – as should again be clear from the preceding section. Further weakening of aspects (2) and (3) would simply weaken condition L into being an uninteresting condition in social choice.

But what about aspect (1)? In the devolution example cited earlier the issue framework does seem the appropriate way to formulate a rights assignment. Are all case examples so well suited to an issue framework? Consider the following example taken from Barnes (1980).

There are two individuals, Mr Box and Mr Cox, who are the sole members of the 'Tolpuddle Philanthropical Association'. Mr Cox, who is steward of the wine cellar, is decisive when it comes to choosing wines; and Mr Box, being secretary for local charities, is decisive in matters of making donations to worthy Tolpuddle causes. At the annual general meeting the association must decide how to allocate its few remaining funds. Four proposals are listed on the agenda:

A   That monies be donated to the Tolpuddle Martyrs memorial fund.
B   That monies be donated to the Tolpuddle Arts Council.
C   That a good bottle of malmsey be bought and drunk.
D   That a good bottle of Quninto du Noval be bought and drunk.

'Natural' considerations of rights would construct the following rights system for this committee:

$\langle A, B; \text{Mr Box} \rangle$ $\langle D, C; \text{Mr Cox} \rangle$

$\langle B, A. \text{Mr Box} \rangle$ $\langle C, D; \text{Mr Cox} \rangle$

It should be clear that in this case, and conceivably many others, the natural assignment of rights and the definition of alternatives do *not* fit well into the issue framework as formalised by Gibbard. There is no possibility of forming the notion of j-variants in this case. Note also that in the above case the rights system, together with SRI, will not lead to an empty choice set for any logically possible set of preferences of the two individuals.

Thus in some cases at least, a solution to the Gibbard paradox can be well constructed by not defining a rights system with respect to issues but over the social alternatives themselves. This is the approach that Sen (1970a, b) uses in constructing his libertarian condition. Consider the rights system that Sen adopts.[1]

Sen's rights system (SENRS) For each person b there is at least one pair of social alternatives x and y such that $\langle x, y; b \rangle$ and $\langle y, x; b \rangle$ are in $\mathscr{R}$.

SENRS together with SRI becomes Sen's 'liberalism' condition:

Condition L^S (Sen's liberalism condition, Sen (1970a, b)). SENRS and SRI respectively exist and operate in society.

By assigning rights directly over pairs of social alternatives, rather than indirectly via issues, a greater degree of freedom is gained in the specification of the rights system. With the definition of SENRS no stipulation is made over the relationship between the alternatives people are decisive over. Thus we can assume, to take an unnecessarily restrictive example, that no alternative in a pair over which a person b is decisive is in a pair of alternatives over which another person c is decisive. It follows that condition L^S, with any configuration of preferences, cannot dismiss all the alternatives from the choice set.

In fact, there are many types of rights assignments, consistent with SENRS, that will guarantee possibility. All we need to be careful about is that they are 'coherent'.

Coherent rights assignment (Suzumura (1978), p. 331, and Sen (1976), p. 243) Each person b is assigned pairs of alternatives $\{x, y\}$ such that no matter how they order them there is a full ordering R of X of which each b's preference over each respective $\{x, y\}$ is a subrelation.

Suzumura (1978) proves that coherent rights assignments are necessary and sufficient for the resolution of the Gibbard paradox, given SRI.[1] The

---

[1] Sen does not construct his libertarian condition specifically to avoid the Gibbard paradox, but to illustrate the paradox of the 'Paretian–Liberal'. What is important here is that his rights system can be seen explicitly to avoid the Gibbard paradox. Sen's result can thus be seen as a conflict between a consistent formulation of rights and the Pareto principle. Note also that it is not necessary to use *either* the SRS *or* SENRS but we can construct a rights system which is a mixture of the two, e.g. one person's rights may be allocated to be consistent with SENRS only, and another allocated rights also consistent with SRS. Possibility *may* still be assured so long as only one person is allocated rights that are also consistent with SRS.

trouble with Gibbard's SRS is that rights are assigned incoherently by stipulation. Given that at least two people have two features each in their respective M_j there will *always* exist a configuration of preferences (like in the devolution example) such that there will *not* exist an ordering R of X of which every person b's preferences over respective assignment pairs is a sub-relation.[2]

We have found that by moving away from the issue framework, and defining rights over pairs of social alternatives there is a possible way out of the Gibbard paradox. For some cases, e.g. Barnes' Tolpuddle example, this does seem an appropriate solution. However, we are left with the cases of which there must be a multitude, that do conform to Gibbard's issue framework. In these cases SRS is the most natural way to assign rights. For these cases relaxing SRS might not be so appropriate. One thus turns to look at the other aspects of Condition L, i.e. SRI.

2.3.2 *Rights implementation modification*

Let us accept SRS and consider possible modifications of SRI that will resolve the Gibbard paradox. Discussion of the motivation underlying these approaches and detailed comparison under different criteria will be left until Section 2.4.

2.3.2.1 Gibbard's solution procedure seeks a solution by examining, for each individual, his preferences as a whole. SRS assigns rights with respect to issues, i.e. assigns each person pairs of j-variants. Consider a pair of j-variants, $\{x, y\}$ assigned to b. If xP_by then 'apparently' person b is revealing a preference for feature x_j over y_j, i.e. since x and y only differ with respect to their

---

[1] See Suzumura (1978), Lemma 1, pp. 331–341. This is based on a result given by Farrell (1976).

[2] It should be noted that an available set of alternatives can be constructed such that each person b has an issue j and such that each person b has rights over their respective j-variants and obtain possibility:

$(w_1 w_2) =$ (person 1 wears white, person 2 wears white)

$(r_1 w_2) =$ (person 1 wears red, person 2 wears white)

$(y_1 w_2) =$ (person 1 wears yellow, person 2 wears white)

Each person has an issue, the colour of his own clothes, but, with this available set, person 2 has no j-variants over which he can be decisive according to SRI. Gibbard (and I have assumed this also) insists that in the set X of all alternatives ('available and unavailable') $M_j \geqslant 2$, $\forall j$. He does not stipulate that $M_j \geqslant 2$ for each available set. Thus conceivably we can construct an available set as above, apply SRS and SRI and be assured of possibility given any configuration of preferences. However, our choice function is defined over all possible subsets of X, and we require that the choice be non-empty for every subset S of X. Thus it must be non-empty (for all possible preference profiles) for subsets where there exists two people, each with two feature alternatives in their respective values of M_j – this is not possible by Gibbard (1974), Theorem 1.

jth feature then surely such a strict preference for x over y implies, indirectly, a strict preference for x_j over y_j? However, consider a person b ordering over the following four alternatives:

$$(x_1, x_2, z) \, P_b \, (y_1, x_2, z) P_b \, (y_1, y_2, z) P_b \, (x_1, y_2, z)$$

where $z = x_3, \ldots, x_n$, the same for all four alternatives. Assume person b is assigned issue 1. Since $(x_1, x_2, z) \, P_b \, (y_1, x_2, z)$ then it seems he prefers x_1 to y_1. However, since $(y_1, y_2, z) \, P_b \, (x_1, y_2, z)$ it seems he prefers y_1 to x_1.

Given an ordering over the social alternatives by person b above, we find no straightforward way of deducing an order over his feature alternatives Such a 'private' ordering is masked by a conditional preference over his feature alternatives in his ordering of social alternatives. It is precisely these types of preference that Scotland and Wales exhibit in the example used to illustrate the Gibbard paradox.

Gibbard (1974) suggested that a person's right to choose a feature alternative x_j over another y_j should only be respected (implemented) if and only if he orders x_j over y_j for *all j-variants x and y*, which include x_j and y_j respectively. He formulates this idea via his definition of 'unconditional preferences'.

Unconditional preferences A person b prefers x_j to y_j *unconditionally* if and only if for every pair of j-variants x and y, which include x_j and y_j respectively, xP_by.

The strict unconditional preference of person b over feature alternatives will be represented by the relation P_b^u. Thus if $x_j P_b^u y_j$, then person b reveals a strict unconditional preference for x_j over y_j.

Gibbard's 'self-consistent' rights implementation rule (GRI) If for any two features $x_j, y_j \in M_j$, $x_j P_b^u y_j$, then for all alternatives y that include y_j as their jth feature, and that are j-variants of an x which includes x_j as its jth feature, then $y \notin C(S : x \in S, \{R_b\})$.

Condition L^G (Gibbard's 'self-consistent' libertarian condition, Gibbard (1974), p. 393). SRS and GRI respectively exist and operate in society.

In the light of the above discussion it should not be too surprising to find the following result holds.

Theorem 2.3.1 *There exists a choice function $C(S, \{R_b\})$ which satisfies condition L^G.*

Proof: See Gibbard (1974), Theorem 3, p. 395.

2.3.2.2 A solution procedure based on the use of 'non-preference' information
(Wriglesworth (1985)) In Gibbard's resolution scheme a 'private' ordering
P_b^u is deduced for each individual over feature alternatives. However, when an
individual b does not display unconditional preferences in his ordering over
social alternatives, the private ordering P_b^u becomes void, and *no* rights will be
implemented for person b. This secures possibility but at the expense of
restricting the implementation of rights to quite a large extent. For example,
in the devolution case presented in Section 2.2, P_b^u is void for both parties, and
each will forfeit *all* their rights. Maybe this restriction of SRI is too strong.

I wish now to formulate a new approach. This shares with Gibbard a desire
to formulate a transitive 'private' ordering over feature alternatives, but differs with respect to the formulation of this private ordering. The method I
wish to construct seeks to formalise a relation over feature alternatives which
may still hold when individuals do not display unconditional preferences;
thus in essence we may be able to deduce a more complete private ordering
over features for each person b, with the possibility of allowing more rights
to be implemented.

The method relies on allowing each individual b, if he so wishes, to state
a subrelation R_b^* of his own original ordering R_b, which will be used instead
of R_b in deducing his private ordering over feature alternatives. Let us consider the method more formally.

Let R_b^* be a subrelation of R_b representing a preference ordering (very
likely a partial ordering) over alternatives that individual b wishes to have
respected in the procedure to decide on rights implementation. Let P_b^* and
I_b^* be the asymmetric and symmetric factors of R_b^* respectively.

Private preferences A person b *privately* prefers x_j to y_j where $x_j, y_j \in M_j$ if
and only if:
(1) For some available j-variants and x and y, which include x_j and y_j res-
    pectively, xP_b^*y
and
(2) For all available j-variants x and y, which include x_j and y_j respectively,
    (not yP_b^*x)
Let the relation P_b^p represent person b's 'private' preference over his feature
alternatives.

The 'private preference' rights implementation rule (PRI) If for any two features $x_j, y_j \in M_j, x_jP_b^p y_j$, then for all alternatives y that include y_j as their jth
feature, and that are j-variants of an x which includes x_j as its jth feature, if
xP_b^*y, then $y \notin C(S:x \in S, \{R_b\})$.

Condition L^P ('Private preference' libertarian condition, Wriglesworth (1985),
p. 107) SRS and PRI respectively exist and operate in society.

Theorem 2.3.2 *There exists a choice function $C(S, \{R_b\})$ which satisfies condition L^P.*

Proof: (This proof will use Theorem 2.3.1.) For *any* two features x_j and y_j assigned to individual b, let $x_j P_b^p y_j$ without loss of generality. If this was not the case for any two features in any assigned issue set M_j, then b would have no rights implemented by PRI and hence could be safely discounted from the analysis. (The preferences of b would not be able to contribute towards dismissing any alternatives from any choice set via condition L^P.)

Given $x_j P_b^p y_j$ then if $x P_b^* y$, where x and y are any pair of j-variants including x_j and y_j respectively, we have by condition L^P, for $x \in S, y \notin C(S, \{R_b\})$. By the definition of private preferences it can *not* be the case that for any such j-variants x and y that we can also have $y P_b^* x$ or $y_j P_b^p x_j$.

Consider now all such pairs of j-variants x and y strictly ordered by R_b^*. We can view P_b^* over these pairs as a strict partial ordering of the alternatives in these pairs. Because we can only have $x P_b^* y$, and *not* $y P_b^* x$, for any such j-variants, there must exist a *complete order extension* of this partial ordering (over all social alternatives), call it R_b^E, such that according to this ordering $x_j P_b^u y_j$, i.e. such that x_j is unconditionally preferred to y_j in the Gibbardian sense.

Given this R_b^E, Gibbard's rights implementation rule GRI will implement all those rights for such j-variants which PRI would, given R_b^* (and possibly more).

The argument extends straightforwardly given that individual b has more than two features in his issue set, or given that b has more than one assigned issue: for any revealed preferences R_b and subrelation R_b^* we can, for any set of alternatives S, replace them with another complete ordering R_b^E, such that all those alternatives dismissed by L^P given R_b^* will also be dismissed by Gibbard's condition L^G, given R_b^E. This occurs because R_b^E is constructed such that features are ordered unconditionally, and such that individual b's strict partial ordering P_b^*, over assigned pairs for which PRI implements rights, is a subrelation.

What is true for individual b is also true for any other individual. Generally, then, any set of alternatives dismissed by condition L^P, given any profile $\{R_b^*\}$, can also be dismissed by Gibbard's condition L^G given suitable choice of $\{R_b^E\}$. Given that there exists a choice function satisfying condition L^G by Theorem 2.3.1, there must exist a choice function satisfying condition L^P.

Consider an example which will help to clarify the above proof. Consider the following preference ordering over six alternatives and assume b is assigned issue j:

$$(x_j, z) P_b (y_j, z) P_b (y_j, z') P_b (x_j, z') P_b (x_j, z'') P_b (y_j, z'').$$

Assume $x_j P_b^P y_j$, with $(x_j, z) P_b^* (y_j, z)$ and $(x_j, z'') P_b^* (y_j, z'')$. In this case we can view P_b^* as strictly partially ordering these four alternatives. Now there must exist a complete order extension R_b^E such that $x_j P_b^u y_j$, for example the following strict ordering:

$$(x_j, z) P_b^E (y_j, z) P_b^E (x_j, z') P_b^E (y_j, z') P_b^E (x_j, z'') P_b^E (y_i, z'')$$

Given this ordering, Gibbard's GRI will implement all those rights which PRI would, given R_b^*, and more.

If all members of society display unconditional preferences with respect to their features and if $R_b^* = R_b$, then condition L^P becomes equivalent to Gibbard's condition L^G. Note that in this case, if $R_b^* \neq R_b$ some rights may not be implemented by L^P that would be implemented by L^G; but this would be a result of an individual deliberately and voluntarily withholding his rights. Cases where this might occur are difficult to think of but most will agree that an individual should not be forced to have his rights implemented if he does not wish them to be.

It is important to realise that even if $R_b^* = R_b$, and a person does not display unconditional preferences, L^P may still implement rights. For example, consider the following preferences for person b over four alternatives and assume $R_b^* = R_b$:

$$(x_1, z) P_b (y_1, z) I_b (y_1, z') I_b (x_1, z')$$

Individual b, who is assigned 1, does not exhibit unconditional preferences with respect to x_1 and y_1. Thus P_b^u is void. However, $x_1 P_b^P y_1$, and with L^P, rights over $\langle(x_1, z), (y_1, z); b\rangle \in \mathscr{R}$ will be implemented.

Consider now the following preferences for individual b:

$$(x_1, z) P_b (y_1, z) P_b (y_1, z') P_b (x_1, z')$$

In this case, if $R_b^* = R_b$ then P_b^P would be void. However, an individual could still secure some rights by an alternative choice of R_b^*. He could state $(x_1, z) P_b^* (y_1, z)$. In this case his rights over $\langle(x_1, z), (y_1, z); b\rangle \in \mathscr{R}$ would be implemented by L^P. Instead, individual b could state $(y_1, z') P_b^* (x_1, z')$. In this case rights over $\langle(y_1, z'), (x_1, z'); b\rangle \in \mathscr{R}$ would be implemented by L^P.

This solution method uses non-preference information to enable us to formulate an alternative 'private' ordering over feature alternatives. What is the non-preference information we are using? Basically, it is R_b^*; R_b^* is not the preferences of the individual but a specific subset of his preferences that he has decided he wants to count in rights implementation. Given $\langle x, y; b\rangle \in \mathscr{R}$, then $x P_b^* y$ means that person b prefers x to y (preference information) *and* he wants his right to be implemented in social choice (non-preference information).

2.3.2.3 Resolution procedures based on additional utility information Let us extend the framework in order to allow more individual utility information. The idea here is to use the extra information available to restrict SRI in a 'fair' or 'just' way so as to secure possibility. Kelly (1976a) and Suzumura (1978) have used such an approach in the context of the Sen paradox (Sen (1970a, b). However, neither author uses the extended information framework to tackle the Gibbard paradox. We will see here (and in the later chapters dealing with the Sen paradox) that both Kelly and Suzumura do not make full use of the extra information available in this framework. Let us now formalise our extended framework.

Let (x, b) stand for being in the position of individual b in state x. Let $\tilde{R}_b$ be the ordering of individual b defined over the cartesian product $X \times H$, where X is the set of social states and H the set of individuals $b = 1, 2, \ldots, m$.

In the discussion so far, we have used R_b over such alternatives as (x, b), (y, b), (z, b) etc. $\tilde{R}_b$ is an 'extended ordering' in that we can now have (x, b) $\tilde{R}_b$ (y, a), which can be interpreted as: individual b finds it at least as good to be himself in state x than to be individual a in state y.

Let $C^*(S, \{\tilde{R}_b\})$ be a generalised choice function that specifies a non-empty choice set $C^* \subseteq S$ for every non-empty subset $S \subseteq X$ and for every logically possible set of individual extended orderings $\{\tilde{R}_b\}$.

In this framework we can redefine SRI.

Standard rights implementation rule in extended framework (SRI*) If $\langle x, y; b \rangle \in \mathscr{R}$ and $(x, b) \tilde{P}_b (y, b)$ then $y \notin C^*(S: x \in S, \{\tilde{R}_b\})$

Condition L* (cf. condition L, p. 7) SRS and SRI* respectively exist and operate in society.

That condition L^* implies an incoherent rights system should be obvious, and the Gibbard paradox holds for L^* in an analogous way to that of L.

But now we want to make use of the extra utility information available in order to modify SRI*. Let us consider some well-known principles of justice and fairness.

Let us first consider the 'Suppes relation of justice'. It involves one-to-one correspondence between H and H, such that $k = \rho(b)$, where person b is mapped on to person k. Let the set of all such one-to-one correspondences be called λ. Let $xJ_b y$ be read as: x is more just than y, according to individual b, in the Suppes sense.

Suppes criteria for justice

$$\forall\, x, y \in X$$

$$xJ_b y \leftrightarrow \exists\, \rho \in \lambda:$$

$$[\{\forall a\colon (x, a)\,\tilde{R}_b\,(y, \rho(a))\} \text{ and } \{\exists a\colon (x, a)\,\tilde{P}_b\,(y, \rho(a))\}]$$

In words, according to person b, x is more just than y if there is a one-to-one correspondence from the set H of individuals to itself such that he/she would prefer to be in the position of someone in x rather than in the position of the corresponding person in y, and also would prefer, or be indifferent to, being in the position of each person in x than to be in the position of the corresponding person in y.

It is a well known property of J_b that it is transitive and asymmetric for every logically possible extended ordering $\tilde{R}_b$. For proof see Sen (1970a), Chapter 9*, Theorem 9*1.

Next we consider Rawls' 'maximin relation of justice'. Let $xM_b y$ be read as: x is at least as just as y, according to person b, in the Rawlsian maximin sense.

Rawls' maximin criteria for justice

$$\forall x, y \in X$$

$$xM_b y \leftrightarrow [\exists k\colon \{\forall a\colon (x, a)\,\tilde{R}_b\,(y, k)\}]$$

In words; according to person b, if it is no worse to be anyone in state x than to be individual k in state y, then x is at least as just as y.

It is a well-known property of M_b that it is reflexive, transitive, and complete for every logically possible extended ordering $\tilde{R}_b$. For proof see Sen (1970a), Chapter 9*, Theorem 9*4.

Finally we will consider a lexicographic version of the maximin criteria, 'leximin' for short. I will define strict ranking leximin. Let $xL_b^{ex}y$ be read as: x is more just than y, according to person b, in the leximin sense.

Leximin criteria for justice Define $r(x)$ as the rth worst off individual in state x, (in cases of ties, the tied persons may be ranked in any arbitrary strong order for doing the numbering $r(x)$).

$$\forall x, y \in X$$

$$xL_b^{ex}y \leftrightarrow [\exists k\colon \{1 \leqslant k \leqslant m\colon (x, k(x))\,\tilde{P}_b\,(y, k(y))\}$$

$$\text{and } \{\forall r < k\colon (x, r(x))\,\tilde{I}_b\,(y, r(y))\}]$$

It is a well-known property of L_b^{ex} that it is transitive and asymmetric for every logically possible individual extended ordering $\tilde{R}_b$. See Sen (1977) Section 4.

It is easily checked that, for any $x, y \in X$, and for any logically possible individual extended ordering $\tilde{R}_b$:

(1) $xJ_b y \rightarrow xL_b^{ex}y \rightarrow xM_b y$

(2) not $yM_b x \rightarrow$ not $yL_b^{ex}x \rightarrow$ not $yJ_b x$

(3) not $yM_b x \rightarrow xL_b^{ex}y \rightarrow$ not $yL_b^{ex}x$

The problem now is how best to incorporate the justice principles into the extended framework in order to seek a solution. Consider the following modifications to SRI*.

If $\langle x, y; b \rangle \in \mathscr{R}$, then if $(x, b) \tilde{P}_b (y, b)$ and:

(i) $\{\forall a : xJ_a y\}$ then $y \notin C^*(S : x \in S, \{\tilde{R}_b\})$. I will call this implementation rule SRI*(J).

(ii) $\{\forall a : \text{not } yJ_a x\}$ then $y \notin C^*(S : x \in S, \{\tilde{R}_b\})$. I will call this implementation rule SRI*(J^*).

(iii) $\{\forall a : xM_a y\}$ then $y \notin C^*(S : x \in S, \{\tilde{R}_b\})$. I will call this implementation rule SRI*(M).

(iv) $\{\forall a : \text{not } yM_a x\}$ then $y \notin C^*(S : x \in S, \{\tilde{R}_b\})$. I will call this implementation rule SRI*(M^*).

(v) $\{\forall a : xL_a^{ex}y\}$ then $y \notin C^*(S : x \in S, \{\tilde{R}_b\})$. I will call this implementation rule SRI*(L^{ex}).

(vi) $\{\forall a : \text{not } yL_a^{ex}x\}$ then $y \notin C^*(S : x \in S, \{\tilde{R}_b\})$. I will call this implementation rule SRI*(L^{ex*}).

Combining each of the above rights implementation rules with the standard rights system (SRS) we can respectively define:

(i) L^*J (ii) L^*J^* (iii) L^*M (iv) L^*M^* (v) L^*L^{ex} (vi) L^*L^{ex*}

as six possible libertarian conditions that we can use in social choice in this extended framework.[1]

Theorem 2.3.3 *There does not exist a choice function $C^*(S, \{\tilde{R}_b\})$ satisfying either L^*M, L^*J^*, or L^*L^{ex*}.*

Proof: Define four alternatives as

$$x = (x_1, x_2, z) \qquad\qquad y = (x_1, y_2, z)$$
$$w = (y_1, x_2, z) \qquad\qquad v = (y_1, y_2, z)$$

Let
$x_1, y_1 \in M_1$ and individual 1 is assigned issue 1.

$x_2, y_2 \in M_2$ and individual 2 is assigned issue 2

[1] These rights implementation rules and associated libertarian conditions will be referred to frequently in later chapters.

For all individuals b, let preferences be

$$(x, 1) \tilde{I}_b (v, 1) \tilde{I}_b (y, 2) \tilde{I}_b (w, 2) \tilde{P}_b (w, 1) \tilde{I}_b (y, 1) \tilde{I}_b (x, 2) \stackrel{\sim}{}$$
$$\tilde{I}_b (v, 2)$$

and for any other alternatives, e.g. (x, b), $b = 3, \ldots, m$, assume that every individual finds them indifferent to $(x, 1)$. It is easily checked that with $L*M$, $L*J*$ or $L*L^{ex}*$ individuals 1 and 2 will be allowed to implement all their rights and the choice set over the four alternatives will be empty.[1]

Theorem 2.3.4   *There exist choice functions $C*(S, \{\tilde{R}_b\})$ which can satisfy $L*M*, L*L^{ex}$, or $L*J$.*

Proof: Due to the completeness of the maximin relation M (not $xM_b y$) $\rightarrow$ $yM_b^A x$. where M_b^A is the asymmetric factor of M_b.

Given this and the properties of J_b and L_b^{ex} we know that J_b, L_b^{ex} and M_b^A are all transitive and asymmetric for any extended preference ordering $\tilde{R}_b$.

By the definition of $L*M*$ if all alternatives in a set $S = \{x^1, x^2, \ldots, x^h\}$ are to be dismissed from the choice set by the implementation of rights it must be the case that a cycle of the form $\forall a : x^1 M_a^A x^2 M_a^A x^3 \ldots x^h M_a^A x^1$, exists.

Analogously, if $L*L^{ex}$ and $L*J$ are to dismiss all the alternatives from the same set S then there must exist cycles of the form

$$\forall a : x^1 L_a^{ex} x^2 L_a^{ex} x^3 \ldots x^h L_a^{ex} x^1 \text{ and } \forall a : x^1 J_a x^2 J_a x^3 \ldots x^h J_a x^1$$

for $L*L^{ex}$ and $L*J$ respectively.

However, such cycles contradict the asymmetry and transitivity of these justice relations.

In general, if we formulate a 'justice' or 'fairness' or 'equity' relation, call it P_b^J which is transitive and asymmetric then we know that constraining SRI* such that if $\langle x, y : b \rangle \in \mathcal{R}$, we must have $(x, b) \tilde{P}_b (y, b)$ and $\{\forall a: xP_a^J y\}$ for $y \notin C*(S : x \in S, \{\tilde{R}_b\})$, then we know that the corresponding libertarian condition will not be vulnerable to the Gibbard paradox.

---

[1] Note that individuals' preferences in Theorem 2.3.3 satisfy the 'axiom of complete identity'. This axiom states that, $\forall a, b \in H: \tilde{R}_a = \tilde{R}_b$ (see Sen (1970a), p. 156). This impossibility result is thus robust to a very strong restriction on the extended orderings. This axiom will be introduced on p. 50.

2.4   Evaluation of rights implementation modification procedures

2.4.1   *Motivation*

2.4.1.1 Gibbard's 'consistent' rights implementation rule (GRI) (see p. 11) Gibbard (1974) appeals to an 'apparent truism': that rights should allow a person to choose the feature alternative in his set M_j, everything else equal. However, according to Gibbard, SRI grants something stronger in that it allows individuals the rights to choose a feature conditional on others' feature alternatives. He argues:

> The libertarian claim as given [SRS and SRI] lets this mere conditional preference govern: it says that if I want my walls to differ from Grundy's, then it is better to have my walls white and Grundy's yellow than to have both our walls yellow. In saying that, it may read too much into the truism it was supposed to formulate.

> Perhaps, then, a reasonable libertarian claim would disregard such conditional preferences. (Gibbard, 1974, p. 393).

Consider the following set of alternatives:

$$wy = (w_1, y_2, x_3, \ldots, x_n)$$

$$ww = (w_1, w_2, x_3, \ldots, x_n)$$

$$yy = (y_1, y_2, x_3, \ldots, x_n)$$

$$yw = (y_1, w_2, x_3, \ldots, x_n)$$

Let issue 1 be person 1's wall colour. Assume he has a choice between white (w_1) or yellow (y_1). Let issue 2 be person 2's wall colour and he also has a choice between white (w_2) and yellow (y_2), i.e. $w_1, y_1 \in M_1$ and w_2, $y_2 \in M_2$. Now, say person 1 who is assigned issue 1 prefers wy to yy. Given SRI, his rights over this pair will be implemented. However, Gibbard claims this should not necessarily occur. It depends on the motivation behind this preference. Does person 1 actually prefer white walls to yellow, or is it because he wants his walls to be different to person 2's? Gibbard claims that in this latter case it 'is not the same thing as an intrinsic preference for white walls' and, as such, rights should not be implemented. To infer such 'intrinsic' preference one must examine the individual's preference as a whole. According to Gibbard, if a person is seen to be displaying 'unconditional' preference for one feature over another, then and only then should his rights be respected.

Given this motivation it is clear that one *should* look at a person's preferences over all of X (the set of all technologically feasible alternatives, 'available and unavailable').[1] This is clear if we assume the set $\{wy, yy\}$ is the 'available' set. In this case if person 1 prefers wy to yy, then over this set he is exhibiting unconditional preferences. But Gibbard's motivation implies that one wants to inquire whether person 1 is preferring white walls because he 'intrinsically' likes white walls or because he wants different walls to person 2. To be consistent with Gibbard's motivation one must look at person 1's preferences over other alternatives. Gibbard does not make clear in his definition of unconditional preferences, which set of alternatives (the available set or the total set) such preferences should apply to. It does seem clear that to be consistent with his motivation one should look at preferences over the total set X.

Consider an alternative motivation. Some might argue that rights implementation should not be conditional on the reasons why a person prefers one alternative to another. If two alternatives differ solely with respect to a person's issue then he *should* have rights over this pair independently of why he actually prefers one to the other. Thus we can take the view that SRI should operate in society. So long as person 1 prefers wy to yy then rights should be implemented over this pair, independently of his motivation. However, SRI together with SRS can result in a conflict in that in some cases not all rights can be implemented. Given that some rights have to be axed to secure possibility GRI can be considered as one method which achieves this. Given this motivation then only the available set of alternatives should be viewed when deducing whether an individual displays conditional preferences with respect to features, for this would allow more rights to be implemented.

3.4.1.2 The 'private preference' rights implementation rule (PRI) (see p. 13)

Despite individuals displaying conditional preferences it is not the case that they can have no 'intrinsic' preference over features. I might prefer to have different colour walls to my neighbour yet still basically prefer the colour white to yellow. Given that one wishes to implement rights over pairs of j-variants, preferences over which reflect intrinsic preference, then axing all rights in the face of conditional preferences might be too extreme. Consider the following preferences:

$$ywP_1wwP_1wyP_1yy$$

where alternatives are the same as defined before. Individual 1 is displaying

---

[1] See Gibbard (1974), p. 390. Gibbard makes an explicit distinction between the set of all alternatives and the set of available alternatives over which choice is actually being made.

conditional preferences in that he wishes to have a different wall colour to his neigbour. However, consistent with the above preferences, person 1 might still intrinsically prefer white to yellow. If individual 1 is of the same moral suasion as Gibbard then he should think he is justified in having his right over the pair $\{wy, yy\}$ implemented (though he should have no rights over $\{yw, ww\}$). Gibbard's GRI will not allow him such rights. However, PRI can. The individual, by revealing wyP_1^*yy as the only preference that he wants to count in rights implementation, will have his rights over this pair implemented by PRI. If individuals do have an 'intrinsic' preference over features then this can be better inferred from P^P, rather than Gibbard's P^u, given that individuals choose their R_b^* consistent with such intrinsic preferences.

However, it might *not* be the case that individuals *will* choose to reveal an R_b^* that is consistent with such intrinsic preference over features, even if they are able to intrinsically order their features. In this case, and given that society still wants to deduce a person's intrinsic preference (society approves of Gibbard's motivation) then it must somehow persuade individuals to reveal their R_b^* such that this can be ascertained.

I do not wish to motivate the procedure, embodied in PRI, in this way. Given SRS is an acceptable assignment of rights, then I think SRI is the natural rights implementation rule to use. If two alternatives differ solely with respect to a person's issue then he should have rights over this pair independently of why he prefers one to another. Given this, there are only two possible reasons to amend SRI:

(1) To avoid the Gibbard paradox.
(2) The rights implemented by SRI, though desirable, conflict with some
     other more desirable criteria in social choice (e.g. Pareto or justice).
For the moment I will ignore the second reason, but I will discuss it later. For now, assume that rights outrank other social criteria in social choice.

Thus we wish to amend SRI so as to avoid the Gibbard paradox. PRI can be seen under this interpretation as a constraint which individuals must consider when assessing what R_b^* to reveal. If an individual b exhibits conditional preferences and reveals $R_b^* = R_b$, he might find all his rights will be axed under PRI. In this situation an individual might find it in his best interest to restrict R_b^* so as at least to guarantee himself some rights. In this sense PRI effectively allows individuals to choose (to a certain extent) which rights should be axed in conflict situations, given that rights must be axed to secure possibility.

In the devolution example given at the end of Section 2.2 each country has conditional preferences. It seems to me that even if each country cannot honestly say that it can 'intrinsically' order their respective features, this is not enough grounds to axe all rights. Whether, for example, Wales is devolving from England, or England *and* Scotland, is a relevant piece of information that should be considered by Wales. Motivationally each should be allowed to implement their rights according to SRI. However, this is impossible. Given PRI, each can at least ensure some rights. For example, each can dismiss their respective 'worst' alternative, i.e. $\{D_1D_2, N_1D_2\}$. The choice function will then choose between the remaining two alternatives. Given such a conflict situation, surely such rights implementation as allowed by PRI is useful in obtaining a best alternative.

Though individuals, under PRI, are free to choose R_b^* in any way they like, R_b^* must be a subrelation of R_b, the true preferences. Thus rights that will be implemented by PRI will always be those that SRI would implement.

2.4.1.3 Justice constrained rights implementation rules (see p. 18) As said before, one reason to amend SRI is that rights using this implementation rule might conflict with some other criteria in social choice that should be valued more highly. This does not imply that SRI is a priori undesirable, only that full implementation of rights, given SRI, might lead to a conflict with yet more desirable criteria. Solution procedures that constrain rights to conform to justice principles are thus not motivated by reasoning similar to Gibbard's, i.e. that SRI is prima facie undesirable in its unqualified form, or my motivation, i.e. that SRI *must* be amended since it can lead to a conflict of rights.

Consider the following quotation from Berlin (1958, pp. 54, 55):

The extent of man's or peoples' liberty to choose to live as they desire must be weighed against the claims of many other values, of which equality, or justice, or happiness, or security, or public order, are perhaps the most obvious examples. For this reason, it cannot be unlimited . . . [R]espect for the principles of Justice, or shame at gross inequality of treatment, is as basic in man as the desire for liberty.

The solution concepts that use justice principles to constrain liberty are most appropriate in case examples when the desire for justice (as formalised by the particular justice relation used) outweighs the desire for liberty (in the sense that SRS and SRI should exist and operate).

The Gibbard paradox is solved in these cases as a 'by-product' of what one is motivationally aiming to do, i.e. constrain rights to be consistent with a more important justice criterion.

In some cases, such procedures might form a morally appropriate solution to the Gibbard paradox. But is it the case that in all circumstances liberty should be constrained by justice as formulated by some specific relation? Justice and liberty might conflict, but which, in society, should give way to the other depends on the nature of the case in question. For example, consider SRI*(M^*), (cf. p. 18). Given $\langle x, y; b \rangle \in \mathscr{R}$ and $(x, b)\, \tilde{P}_b\, (y, b)$ then rights will only be implemented if $\{\forall a : xM_a^A y\}$, where M^A is the asymmetric factor of the Rawlsian maximin justice relation M. Thus rights, as would be implemented by SRI*, must be endorsed by everybody in society considering that x is strictly more just than y in the maximin sense. If just one person considers y at least as just as x then person b's rights will be axed over the pair, given SRI*(M*). It is hard to think of cases when rights should be curtailed on the basis of such an insignificant violation of justice.

2.4.2 Information

I will now state the informational requirements for the procedures discussed in Section 2.3. These 'costs' must be weighed against the other criteria for comparison presented in this Chapter (e.g. the discussion on motivation discussed in the previous subsection).

2.4.2.1 Gibbard's 'consistent' rights implementation rule (GRI) (p. 11) Under Gibbard's motivational interpretation it is necessary to know each person's true preferences over *all* alternatives in X (available and unavailable). The question of defining X precisely is immensely difficult even before a truthful set of preferences is obtained. Under my alternative motivational interpretation of GRI, it is only necessary to know the true set of preferences over the subset S of X that is *available*.

2.4.2.2 The 'private preference' rights implementation rule (PRI) (p. 13) For rights implementation only R_b^* is needed for each b, and that regarding to the available set $S \subseteq X$. R_b^*, as I have said, is a subrelation of R_b that b has decided he wishes to see count in rights implementation. Thus it must be ensured that R_b^* is indeed a subrelation of b's true preferences R_b over the available set of alternatives.

2.4.2.3 Justice constrained rights implementation rules (p. 18) This set of procedures demands much information. Apart from the problem of honest revelation of (extended) preferences there is the additional problem of whether individuals themselves have enough information to formulate such (honest) extended comparisons. For me to say honestly that I prefer to be myself in a state x, rather than some other person in a state y, necessitates that I have a lot of information as regards the position of the other person. Obtaining a full set of extended preferences requires each person in society to know who is who, and how well off they are (relatively) compared with others. Such an informational requirement is plainly not going to be met in many cases and, as such, the 'costs' of implementing a procedure with such extended ordering may be prohibitively high. It should be noted that preferences over the available set, not the total set, are required for these procedures, but this informational advantage hardly outweighs the informational disadvantage.

2.4.3 *Efficiency*

A resolution method that solves the Gibbard paradox yet allows more rights to be implemented than another method will be deemed more 'efficient'. This criterion is most relevant when, given SRS, SRI is accepted as primà facie desirable. Given this interpretation SRI is only modified because (1) the Gibbard paradox must be avoided, and (2) there are yet more desirable social criteria that conflict with SRI in social choice. Given (1) it would be desirable to solve the conflict in a fair way, yet preserve rights as much as possible. Given (2) one would only want to modify rights when they conflict with each other or with the other desirable social criteria — in cases where there is no conflict one would wish to retain rights according to SRI. Given Gibbard's motivation behind GRI, and also the motivation behind the solutions that use justice principles to restrict rights, then efficiency is not so relevant: rights are being restricted because they should, not because they must. Nevertheless, these approaches can be looked upon as a way to solve the Gibbard paradox, independent of the original motivations.

Let us now define precisely what we mean by efficiency in this context: Given

(a) a particular subset S of X,
(b) a particular set of preferences $\{R_b\}$,
(c) other associated relevant information θ,

let $\mu_{RI}^{SRS} (S, \{R_b\}, \theta)$ be the number of pairs of alternatives for which a libertarian condition, defined as the combination of SRS and a particular rights implementation rule RI, would desire to implement rights.

Examples

If RI = SRI we have $\mu_{SRI}^{SRS} (S, \{R_b\})$

If RI = PRI we have $\mu_{PRI}^{SRS} (S, \{R_b\}, \{R_b^*\})$

If RI = SRI*(M) we have $\mu_{SRI*(M)}^{SRS} (S, \{R_b\}, \{\tilde{R}_b\})$

In formulating an efficiency measure $\mu_{SRI}^{SRS} (S, \{R_b\})$ will be used as a reference base. Given certain $\{R_b\}$ and S we know that SRS and SRI can result in an empty choice set. This is why in the general definition of $\mu_{RI}^{SRS} (S, \{R_b\}, \theta)$ we determine the number of pairs the rights implementation rule RI 'desires' to implement.

Given a subset of available alternatives S, a set of preferences $\{R_b\}$ and associated other relevant information θ, the efficiency of a rights implementation modification procedure will be defined as

$$\Pi_{RI}^{SRS}(S,\{R_b\},\theta) = \frac{\mu_{RI}^{SRS}(S,\{R_b\},\theta)}{\mu_{SRI}^{SRS}(S,\{R_b\})} \text{ if } \mu_{SRI}^{SRS}(S,\{R_b\}) \neq 0$$

$$= 1 \text{ otherwise}$$

For all possible S, $\{R_b\}$ and associated θ

$$1 \geqslant \Pi_{RI}^{SRS}(S,\{R_b\},\theta) \geqslant 0$$

If $\Pi_{RI}^{SRS}(S,\{R_b\},\theta) = 1$ then $\mu_{RI}^{SRS}(S,\{R_b\},\theta) = \mu_{SRI}^{SRS}(S,\{R_b\})$

We have absolute efficiency but of course impossibility for some $\{R_b\}$ and $S \subseteq X$.

If $\Pi_{RI}^{SRS}(S,\{R_b\},\theta) = 0$ then $\mu_{RI}^{SRS}(S,\{R_b\},\theta) = 0$

In this case no rights are implemented.

Given that SRI is accepted as the correct rights implementation procedure then we might choose an amended rights implementation rule that, for each S, $\{R_b\}$ and associated θ, maximises efficiency subject to the constraint that there will always exist a choice function $C(S,\{R_b\})$ satisfying the libertarian condition.

If a rights implementation rule RI^0 is 'at least as efficient' as another rights implementation rule RI^1 we will write

$$RI^0 \geqslant_E RI^1$$

This is defined as

$$RI^0 \geqslant_E RI^1 \leftrightarrow [\forall S \subseteq X, \forall \{R_b\}: \Pi_{RI^0}^{SRS}(S,\{R_b\},\theta^0)$$
$$\geqslant \Pi_{RI^1}^{SRS}(S,\{R_b\},\theta^1)]$$

where θ^0 and θ^1 represent other relevant information, associated with S and $\{R_b\}$, for RI^0 and RI^1 respectively. If a rights implementation rule RI^0 is 'more efficient' than another, RI^1, we will write

$$RI^0 >_E RI^1$$

where

$$RI^0 >_E RI^1 \leftrightarrow [RI^0 \geqslant_E RI^1 \text{ and for some } S \subseteq X, \text{ and some } \{R_b\}:$$
$$\{\Pi_{RI^0}^{SRS}(S,\{R_b\},\theta^0) > \Pi_{RI^1}^{SRS}(S,\{R_b\},\theta^1)\}]$$

$\geqslant_E$ is reflexive and transitive. $>_E$ is transitive and asymmetric. Neither is necessarily complete.

2.4.3.1 PRI versus GRI (see pp. 11, 13) In making an efficiency comparison between PRI and GRI a difficulty arises in that, under PRI, the value that $\Pi_{PRI}^{SRS}(S,\{R_b\},\{R_b^*\})$ takes, for each $\{R_b\}$ and S, depends on $\{R_b^*\}$. Individuals could decide not to wish any of their rights to count in social choice.

However, such inefficiency is brought about by the individuals' own choice. It is inefficiency that comes with the axing of rights, when individuals would otherwise wish their rights respected, that is troublesome. Thus for an efficiency comparison I will assume a desire on behalf of individuals to implement rights according to SRI but each realising that this is constrained by the operation of PRI.

Theorem 2.4.1 *If individuals 'b' choose $R_b^* = R_b$ in cases when PRI, given this R_b^*, implements all those rights which SRI will implement, then PRI $>_E$ GRI.*

Proof: When individuals exhibit unconditional preferences, whether over the feasible set or the total set X, PRI will implement all rights that GRI does. In addition, if say $\langle(x_1, z), (y_1, z); b\rangle \in \mathcal{R}$, and $(x_1, z)P_b(y_1, z)$ for some $z = (x_2, x_3, \ldots, x_n)$, and $\forall z' \neq z: (x_1, z')I_b(y_1, z')$, then PRI will implement rights over the pair $\{(x_1, z), (y_1, z)\}$ but GRI will not.[1]

2.4.3.2 Justice constrained rights implementation rules On p. 18 it was noted that

(1) $xJ_by \rightarrow xL_b^{ex}y \rightarrow xM_by$
(2) not $yM_bx \rightarrow xL_b^{ex}y \rightarrow$ not $yL_b^{ex}x \rightarrow$ not yJ_bx

Thus

(1) $L*M \rightarrow L*L^{ex} \rightarrow L*J$
(2) $L*J* \rightarrow L*L^{ex*} \rightarrow L*L^{ex} \rightarrow L*M*$

(Assuming $A \rightarrow B$, then $L*$ restricted to conform to condition A is weaker than $L*$ restricted to conform to condition B.) Note also that, for no pairs of the above libertarian conditions does the implication also go the other way round. Thus

(1) SRI*$(M) >_E$ SRI* $(L^{ex}) >_E$ SRI*(J)
(2) SRI*$(J*) >_E$ SRI* $(L^{ex*}) >_E$ SRI* $(L^{ex}) >_E$ SRI*$(M*)$

Now from Theorem 2.3.3, the three implementation rules that are more efficient than SRI*(L^{ex}), i.e. SRI*(M), SRI*$(J*)$ and SRI*(L^{ex*}), all fail to resolve the Gibbard paradox. Looking at only those rights implementation rules that do solve the paradox we have

(1) SRI*$(L^{ex}) >_E$ SRI*(J)
(2) SRI*$(L^{ex}) >_E$ SRI*$(M*)$

Thus in terms of efficiency SRI* (L^{ex}) is most efficient out of the set of rights implementation rules above that solve the Gibbard paradox.

---

[1] We also know that with 'strict' conditional preferences individuals can also implement rights under PRI whereas they cannot under GRI.

2.4.3.3 Other comparisons Unfortunately comparisons between PRI (or GRI) and SRI*(L^{ex}) are not possible using the relations $\geqslant_E$ or $>_E$. Given a particular $\{\widetilde{R}_b\}$ (of which $\{R_b\}$ is contained) and a particular $S \subseteq X$ then an efficiency comparison may be made. However, when considering all $S \subseteq X$ and all possible extended ordering $\{\widetilde{R}_b\}$ no general conclusion can be made.

2.4.3.4 Conditional rights implementation rules In order to maximise 'efficiency' it might well be asked, why not make the resolution procedures operable only when conflict situations arise. That is, use SRI (or SRI*) in all cases except those which lead to an empty choice set. Only in such 'paradox' cases should we resort to amend SRI (or SRI*). Doing this will raise the efficiency of all the procedures discussed but the strict rankings under the efficiency relation will still hold.

However, doing such a thing relies on a total acceptance of SRI and the attitude that all amendments to SRI should be made only to secure possibility. As I have said, when considering the motivation behind the justice constrained implementation rules and Gibbard's motivation behind GRI, efficiency is not such a relevant criterion — rights are being axed in those cases because they *should*, not because they *must*.

2.4.4   *Rationality versus minimal rights*

Consider the following two definitions

Contraction consistency $(\alpha)^1$

$$\forall x: x \in S^1 \subseteq S^2 \subseteq X \to [x \in C(S^2, \{R_b\}) \to x \in C(S^1, \{R_b\})]$$

Minimal rights (MR) If the available set is $S = \{x,y\}$ and $\langle x, y; b \rangle \in \mathcal{R}$, then if xP_by then $y \notin C(\{x,y\}, \{R_b\})$

These two conditions can easily be rewritten for the extended framework of Section 2.3.2.3.

At first glance these two conditions are very appealing. Condition α says that if an alternative is chosen given a set S^2 then it should also be chosen, given that it is still available, if the set is reduced in size. Condition MR says that if the available set consists of only two alternatives, assigned to individual b, then b should be allowed to have his rights implemented.

Theorem 2.4.2 *All solution procedures that solve the Gibbard paradox by 'rights implementation modification' methods imply that either condition α or condition MR is violated in social choice.*

---

[1] Also called the 'Chernoff condition' (see Sen (1970a), p. 17).

Proof: Let $S^1 = \{x = (x_1, x_2, z)$

$$y = (x_1, y_2, z)$$
$$u = (y_1, y_2, z)$$
$$w = (y_1, x_2, z)\}$$

Let there be two individuals 1 and 2.

Let person 1 be assigned issue 1 and person 2 assigned issue 2.

Let preferences over this set S^1 be:

1	2	
x	y	
w	x	descending order of
u	w	strict preference
y	u	

Now a solution procedure must choose at least one alternative out of S^1 given these preferences.

Given *MR*, these rights will be implemented over the following different available sets.

$$S^2 = \{x, w\} \rightarrow w \notin C(S^2, \{R_b\})$$
$$S^3 = \{u, y\} \rightarrow y \notin C(S^3, \{R_b\})$$
$$S^4 = \{y, x\} \rightarrow x \notin C(S^4, \{R_b\})$$
$$S^5 = \{w, u\} \rightarrow u \notin C(S^5, \{R_b\})$$

Thus whatever is chosen from S^1 will be dismissed from a smaller subset (either S^2, S^3, S^4 or S^5). This violates condition α.

Accepting SRS we are forced to give up SRI. Giving up SRI means we must either give up α or *MR*. Let us now consider the approaches to solving the Gibbard paradox discussed and consider which condition, *MR* or α will be violated in social choice.

2.4.4.1 GRI Under Gibbard's motivation, minimal rights will be violated and condition α can be satisfied. This is because the total set X is considered when deducing unconditional preferences, not the available set in question. If one was to look just at the available set then condition *MR* will be satisfied but condition α will not.

2.4.4.2 PRI Assuming individuals wish to preserve their rights then with PRI condition α will be violated and condition *MR* will be satisfied. This is because 'private preferences' are deduced from $\{R_b^*\}$ defined over the available set.

2.4.4.3 Justice constrained rights implementation rules All implementation rules discussed in Section 2.3.2.3 will imply violation of MR, and condition α can be satisfied. This is because information only on extended orderings over $\{x, y\}$ is used in deducing whether rights over $\langle x, y; b \rangle \in \mathscr{R}$ for some b, should be implemented.

For resolution procedures that amend SRI, either condition α or condition MR must be violated in social choice. If SRI is accepted as prima facie desirable then procedures should seek to preserve minimal rights, even at the expense of violating the contraction consistency condition. If on the other hand SRI is not morally appropriate, because one does not approve of conditional preferences, or desires that certain justice principles should be satisfied, then violation of MR might then be justified and condition α can be satisfied. Typically to justify violation of MR for an individual, more information is needed − one must look beyond an individual's preferences over the available set of alternatives and, for example, consider the rest of his preferences over unavailable alternatives or examine the preferences of other individuals.

2.5   Conclusion

Various approaches that resolve the Gibbard paradox have been discussed. Each is based on different motivation. Which is the 'best' probably depends on one's notion of what rights should be implemented in particular cases.

If it is accepted that SRI is desirable and rights implementation is more important than other criteria in social choice, then SRI should be amended by a procedure that seeks to preserve rights. If the natural rights system is coherent then SRI can be retained without amendment. If the rights system is incoherent, e.g. SRS, then the Gibbard paradox can arise and SRI cannot operate. Given this situation, then replacing SRI with PRI seems the best of the approaches discussed. In conflict situations PRI allows individuals to implement some rights. It is more efficient than GRI and does not involve the large amount of information needed if the justice constrained libertarian conditions are used. PRI implies that the contraction consistency condition is violated in social choice. Given that one wants to preserve rights, and specifically to preserve minimal rights this is a price one should pay. Further, given that SRI is prima facie desirable, then there is a strong case for retaining SRI in all non-conflict cases, and only replacing SRI with PRI when preferences are such that SRI cannot operate, i.e. when the Gibbard paradox arises.

Gibbard on the other hand, argues that SRI is prima facie inappropriate and should be amended to GRI. I do not accept his motivation. Given that a person's assigned pair differs only with respect to his personal issue then rights should be implemented regardless of motivation. Even if Gibbard's motivation is accepted, then it is not altogether clear that GRI should operate. The preference over features P^u (see p. 12) can only be inferred when individuals exhibit unconditional preferences. Despite a conditional ordering of features in a particular ordering of social alternatives, there might still be an 'intrinsic' preference over features. If individuals could be persuaded honestly to reveal such intrinsic preference via their revelation of R_b^* then PRI would conform to Gibbard's motivation more than Gibbard's own GRI.

Accepting that SRI is desirable, it might be the case that the implementation of rights conflicts with a yet more desirable social criterion. For example, if justice is considered more important than rights, then rights should be constrained to conform to this justice (this is the approach used in section 2.3.2.3). However, the modifications to SRI are very strong and there is the huge informational requirement necessary to implement such procedures.

CHAPTER 3

The Sen paradox

3.1   Introduction

In the previous chapter, different types of approaches were discussed that resolved the conflict of rights presented as the 'Gibbard Paradox'. Given these, we are assured that for any subset of available social states, and for any given set of individual preferences, implementation of rights will never result in an empty choice set. However, liberty, as formalised (in a very weak sense) by these different approaches is not the only social condition we would want to see satisfied in social choice. It is important to know what other social criteria can coexist in social choice with such libertarian conditions. Put in another way, we would want to know the cost of accepting a mild form of liberty in social choice, in terms of violation of other desirable social criteria.

The previous chapter has already shown that other desirable social criteria may have to be violated if rights are to be implemented. In Section 2.4.4 it was shown that, accepting the standard rights system (SRS), then modifications to the standard rights implementation rule (SRI) that resolve the Gibbard paradox must imply violation of either the minimal rights (MR) or the contraction consistency condition (α) in social choice. Thus, given SRS, the price of accepting MR as a condition on the choice function $C(S, \{R_b\})$ is a violation of the rationality condition α. MR is a weak condition of liberty and it is disturbing to find that, given SRS, a mild rationality condition cannot also be satisfied.

It can be inferred from Section 2.3.2.3 that conditions of justice, formulated within the extended informational framework, can conflict with rights. A condition of justice in social choice might dictate that if everybody ranks an alternative x as strictly more 'just' than another alternative y then y should not be chosen if x is available. We could use the Suppes relation (J), strict ranking maximin (M^A) or leximin (L^{ex}) for example, in such a condition (see pp. 16, 17). To illustrate the possible conflict between rights and justice, consider the following preferences for all individuals over a pair of alternatives $\{x, y\}$

$$\forall a = 1, \ldots, m:$$

$$(y, 2)\,\tilde{P}_a\,(y, 3)\,\tilde{P}_a\,\ldots\,\tilde{P}_a\,(y, m)\,\tilde{P}_a\,(x, 1)\,\tilde{P}_a\,(y, 1)\,\tilde{P}_a\,(x, 2)$$

$$\tilde{P}_a\,(x, 3)\,\tilde{P}_a\,\ldots\,\tilde{P}_a\,(x, m)$$

Let person 1 be assigned the pair $\{x, y\}$ (i.e. $\langle x, y; 1 \rangle \in \mathscr{R}$). Given that he can implement his rights by SRI we can conclude that $y \notin C^*(\{x,y\}, \{\tilde{R}_b\})$. However, from the above preferences we can conclude that all individuals find y to be strictly more just than x in

(i) the 'Suppes sense': $\{\forall a : yJ_a x\}$;
(ii) the strict ranking 'leximin' sense: $\{\forall a : yL_a^{ex} x\}$; and
(iii) the strict ranking 'maximin' sense: $\{\forall a : yM_a^A x\}$.

A justice condition based on such justice relations might reasonably dismiss x from the choice set over $\{x, y\}$. But such a justice condition cannot exist with individual 1's rights over the pair $\{x, y\}$ since the choice set over $\{x, y\}$ would be empty. This conflict can manifest itself given any assignment of pairs to individuals.

Consider now the following two conditions:

Anonymity (*A*) If $\{R_b\}$ is a reordering of $\{R_b'\}$, then $C(S, \{R_b\}) = C(S, \{R_b'\})$.

Neutrality (*N*) If $\forall x, y, w, z \in X$: $[\{\forall b : xR_b y \leftrightarrow zR_b' w\}$ and $\{\forall b : yR_b x \leftrightarrow wR_b' z\}]$ then $C(\{x, y\}, \{R_b\}) = C(\{z, w\}, \{R_b'\})$.

The decision to have a system of rights can be seen as implying a decision that conditions A and N should not hold in social choice.

Anonymity requires that the choice over a set of alternatives should be invariant with respect to permutations of individuals' preferences. Assume a pair of alternatives $\{x, y\}$ is assigned to individual 1, and he has preference $xP_1 y$. Suppose that another individual 2 has preferences $yP_2 x$. Implementation of individual 1's rights would imply that $y \notin C(\{x, y\}, \{R_b\})$. According to condition A, if person 1 took on person 2's preferences, and vice versa, y should still not be chosen. However, given this exchange of preferences, person 1's rights would now imply $x \notin C(\{x, y\}, \{R_b\})$. Clearly, then, anonymity is in complete conflict with the concept of individual rights.

Neutrality demands that if two alternatives x and y respectively have the same relation to each other in each individual's preference in a case 1 as z and w have in a case 2, the choice over the set $\{x, y\}$ must be the same as the choice over the set $\{w, z\}$. Consider now the following preferences for two individuals over the four alternatives $\{x, y, w, z\}$

$$xP_1 yP_1 zP_1 w, \quad yP_2 xP_2 wP_2 z$$

Assigning $\{x, y\}$ to person 1 and $\{w, z\}$ to person 2 implies, given they can implement their rights, that

$$y \notin C(\{x, y\}, \{R_b\}) \quad \text{and} \quad z \notin C(\{w, z\}, \{R_b\})$$

But by neutrality we should have

$$w \notin C(\{w, z\}, \{R_b\})$$ since $y \notin C(\{x, y\}, \{R_b\})$

and

$$x \notin C(\{x, y\}, \{R_b\})$$ since $z \notin C(\{w, z\}, \{R_b\})$

neutrality and rights are clearly in conflict.

In this introduction, we have seen that rights can conflict with 'rationality', 'justice', 'anonymity' and 'neutrality'. The most disturbing result, which is not so obvious as some of the above conflicts, is that rights implementation can conflict with the Pareto condition in social choice.

3.2   The Sen paradox

The Pareto principle, defined as a condition on social choice in its weakest form is as follows:

Weak Pareto condition (P)

$$\forall x, y \in X, \{\forall b : xP_b y\} \rightarrow y \notin C(S : x \in S, \{R_b\})$$

A slightly stronger form is

Strong Pareto condition (P^*)

$$\forall x, y \in X, [\{\forall b : xR_b y\} \text{ and } \{\exists b : xP_b y\}] \rightarrow y \notin C(S : x \in S, \{R_b\})$$

The Pareto principle is at the heart of the so-called 'New Welfare Economics'. That 'perfect competition' under certain conditions can be shown to be 'Pareto efficient' or 'Pareto optimal' has been put forward as a very attractive feature of the model. In fact most welfare literature has accepted that Pareto optimality is a *necessary* condition for 'welfare maximisation'.

That Pareto optimality is a necessary condition for welfare maximisation implies that 'welfare' or choice functions should be 'Pareto inclusive'. If our choice function seeks to choose an alternative or set of alternatives which is 'best' for society, then given this view it should satisfy the Pareto condition. However, the Pareto condition, even in its weak form conflicts with rights in social choice. This result was first established by Sen (1970a, b) and has initiated quite an extensive literature on how best this inherent conflict can be solved.

Theorem 3.2.1 ('The Impossibility of a Paretian Liberal' see Sen (1970a, b))
If the number of individuals is greater than one, there does not exist a choice function $C(S, \{R_b\})$ *satisfying condition P and condition* L^S.[1]

Sen also considers an alternative 'rights system' that implies a weaker libertarian condition than L^S for the case of more than two individuals.

[1] Condition L^S is defined on page 10.

Sen's 'minimal' rights system (SENRS^M) There are at least two individuals b such that for each there is a pair of social alternatives x and y such that $\langle x, y ; b \rangle$ and $\langle y, x ; b \rangle$ are in $\mathscr{R}$.

Condition ML^S (Sen's 'minimal liberalism' condition) SENRS^M and SRI respectively exist and operate in society.

Theorem 3.2.2 *There does not exist a choice function of $C(S, \{R_b\})$ satisfying ML^S and P.*

Proof: See Sen (1970b). An indirect proof will be provided in the next section.

Corollary to Theorem 3.2.2 Theorem 3.2.2 implies Theorem 3.2.1, since with the number of individuals greater than one $L^S \rightarrow ML^S$.

Note that the rights systems SENRS and SENRS^M can be constructed to be 'coherent' and the Sen paradox will still hold. The following illustration, taken from Sen (1970b) serves to show how conflicts between rights and Pareto can occur.

There is a book (e.g. *Lady Chatterley's Lover*) which may be read by Mr A (the prude) or Mr B (the lascivious) or by neither. Given other things, these three alternatives define three social states x, y and w respectively. Consider now the following possibility. The prude A most prefers w (no one reading it), then x ('I'll take the hurt on myself') and lastly y ('imagine that lascivious lapping it up'). The lascivious most prefers x ('it will give that lilywhite baby a nice shock!'), then y ('it will be fun'), and lastly w ('what a waste of a good book'). On grounds of individual freedom, since B wants to read the book rather than not read it, $\langle y, w ; B \rangle \in \mathscr{R}$. Now, yP_Bw and by SRI, $w \notin C(\{x, y, w\}, \{R_b\})$. Similarly since alternatives x and w only differ with respect to A reading it, $\langle w, x ; A \rangle \in \mathscr{R}$. Since wP_Ax, then given SRI, $x \notin C(\{x, y, w\}, \{R_b\})$. However all individuals in this example prefer x to y, and thus by the Pareto condition $y \notin C(\{x, y, w\}, \{R_b\})$. No alternative in the choice set over $\{x, y, w\}$ can be chosen given the two individuals' rights and the Pareto condition applied with the above individual preferences.

3.3   The Paretian epidemic and related results

In this section a proof of Theorem 3.2.2 will be provided. It is not a direct proof but comes via a theorem that highlights the strength of the conditions applied to the choice function, and helps us to see clearly the way the conditions interact so as to result in impossibility. Also some very related results are presented that show quite neatly how the 'Impossibility of a Paretian Liberal' fits into the whole class of 'Arrovian' impossibility theorems that have gained prominence in the economic literature since Kenneth Arrow's classic 'General possibility theorem' (Arrow, 1951).

The results are similar to those presented by Sen (1976), in the appendix with the same title as this section. However, they differ in that my results are presented consistent with the non-binary framework developed in this book. First, some definitions:

Full rights A person b will be said to have 'full rights' over an ordered pair of alternatives (x, y) if for all $S \subseteq X$ and all $\{R_b\}$, $xP_by \to y \notin C(S : x \in S, \{R_b\})$.

Potential full rights A person b will be said to have 'potential full rights' over an ordered pair of alternatives (x, y) if for all $S \subseteq X$ and for any $\{R_b\}$ satisfying some specified restrictions on the rankings of pairs other than (x, y), $xP_by \to y \notin C(S : x \in S, \{R_b\})$.

Semi-rights A person b will be said to have 'semi-rights' over an ordered pair of alternatives (x, y) if for some $S' \subseteq X$ such that $x, y \in S'$, and for all $\{R_b\}$, $xP_by \to \{x\} = C(S', \{R_b\})$.[1]

Potential semi-rights A person b will be said to have 'potential semi-rights' over an ordered pair of alternatives (x, y) if for some $S' \subseteq X$ such that $x, y \in S'$, and for any $\{R_b\}$ satisfying some specified restrictions on the rankings of pairs other than (x, y), $xP_by \to \{x\} = C(S', \{R_b\})$.

Theorem 3.3.1 ('The Paretian epidemic' in the context of a non-binary framework of choice) *For any choice function $C(S, \{R_b\})$, the weak Pareto condition P implies that if a person b has full rights both ways over a single pair $\{x, y\}$, (i.e. full rights over the ordered pair (x, y) and the ordered pair (y, x)), then he has potential semi-rights over all ordered pairs of alternatives.*

Proof: Let person b have full rights both ways over $\{x, y\}$. Take any other ordered pair (z, w). There are three possibilities:

I x, y, w and z are all distinct
II $\{z, w\}$ and $\{x, y\}$ have one element in common
III $\{x, y\} = \{z, w\}$

Case I By the unrestricted domain condition incorporated into the definition of $C(S, \{R_b\})$ let preferences be:

For b: $zP_bxP_byP_bw$

$\forall a \neq b$: zP_ax and yP_aw

---

[1] Full rights $\to$ semi rights. If for all $S \subseteq X$ and for all $\{R_b\}$, $\{xP_by \to y \notin C(S : x \in S, \{R_b\})\}$, then $xP_by \to y \notin C(\{x, y\}, \{R_b\})$, which implies that $\{x\} = C(\{x, y\}, \{R_b\})$. The set $S' = \{x, y\}$ is a particular set which contains x and y, so we have established that full rights over the pair (x, y) implies semi-rights over this pair.

By Pareto $x \notin C(\{x, y, w, z\}, \{R_b\})$ and $w \notin C(\{x, y, w, z\}, \{R_b\})$

By b's full rights $y \notin C(\{x, y, w, z\}, \{R_b\})$

Thus $\{z\} = C(\{x, y, z, w\}, \{R_b\})$

We have zP_bw, $\{z\} = C(S' = \{x, y, w, z\}, \{R_b\})$ and preferences of other individuals over z and w have not been specified. Thus b has potential semi-rights over (z, w).

Case II There are four possible sub cases. Say $z = x$.

Let preferences be

$$b : xP_b yP_b w$$

$$\forall a \neq b : yP_a w$$

By Pareto, $w \notin C(\{x, y, w\}, \{R_b\})$

By b's full rights, $y \notin C(\{x, y, w\}, \{R_b\})$

Thus $\{x\} = C(\{x, y, w\}, \{R_b\})$. But preferences of individuals other than b over x *vis-à-vis* w have not been specified. Thus b has potential semi-rights over the pair $(x, w) = (z, w)$.

The other cases $(y = z, y = w, x = w)$ can be illustrated analogously.

Case III Trivial: b's full rights over $\{x, y\}$ must imply potential semi-rights over the same pair, i.e.

$$xP_b y \to y \notin C(\{x, y\}, \{R_b\}) \to \{x\} = C(\{x, y\}, \{R_b\})$$

Corollary to Theorem 3.3.1 (cf. Theorem 3.2.2) Any choice function $C(S, \{R_b\})$ satisfying condition P implies that if any one person b has full rights both ways over a pair of alternatives $\{x, y\}$ then no other individual can have full rights both ways over any pair of alternatives.[1]

Theorem 3.3.1 states that given b's full rights both ways over a pair $\{x, y\}$, the Pareto condition implies he has potential semi-rights over every ordered pair, including a pair (z, w) which we may wish to give another person c full rights both ways over. Individual b's potential semi-rights over (z, w) implies that there exists some subset $S' \subseteq X$ (such that $z, w \in S'$) and some set of preferences $\{R_b\}$ (which leaves the ranking of other individuals over $\{z, w\}$ unspecified), such that: $zP_bw \to \{z\} = C(S', \{R_b\})$. But if another person c

---

[1] Note that no rationality property is imposed on the choice function in this result. In Sen's original theorem (Sen, 1976, Theorem 2.1) his binary choice function (called a social decision function) satisfies the contraction consistency condition α.

has full rights over $\{w, z\}$ then if $wP_c z$ then $z \notin C(S : w \in S, \{R_b\})$ including the case when $S = S'$, and for the set of preferences that gave rise to $\{z\} = C(S', \{R_b\})$. This is not possible, for if c's rights were implemented fully in this case the choice set over S' would be empty.

Following Sen (1976) I have called Theorem 3.3.1 'the Paretian epidemic'. It shows that for a choice function $C(S, \{R_b\})$, the weak Pareto condition is sufficient to spread full rights from one pair of alternatives to all in the weaker form of potential semi-rights. Sen stresses that the Pareto condition is not the same as saying preferences unanimously held over all social states must be reflected in social judgement. The Pareto condition is saying more. It says that if there is unanimous preference over a *pair* of alternatives then the least preferred alternative should be dismissed from the choice set over any $S \subseteq X$ such that the pair is included in S. Thus the alternative is being dismissed independently of preferences over other alternatives. This implicit element of 'independence' plays a large role in the preceding results.

While Sen is right to stress the strength of the Pareto condition in this way, we must not forget that it is not just Pareto doing the work. Condition P and b's full rights both ways over a pair both combine to produce the spread of rights. Letting b have full rights both ways over a pair is also a very strong condition (but a very mild libertarian condition that allows one person rights over a single pair). The full rights of b over a pair also has an 'independence' property as stressed by Blau (1975), i.e. the dismissal of b's least preferred alternative in his assigned pair is due to b's preferences over that pair alone, independent of anybody's preference over any other pair, and independent of anybody else's preferences over the assigned pair itself. Theorem 3.3.1 could well be called the 'libertarian epidemic' since it shows that even a weak form of liberty (i.e. only one person being granted rights over one pair), when combined with the condition that there exists a choice function $C(S, \{R_b\})$ satisfying Pareto, is sufficient to spread rights to all pairs, albeit in a weakened form.

Consider now some related results that help put Theorem 3.3.1 into context with a very general class of impossibility results.

If a weak form of 'rationality' is imposed on the choice function the 'semi' aspect of Theorem 3.3.1 can be ignored. Consider two mild rationality conditions. Firstly we reintroduce the contraction consistency condition α.

Condition α (Contraction consistency)

$$\forall x \in X: [x \in C(S^2, \{R_b\}) \text{ and } x \in S^1 \subseteq S^2] \rightarrow x \in C(S^1, \{R_b\})$$

Secondly, we can impose a weak 'expansion consistency' requirement:

Condition δ (Expansion consistency)

$$\forall x, y \in X: [x, y \in C(S^2, \{R_b\}) \text{ and } S^2 \subseteq S^1] \rightarrow \{y\} \neq C(S^1, \{R_b\})$$

In words, if both x and y are chosen in S^2, a subset of S^1, then one of them (say y) cannot be chosen exclusively in S^1.

Theorem 3.3.2 *Any choice function satisfying condition P, condition α and condition δ implies that if a person b has full rights both ways over a single pair of alternatives $\{x, y\}$ then he has potential full rights over all ordered pairs of alternatives.*

Sketch of Proof: To illustrate the proof consider any other ordered pair (z, w) and assume that it is totally distinct from b's assigned pair.

From the proof of Theorem 3.3.1 we observed that with preferences

$$b: zP_b xP_b yP_b w$$

$$\forall a \neq b: xP_a x \text{ and } yP_a w$$

then $\{z\} = C(\{x, y, w, z\}, \{R_b\})$ (see case I)
By condition α

$$z \in C(\{w, z\}, \{R_b\})$$

By condition δ

$$w \notin C(\{w, z\}, \{R_b\})$$

since if $\{z, w\} = C(\{w, z\}, \{R_b\})$ then $\{z\} \neq C(\{x, y, w, z\}, \{R_b\})$
By condition α again

$$w \notin C(S : z \in S, \{R_b\})$$

Thus given that preferences of others $(a \neq b)$ over $\{w, z\}$ have not been specified, person b has potential full rights over the ordered pair (z, w).

Other cases can be dealt with analogously.

Instead of imposing the two conditions α and δ we can replace them with the following rationality condition taken from the results of Karni (1978).

Independence of non-optimal alternatives (INOA) For all pairs of subsets $S^1, S^2 \subseteq X$

$$C(S^1, \{R_b\}) = C(S^2, \{R_b\}) \quad \text{whenever}$$

$$C(S^1, \{R_b\}) \in S^2 \text{ and } S^2 \subseteq S^1$$

In words, if the choice from a set S^1 is contained in a set S^2 which itself is contained in S^1, then choice over set S^2 should be the same as the choice over S^1.

That condition α is implied by INOA is obvious. To show that INOA implies condition δ consider the analogous implication: *not* $\delta \rightarrow not$ INOA. Suppose δ does not hold. Therefore for some $x, y \in X$

$$x, y \in C(S^2, \{R_b\}) \quad \text{and} \quad S^2 \subseteq S^1 \rightarrow \{y\} = C(S^1, \{R_b\})$$

By INOA, $\{y\} = C(S^2, \{R_b\})$ since $S^2 \subseteq S^1$, but this is not true since $x, y \in C(S^2, \{R_b\})$. Thus *not* $\delta \rightarrow not$ INOA, thus INOA $\rightarrow \delta$.

I have stressed that both Pareto and b's full rights over a pair have 'independence' properties, but at no point have I invoked Arrow's condition of 'independence of irrelevant alternatives'.

Condition I (Independence of irrelevant alternatives, see Arrow (1951))

$$\forall b : (\forall x, y \in S : xR_b y \leftrightarrow xR_b' y) \rightarrow C(S, \{R_b\}) = C(S, \{R_b'\})$$

Given any two profiles $\{R_b\}$ and $\{R_b'\}$, if for any subset S of X the preference orderings are the same in each of these profiles, then the choice set for S should be the same in each case.

Theorem 3.3.3 *For any choice function $C(S, \{R_b\})$, the weak Pareto principle P and the independence of irrelevant alternatives condition I together imply that if a person b has full rights both ways over any pair in X then b has semi-rights over every ordered pair of alternatives from X.*

Theorem 3.3.4 *For any choice function $C(S, \{R_b\})$, the weak Pareto condition P, condition I, condition α and condition δ collectively imply that if any person b has full rights over any ordered pair of alternatives in X, then b has full rights over every ordered pair in X.*

The added 'condition I' enables us to ignore the 'potential' aspects of the previous theorems. This is because, having deduced that a person b has rights (semi or full) over a pair of alternatives (x, y) under some configuration of preferences which leaves the ordering of other individuals over (x, y) unspecified, condition I enables us to state that person b must have rights (semi or full) for *any* configuration of preferences.

Conditions α and δ can be replaced by INOA in Theorem 3.3.4. Theorem 3.3.4 is a particular non-binary equivalent of the central lemma in Arrow's 'general possibility theorem' (see Sen (1970a), Lemma 3*a, called the 'field expansion lemma' in Sen (1983b)).

Consider the following summary of Theorems 3.2.1 to 3.3.4 in the context of the stipulated existence of a choice function $C(S, \{R_b\})$.

Theorem 3.2.1 $P +$ 'every person having full rights both ways over a pair of social alternatives each'
→ *impossibility*

Theorem 3.2.2 $P +$ 'two persons having full rights both ways over a pair of social alternatives each'
→ *impossibility*

Theorem 3.3.1 $P +$ 'one person having full rights both ways over a pair of social alternatives'
→ *that one person has 'potential semi-rights' everywhere*

Theorem 3.3.2 $P + \alpha + \delta +$ 'one person having full rights both ways over a pair of social alternatives'
→ *that one person has 'potential full rights' everywhere*

Theorem 3.3.3 $P + I +$ 'one person having full rights both ways over a pair of social alternatives'
→ *that one person has 'semi-rights' everywhere*

Theorem 3.3.4 $P + I + \alpha + \delta +$ 'one person having full rights over an ordered pair of social alternatives'
→ *that one person has 'full rights' everywhere (dictator)*

Theorems 3.2.1 and 3.2.2 represent the 'Sen paradox'. Theorem 3.3.1 shows that one person's full rights over a pair of alternatives, in the context of a choice function satisfying Pareto, will spread to all pairs in a specific, weakened form, but strong enough to stop anybody else having full rights over any other ordered pair. Theorems 3.3.2, 3.3.3 and 3.3.4 show that adding some other seemingly reasonable and well-known conditions of social choice, makes the spread of decisiveness more exacting, with Theorem 3.3.4 showing that the individual, given full rights over an ordered pair of alternatives, will become a dictator. If one additionally imposes a non-dictatorship condition in Theorem 3.3.4 we will then, of course, have impossibility.

3.4   The Sen paradox with the standard rights system

In Chapter 2 it was shown that the following libertarian conditions that assigned rights according to SRS were not vulnerable to the Gibbard paradox: L^G (see p. 12), L^P (see p. 13), $L*L^{ex}$ (see p. 18), $L*M*$ (see p. 18) and $L*J$ (see p. 18). All these conditions are inconsistent with the weak Pareto condition in social choice given $C(S, \{R_b\})$.

Theorem 3.4.1 *There exists a set of profiles $\{R_b^*\}$, consisting of subrelations of a set of individuals' preferences $\{R_b\}$ (which individuals want to count in rights implementation) such that if the number of individuals is greater than one, there does not exist a choice function $C(S, \{R_b\})$ satisfying condition L^P and condition P.*

Proof: Consider the following set of four alternatives:

$$\{(x_1, x_2, z), (x_1, y_2, z), (y_1, y_2, z), (y_1, x_2, z)\}$$

where $z = x_3, \ldots, x_n$, the same for all four alternatives. Let individual 1 be assigned issue 1 and individual 2 be assigned issue 2. Thus $x_1, y_1 \in M_1$ and $x_2, y_2 \in M_2$. Let preferences of individuals be:

$$1: (x_1, x_2, z) P_1 (y_1, x_2, z) P_1 (x_1, y_2, z) P_1 (y_1, y_2, z)$$

$$2: (y_1, y_2, z) P_2 (y_1, x_2, z) P_2 (x_1, y_2, z) P_2 (x_1, x_2, z)$$

Others (if any): $(y_1, x_2, z) P_b (x_1, y_2, z), b \neq 1,2$

Let $R_b^* = R_b, \forall b$.

Individual 1's rights, given by L^P will result in the alternatives $\{(y_1, x_2, z), (y_1, y_2, z)\}$ being dismissed from the choice set over the four alternatives. Individual 2's rights will result in the dismissal of alternatives $\{(y_1, x_2, z), (x_1, x_2, z)\}$. The Pareto condition will dismiss the alternative (x_1, y_2, z) from the choice set. Thus the choice set over these four alternatives will be empty.

Theorem 3.4.2 *No choice function $C(S, \{R_b\})$, with number of individuals greater than one satisfies condition L^G and condition P.*

Proof: Assume there exist the same alternatives and preferences as in the proof of Theorem 3.4.1. Given the same rights assignments, individuals 1 and 2 will dismiss the same alternatives from the choice set with L^G as with L^P.

Let us now turn to the conditions that are set up in the context of the extended informational framework that allows more utility information. (see p. 16). The Pareto condition in this framework will be:

Condition P'

$$[\forall x, y \in X, \{\forall b : (x, b) \widetilde{P}_b (y, b)\} \rightarrow y \notin C^*(S : x \in S, \{\widetilde{R}_b\})]$$

Theorem 3.4.3 *No choice function $C^*(S, \{\widetilde{R}_b\})$, satisfies condition L^*M^* and condition P'.*

Proof: Consider the four alternatives and rights assignment in the proof of Theorem 3.4.1. Let the extended preferences be:

1	2 (and others)	
$((x_1, y_2, z), 2)$	$((x_1, y_2, z), 1)$	
$((x_1, x_2,, z), 1)$	$((y_1, y_2, z), 2)$	
$((y_1, y_2, z), 2)$	$((x_1, x_2, z), 1)$	descending
$((y_1, x_2, z), 1)$	$((y_1, x_2, z), 2)$	order of
$((x_1, y_2, z), 1)$	$((x_1, y_2, z), 2)$	strict
$((x_1, x_2, z), 2)$	$((x_1, x_2, z), 2)$	preference
$((y_1, y_2, z), 1)$	$((y_1, y_2, z), 1)$	
$((y_1, x_2, z), 2)$	$((y_1, x_2, z), 1)$	

Let all other alternatives, e.g. $((x_1, x_2, z), 3)$, if any, be ranked in higher order in each individual's preference orderings with

$$[\forall b : ((y_1, x_2, z), b) \, \widetilde{P}_b \, ((x_1, y_2, z), b)]$$

(1) $\langle (x_1, x_2, z), (y_1, x_2, z) ; 1 \rangle \in \mathscr{R}$

and $((x_1, x_2, z), 1) \, \widetilde{P}_1 \, ((y_1, x_2, z), 1)$

Also $[\forall b : ((x_1, x_2, z), b) \, \widetilde{P}_1 \, ((y_1, x_2, z), 2)]$

and $[\forall a \neq 1 \{\forall b : ((x_1, x_2, z), b) \, \widetilde{P}_a \, ((y_1, x_2, z), 1)\}]$

→ $[\forall b : (x_1, x_2, z) \, M_b^A \, (y_1, x_2, z)]$ where M_b^A is the asymmetric factor of the Rawlsian maximin relation M_b (see p. 17).

Thus $(y_1, x_2, z) \notin C^*(S : (x_1, x_2, z) \in S, \{\widetilde{R}_b\}$

(2) $\langle (x_1, y_2, z), (x_1, x_2, z); 2 \rangle \in \mathscr{R}$

and $((x_1, y_2, z), 2) \, \widetilde{P}_2 \, ((x_1, x_2, z), 2)$

It is easily checked that

$$[\forall b : (x_1, y_2, z) \, M_b^A \, (x_1, x_2, z)]$$

Thus $(x_1, x_2, z) \notin C^*(S : (x_1, y_2, z) \in S, \{\widetilde{R}_b\})$

(3) $\langle (x_1, y_2, z), (y_1, y_2, z); 1 \rangle \in \mathscr{R}$

and $((x_1, y_2, z), 1) \, \widetilde{P} \, ((y_1, y_2, z), 1)$

and $[\forall b : (x_1, y_2, z) \, M_b^A \, (y_1, y_2, z)]$

Therefore by $L*M*$

$(y_1, y_2, z) \notin C^*(S : (x_1, y_2, z) \in S, \{\widetilde{R}_b\})$

(4) $[\forall b : ((y_1, x_2, z), b) \, \widetilde{P}_b \, ((x_1, y_2, z), b)]$

Thus by condition P'

$$(x_1, y_2, z) \notin C^*(S : (y_1, x_2, z) \in S, \{\tilde{R}_b\})$$

Thus no alternative is chosen from the set of four alternatives.

Corollary to Theorem 3.4.3 No choice function $C^*(S, \{\tilde{R}_b\})$, satisfies condition $L*L^{ex}$ and condition P'. (Note that $L*L^{ex} \to L*M^*$, see p. 27).

Theorem 3.4.4 *No choice function $C^*(S, \{\tilde{R}_b\})$ satisfies condition $L*J$ and condition P'.*

Proof: Let $xx = (x_1, x_2, z)$
$\qquad yy = (y_1, y_2, z)$
$\qquad xy = (x_1, y_2, z)$
$\qquad yx = (y_1, x_2, z)$

and let the rights assignment be the same as in the proof of Theorem 3.4.1.

Let preferences be:

1	2 (and others)
$(xy, 2)$	$(xy, 1)$
$(yy, 3) (xx, 3) (yx, 3)$	$(yy, 3) (xx, 3) (yx, 3)$
$(xy, 3)$	$(xy, 3)$
$(yy, 3) (xx, 4) (yx, 4)$	$(yy, 4) (xx, 4) (yx, 4)$
$(xy, 4)$	$(xy, 4)$
.	.
.	.
.	.
$(yy, m) (xx, m) (yx, \text{m})$	$(yy, m) (xx, m) (yx, m)$
(xy, m)	(xy, m)
$(xx, 1)$	$(yy, 2)$
$(yy, 2)$	$(xx, 1)$
$(yx, 1)$	$(yx, 2)$
$(xy, 1)$	$(xy, 2)$
$(xx, 2)$	$(xx, 2)$
$(yy, 1)$	$(yy, 1)$
$(yx, 2)$	$(yx, 1)$

The above is in order of strict preference, reading down the list. Alternatives on the same line are alternatives which an individual is indifferent between. It may be the case that there only exist two individuals, in which case the alternatives $(yy, 3)$, $(yy, 4)$, $(xy, 3)$ etc. should be ignored.

(1) $(xx, 1) \tilde{P}_1 (yx, 1)$ and $(xx, 2) \tilde{P}_1 (yx, 2)$

and $\forall a \geqslant 3: (xx, a)\, \tilde{I}_1\, (yx, a)$

$\forall b \geqslant 2: \{(xx, 1)\, \tilde{P}_b\, (yx, 2) \text{ and } (xx, 2)\, \tilde{P}_b\, (yx, 1) \text{ and}$

$\qquad [\forall a \geqslant 3: (xx, a)\, \tilde{I}_b\, (yx, a)]\}$

Therefore by condition $L*J$

$yx \notin C*(S: xx \in S, \{\tilde{R}_b\})$

(2) $[(xy, 1)\, \tilde{P}_1\, (yy, 1) \text{ and } (xy, m)\, \tilde{P}_1\, (yy, 2)$

and $(xy, m-1)\, \tilde{P}_1\, (yy, m) \text{ and } (xy, m-2)\, \tilde{P}_1\, (yy, m-1)$

and $(xy, m-3)\, \tilde{P}_1\, (yy, m-2) \text{ and } \ldots$

and $(xy, 3)\, \tilde{P}_1\, (yy, 4) \text{ and } (xy, 2)\, \tilde{P}_1\, (yy, 3)]$

Thus, $xyJ_1 yy$.

$\forall b \geqslant 2: [(xy, 2)\, \tilde{P}_b\, (yy, 1) \text{ and } (xy, m)\, \tilde{P}_b\, (yy, 2)$

and $(xy, m-1)\, \tilde{P}_b\, (yy, m) \text{ and } (xy, m-2)\, \tilde{P}_b\, (yy, m-1)$

and $(xy, m-3)\, \tilde{P}_b\, (yy, m-2) \text{ and } \ldots$

and $(xy, 3)\, \tilde{P}_b\, (yy, 4) \text{ and } (xy, 1)\, \tilde{P}_b\, (yy, 3)]$

Thus $\forall b \geqslant 2: xyJ_b yy$.

Thus by condition $L*J$

$yy \notin C*(S: xy \in S, \{\tilde{R}_b\})$

(3) $(xy, 2)\, \tilde{P}_2\, (xx, 2)$

$[(xy, 2)\, \tilde{P}_1\, (xx, 3) \text{ and } (xy, 1)\, \tilde{P}_1\, (xx, 2) \text{ and}$

$(xy, 3)\, \tilde{P}_1\, (xx, 4) \text{ and } \ldots \text{ and } (xy, m-1)\, \tilde{P}_1\, (xx, m)$

and $(xy, m)\, \tilde{P}_1\, (xx, 1)]$

$\forall b \geqslant 2: [(xy, 1)\, \tilde{P}_b\, (xx, 3) \text{ and } (xy, 3)\, \tilde{P}_b\, (xx, 4)$

and $\ldots \text{ and } (xy, m-1)\, \tilde{P}_b\, (xx, m) \text{ and } (xy, m)\, \tilde{P}_b\, (xx, 1)$

and $(xy, 2)\, \tilde{P}_b\, (xx, 2)]$

Thus by condition $L*J$

$xx \notin C*(S: xy \in S, \{\tilde{R}_b\})$

(4) $\forall b : (yx, b) \, \widetilde{P}_b \, (xy, b)$

Thus, by condition P'

$$xy \notin C^*(S : \mathrm{yx} \in S, \{\widetilde{R}_b\})$$

Thus all the alternatives from the set $\{xy, xx, yy, yx\}$ are dismissed.

Theorems 3.4.1, 3.4.2, 3.4.3 and 3.4.4 tell us that the rights implementation modification methods of solving the Gibbard paradox developed in Chapter 2, fail to resolve the Sen paradox. The following three chapters discuss various ways of resolving this additional conflict.

CHAPTER 4

Rights implementation modification approaches to resolving the Sen paradox

4.1   Introduction

All the libertarian conditions that were formulated in Chapter 2 fail to be consistent with the Pareto condition in social choice, including those that are not vulnerable to the Gibbard paradox. How can this new paradox best be resolved? Consider the following two approaches:

(a) Modify the libertarian condition such that a choice function $C(S, \{R_b\})$, that satisfies it and the Pareto condition, exists.

(b) Modify the Pareto condition such that a choice function $C(S, \{R_b\})$, that satisfies it and a libertarian condition (which is not vulnerable to the Gibbard paradox) exists.

Approaches which fall under the classification of (a) will be discussed in this Chapter, while approaches which fall under the classification of (b) will be discussed in Chapter 5. These two broad classifications of approaches (and others) will be compared and evaluated in Chapter 6.

A modification to the libertarian condition consistent with approach (a) can be viewed as a weakening of condition L, and this by a weakening of the standard rights system (SRS), or by a weakening of the standard rights implementation rule (SRI), or a weakening of both. In this chapter I will mainly consider methods that weaken SRI and retain SRS. Some of the discussed weakening of SRI can easily be used in conjunction with other rights systems, e.g. SENRS or SENRS^M (see p. 10, 35), others will be seen to rely exclusively on the specification of SRS. This will be made clear in the course of this chapter's analysis. Though a weakening of SRS was seen, in some cases, to be an appropriate way of resolving the Gibbard paradox, such weakenings by themselves are not so appropriate for resolving the Sen paradox. Suffice to note that weakening SRS to SENRS^M does not resolve the Sen paradox given SRI; indeed it was within the context of SENRS^M that Sen first formulated his paradox (see p. 35). SENRS^M is probably the weakest rights system that should possibly be considered (further weakening resulting in a libertarian condition of no analytical or practical interest). Note that the 'rights system' is considered here as an assignment of rights formulated on the basis of non-utility information, i.e. on the basis of the nature of the social alternatives, and is thus constructed independently of individuals' preferences.[1]

In the following 'Methods' section, three different types of modifications of SRI will be outlined, that when combined with SRS will yield a libertarian condition that is consistent with the Pareto condition in social choice. Discussion of the motivation underlying these approaches, informational requirements, efficiency, etc., will be left to later sections.

4.2   Methods

4.2.1   *Gibbard's solution procedure* (see Gibbard (1974))

Given $\langle x, y; b \rangle \in \mathscr{R}$ then b's rights to x over y will be implemented if $xP_b y$ and 'b's rights are not waived'. Thus the heart of Gibbard's approach to resolving the Sen paradox lies in his criteria for rights waiving. This is quite complicated and is given by the following condition:

Gibbard's condition for rights waiving for individual b   For a given set of profiles for society $\{R_b\}$, and a given available set $S \subseteq X$, an individual b's right to x over y is waived under $\mathscr{R}$ if and only if for some $z, (z \neq y), yR_b z$, and for some available sequence of alternatives in S, $\Sigma = y^1, y^2, \ldots, y^\lambda$,

(i) $y^1 = z$

(ii) $y^\lambda = x$

(iii) $\forall i = 1, 2, \ldots, 1 - \lambda$, at least one of the following holds:

either (a) $\forall c : y^i P_c y^{i+1}$

or (b) $\exists c [(c \neq b): \langle y^i, y^{i+1}; c \rangle \in \mathscr{R}$ and $y^i P_c y^{i+1}]$

If b's rights to x over y are waived, I will, following Gibbard, write $xW_b y [\mathscr{R}]$.

---

[1] Austen-Smith (1979) and, following him, Gaertner (1982) have considered making the *assignment* of rights for an individual contingent on his preference over other people's assigned pairs. Thus, in potential conflict situations between rights and Pareto, the paradox can be solved by a respecification of the rights system. Operationally this is not very different from keeping the rights system and making the *implementation* of rights contingent on preferences over other people's assigned pairs. I prefer to view the rights system as something that is constructed independently of preferences, on grounds of the *nature* of the social alternatives under consideration. The solution procedures I discuss in this book (that retain a given rights system and weaken SRI by making it contingent on a particular type of preference structure) can easily be reconstructed such that we can retain SRI, but make the assignment of rights contingent on that particular type of preference structure.

Gibbard's Pareto-consistent rights implementation rule (GPRI) If $\langle x, y; b \rangle \in \mathscr{R}, xP_b y$ and (not: $xW_b y[\mathscr{R}]$) then $y \notin C(S : x \in S, \{R_b\})$

Condition L^{GP} (Condition L'', in Gibbard (1974)) SRS and GPRI respectively exist and operate in society.

Theorem 4.2.1 *There exists a choice function $C(S, \{R_b\})$ which satisfies condition L^{GP} and the Pareto condition P.*

Proof: See Gibbard (1974), pp. 401–2.

Note that GPRI can be used with any rights system which does not allocate a particular pair of alternatives to more than one individual.

4.2.2   Gaertner and Krüger's 'self-supporting preferences' procedure[1]
(see Gaertner and Krüger (1981))

Given $\langle x, y; b \rangle \in \mathscr{R}$ then b's rights for x over y will be implemented, with Gaertner and Krüger's approach if $xP_b y$ and 'b has self-supporting preferences'. Before defining formally what is meant by 'self-supporting preferences' some notation will be useful.

Let the social alternative $(z_1, z_2, \ldots, z_{i-1}, x_i, z_{i+1}, \ldots, z_n)$ be denoted more briefly as $(x_i, \mathbf{z})$

Let $Z_{)i(} = M_1 \times M_2 \times \ldots \times M_{i-1} \times M_{i+1} \times \ldots \times M_n$ (a cartesian product). Thus a list of feature alternatives other than for issue i is an element of the set $Z_{)i(}$.

Gaertner and Krüger's condition for an individual b to have 'self-supporting preferences' (SSP) An individual b has 'self-supporting preferences' (SSP) with respect to his issue j if and only if for all pairs $(x_j, y_j) \in M_j \times M_j$ with $x_j \neq y_j$, if $(x_j, \mathbf{z}) P_b (y_j, \mathbf{z}')$ for some $(\mathbf{z}, \mathbf{z}') \in Z_{)i(} \times Z_{)j(}$, then $(x_i, \mathbf{z}) R_b (y_j, \mathbf{z}')$, for all $(\mathbf{z}, \mathbf{z}') \in Z_{)j(} \times Z_{)j(}$.

Gaertner and Krüger's 'self-supporting preference' rights implementation rule (SSPRI) For any pair of j-variants x and y such that $\langle x, y; b \rangle \in \mathscr{R}$, if $xP_b y$ and individual b has an ordering R_b which satisfies SSP with respect to his issue j, then $y \notin C(S ; x \in S, \{R_b\})$.

---

[1] This presentation of Gaertner and Krüger's procedure is a truncated version in which the explicit definition of what they call 'collective features' constituting a part of each social state are entirely neglected. This simplified version follows closely their own presentation in Krüger and Gaertner (1983). This simplification is made to facilitate easier comparison with other approaches. I feel the important characteristics of their approach are still fully retained in the present truncated version.

Condition L^{SSP} SRS and SSPRI respectively exist and operate in society.

Theorem 4.2.2 (see Gaertner and Krüger (1981), Theorem 1) *There exists a choice function* $C(S, \{R_b\})$ *which satisfies condition* L^{SSP} *and condition P.*

Proof: See Gaertner and Krüger (1981).

Note that SSPRI can only be operated in conjunction with a rights system which assigns rights with respect to issues.

4.2.3   *Solution procedures based on extra utility information*

I will now consider extending the informational framework in order to allow extra individual utility information. This extended framework was developed in Chapter 2, Section 2.3.2.3 and the notation and definitions formulated there will be retained.

In Chapter 2 it was proved that the libertarian conditions $L*L^{ex}$, $L*M*$ and $L*J$ all resolved the Gibbard paradox (see p. 19). However, in Chapter 3, Section 3.4, it was shown that none of these helped resolve the Sen paradox (see pp. 42–6).

Consider now two well-known restrictions on individual's extended orderings $\{\tilde{R}_b\}$ (see Sen (1970a) p. 156).

Axiom of identity (I^A)

$$\forall b : \{(x, b)\, \tilde{R}_b\, (y, b) \leftrightarrow \forall a : (x, b)\, \tilde{R}_a\, (y, b)\}$$

Axiom of complete identity (I^C)

$$\forall a, b : \tilde{R}_a = \tilde{R}_b$$

The axiom of identity states that each individual a in placing himself in the position of person b takes on the tastes and preferences of b. The stronger axiom of complete identity states that all individuals share the same extended ordering. It should be noted that there exists extended orderings $\{\tilde{R}_b\}$ satisfying the axiom of complete identity (and hence the axiom of identity) compatible with every logically possible set of individual orderings $\{R_b\}$, where each individual b is ordering alternatives in the position of himself.

Theorem 4.2.3 *If individuals' extended orderings* $\{\tilde{R}_b\}$ *satisfy the axiom of identity* I^A, *then there exists a choice function* $C*(S, \{\tilde{R}_b\})$ *satisfying* $L*M*$ *(or* $L*L^{ex}$ *or* $L*J$) *and the Pareto condition* P'.

Proof: Define the relation $\bar{\bar{P}}$ such that

$$\forall x, y \in X : [x\bar{\bar{P}}y \leftrightarrow \{\forall b : (x, b) \, \tilde{P}_b \, (y, b)\}]$$

This is, of course, the Pareto relation and is transitive and asymmetric for all logically possible sets of extended orderings.

The first step in this proof is to establish that

(1) $x\bar{\bar{P}}y \rightarrow \{\forall b : xM_b^A y\}$

(2) $x\bar{\bar{P}}y \rightarrow \{\forall b : xJ_b y\}$

(3) $x\bar{\bar{P}}y \rightarrow \{\forall b : xL_b^{\text{ex}} y\}$, given the axiom of identity.

Consider (1)

$$x\bar{\bar{P}}y \rightarrow \{\not\exists (x, k) \text{ such that } \{\forall a : (y, a) \, \tilde{R}_b \, (x, k), \text{ for any } b\}$$

(We use I^A here)

$$\rightarrow \{\exists k : [\forall b \, \{\forall a : (x, a) \, \tilde{P}_b \, (y, k)\}]$$

$$\rightarrow \{\forall b : xM_b^A y\}$$

Consider (2)

$$x\bar{\bar{P}}y \rightarrow \{\forall b \, [\{\forall a : (x, b) \, \tilde{P}_a \, (y, b)]\}$$

(We use I^A here)

$$\rightarrow \{\forall a : xJ_a y\}$$

Consider (3)

$$x\bar{\bar{P}}y \rightarrow \{\forall a : xJ_a y\} \rightarrow \{\forall a : xL_a^{\text{ex}} y\}$$

Consider condition L^*M^* (see p. 18). If rights of any person b are to be implemented for $\langle x, y; b \rangle \in \mathscr{R}$ then it must be the case that $\{\forall a : xM_a^A y\}$. Also if $\{\forall a : (x, a) \, \tilde{P}_a \, (y, a)\}$, then under the axiom of identity we have $\{\forall a : xM_a^A y\}$. Thus if L^*M^* and the Parento condition P' are to dismiss all the alternatives from some subset $\{x^1, x^2, \ldots, x^h\}$ it must be the case that there exists a cycle of the form

$$\forall a : x^1 M_a^A x^2 M_a^A x^3 \ldots x^h M_a^A x^1$$

This violates the transitivity and asymmetry of the relation M^A. (cf. p. 19). An analogous argument can be constructed given L^*L^{ex} or L^*J. Thus L^*M (or L^*J or L^*L^{ex}) and P' cannot dismiss all the alternatives from any subset S of X.

The above possibility result holds for *any* rights system including 'incoherent' ones.

It is clear that the preceding proof works because the justice relation we are using to constrain the implementation of rights is *asymmetric* and *transitive*, and that under the axiom of identity these same justice relations contain the Pareto relation $\bar{\bar{P}}$ as a subrelation. Let us generalise this approach.

Let P_b^J be a justice (or some other fairness or equity relation) allocated to individual b, which for every logically possible extended ordering of individual b, is transitive and asymmetric. Let $\{P_1^J, P_2^J, \ldots, P_m^J\}$ be an m-list of 'ethical orderings', comprising of each individual's ordering of alternatives according to his *particular* relation P_b^J. Note that P_b^J need not be complete for any b, and that individuals may be using different justice or equity relations.

Define the relation $\bar{P}^J$ by

$$\forall x, y \in X : x\bar{P}^J y \leftrightarrow \{\forall b : xP_b^J y\}$$

Obviously the relation $\bar{P}^J$ is transitive and asymmetric, strictly ordering alternatives where there is a unanimous, strict ethical agreement for all individuals.

The next step is to constrain the implementation of rights to be consistent with this ordering $\bar{P}^J$.

$\bar{P}^J$-*constrained rights implementation rule* ($\bar{P}^J$RI) If $\langle x, y; b \rangle \in \mathcal{R}$, then if $(x, b) \, \tilde{P}_b \, (y, b)$ and $x\bar{P}^J y$, then $y \notin C^*(S : x \in S, \{\tilde{R}_b\})$

Combining $\bar{P}^J$RI with any rights system results in a libertarian condition that resolves the Gibbard paradox.

To guarantee a resolution of the Sen paradox we wish to ensure that $x\bar{\bar{P}}y \rightarrow x\bar{P}^J y$. Now one could constrain the allocation of justice or fairness relations P_b^J to ones that, given any set of extended orderings are implied by the relation $\bar{\bar{P}}$. Alternatively, as in Theorem 4.2.3, we can hopefully impose mild restrictions on individuals extended orderings to ensure that with a given set of ethical orderings $\{P_b^J\}$, $x\bar{\bar{P}}y \rightarrow x\bar{P}^J y$. Given this, then combining $\bar{P}^J$RI with any rights system resolves the Sen paradox.

We saw in Chapter 2 that the libertarian conditions L^*J^*, L^*M and L^*L^{ex} all failed to resolve the Gibbard paradox, even when restricting the extended orderings of individuals to conform to the axiom of complete identity (see Theorem 2.3.3, p. 18). Thus trivially they do not seem to be useful in efforts to solve the Sen paradox. However, it will prove interesting to enquire whether these conditions fail to solve the Sen paradox only because of their failure to resolve the Gibbard paradox.

Let L^c be any libertarian condition which is not vulnerable to the Gibbard paradox within the extended framework. The libertarian conditions L^G and L^P, defined in earlier chapters and suitably (and trivially) reformulated for use within the present extended framework could be examples of such an L^c. In an analogous way to the modifications of condition L^* to condition $L*J$ (or $L*L^{\mathrm{ex}}$, $L*M*$ etc.) we can modify L^{c}. Thus, for example, $L^{\mathrm{c}}M$ could be Gibbard's condition L^{G} reformulated for use within the extended utility framework, the rights implementation rule of which is further constrained by insisting that $\{\forall b : xM_b y\}$ before an individual's rights to x over y will be implemented.

Theorem 4.2.4 *If individuals extended orderings $\{\widetilde{R}_b\}$ satisfy the axiom of identity I^{A}, then there exists a choice function $C^*(S, \{\widetilde{R}_b\})$ satisfying any $L^{\mathrm{c}}M$ and the Pareto condition P'.*

Proof: Given any particular $L^{\mathrm{c}}M$, for rights to be implemented for x over y where $\{x, y\}$ assigned to an individual b, it must be the case that $\{\forall b : xM_b y\}$. From the proof of Theorem 4.2.3, $x\bar{P}y \rightarrow \{\forall b : xM_b^{\mathrm{A}} y\}$ given I^{A}. M^{A} is simply the asymmetric factor of M (remember that the Rawlsian maximin relation is transitive, reflexive and complete). Thus $x\bar{P}y \rightarrow \{\forall b : xM_b y\}$. Thus if Pareto and any $L^{\mathrm{c}}M$ are to dismiss all the alternatives from any subset $S = \{x^1, x^2, \ldots, x^h\}$ it must be the case that a cycle of the form: $\{\forall b : x^1 M_b x^2 M_b x^3 \ldots x^h M_b x^1\}$ exists. Such a cycle cannot be caused by the libertarian condition alone since it has been constructed not to be vulnerable to the Gibbard paradox (i.e. by choice of L^{c}). Thus at least one of the above links must be due to Pareto. However, for this link, the asymmetric factor of M, M^{A}, holds. Thus such a cycle violates the transitivity of the relation M.

Theorem 4.2.5 *Given that individuals' extended orderings $\{\widetilde{R}_b\}$ satisfy I^{A}, then there exists a choice function $C^*(S, \{\widetilde{R}_b\})$ satisfying any $L^{\mathrm{c}}L^{\mathrm{ex}}*$ and the Pareto condition P'.*

Proof: Define the relation R_b^{Lex} as

$$xR_b^{\mathrm{Lex}}y \leftrightarrow \{[\forall r : (x, r(x))\,\widetilde{I}_b\,(y, r(y))] \text{ or}$$

$$\exists k : 1 \leqslant k \leqslant m : [(x, k(x))\,\widetilde{P}_b\,(y, k(y)) \text{ and}$$

$$\forall r < k : (x, r(x))\,\widetilde{I}_b\,(y, r(y))]\}$$

where $r(x)$ is the rth worst off individual in state x as in the definition of leximin.

R_b^{Lex} is complete, reflexive and transitive (see Sen (1977), Section 4). L_b^{ex} is simply the asymmetric factor of R_b^{Lex}. Due to the completeness of R_b^{Lex} we have

$$\forall b : \{(\text{not } yL_b^{\mathrm{ex}}x) \leftrightarrow xR_b^{\mathrm{Lex}}y\}$$

If any $L^{\mathrm{c}}L^{\mathrm{ex}}*$ implements rights for x over y for an individual it must therefore be the case that $\{\forall b : xR_b^{\mathrm{Lex}}y\}$. Now $x\bar{P}y \rightarrow \{\forall b : xL_b^{\mathrm{ex}}y\}$ with I^{A} holding. Thus $x\bar{\bar{P}}y \rightarrow \{\forall b : xR_b^{\text{Lex}}y\}$. Thus if Pareto and any $L^cL^{\text{ex}*}$ are to dismiss all the alternatives from subset $S = \{x^1, x^2, \ldots, x^h\}$ it must be the case that a cycle of the form $\{\forall b : x^1R_b^{\text{Lex}}x^2 \ldots x^hR_b^{\text{Lex}}x^1\}$ exists. Such a cycle cannot be caused by $L^cL^{\text{ex}*}$ alone since it is constructed to avoid the Gibbard paradox. Thus at least one of the links must be due to Pareto. But the relation over this link is in fact L^{ex}, the asymmetric factor of R^{Lex}. Thus such a cycle will contradict the transitivity of the relation R^{Lex}.

It is tempting to think that an analogous possibility result will hold when using L^cJ^* but this is not so. There are many libertarian conditions that resolve the Gibbard paradox that, when modified to give L^cJ^*, and given the axiom of identity (or even the axiom of complete identity), will not resolve the Sen paradox. Kelly (1976a) proved this by considering the condition ML^s*J^* which is Sen's condition ML^s suitably adapted for use within the extended framework, the rights implementation rule of which has the added stipulation that $\{\forall b : \text{not } yJ_bx\}$ before any individual's rights to an x over y will be implemented, i.e. it is the combination of SENRS^M and SRI*(J^*) (see Chapter 3, p. 35, and Chapter 2, Section 2.3.2.3, p. 18 respectively).

Theorem 4.2.6 *There does not exist a choice function $C^*(S, \{\tilde{R}_b\})$ satisfying condition ML^s*J^* and P' even when the extended orderings $\{\tilde{R}_b\}$ are restricted to conform to the axiom of complete identity I^C.*

Proof: See Kelly (1976a) Theorem 3.

Though the rights system SENRS^M is general enough to avoid the Gibbard paradox by being constructed to be 'coherent', the above result shows that for all rights assignments consistent with SENRS^M we will still have impossibility. Analogous results will hold for many other L^cJ^*.

Now let us consider why conditions $L^cL^{\text{ex}*}$ and L^cM succeed (with the axiom of identity) to resolve the Sen paradox, but why many L^cJ^* will not.

The key aspects that are used to obtain possibility in Theorems 4.2.4 and 4.2.5 are:

(1) The relations M_b and R_b^{Lex} are transitive, complete and reflexive.
(2) Under the axiom of identity the Pareto relation $\bar{\bar{P}}$ implies the asymmetric factor of these justice relations.
(3) The libertarian condition L^c which is modified by the justice criterion, is not vulnerable to the Gibbard paradox by construction.

The problem with L^cJ^* is that, though the Suppes relation J_b is transitive and asymmetric, the relation 'not J_b' is *not* transitive for all $\tilde{R}_b$.

Apart from Kelly (1976a), Suzumura (1978) has also produced a result in this area and I should put my results in the context of his. In this paper, Suzumura proved a result very similar to my Theorem 4.2.3 here (see

Table 1. *Summary of results presented within the extended utility framework*

| Conditions | None | Restrictions on Extended Orderings | |
		I^A	I^C
$L*J$	√ (See Theorem 2.3.4) →	√ ⟶	√
$L*M*$	√ (See Theorem 2.3.4) →	√ ⟶	√
$L*L^{ex}$	√ (See Theorem 2.3.4) →	√ ⟶	√
$L*J*$	× ⟵	× ⟵	× (See Theorem 2.3.3)
$L*M$	× ⟵	× ⟵	× (See Theorem 2.3.3)
$L*L^{ex}*$	× ⟵	× ⟵	× (See Theorem 2.3.3)
$L*J + P'$	× (See Theorem 3.4.4)	√ (See Theorem 4.2.3) →	√
$L*M* + P'$	× (See Theorem 3.4.3)	√ (See Theorem 4.2.3) →	√
$L*L^{ex} + P'$	× (See Theorem 3.4.3)	√ (See Theorem 4.2.3) →	√
$L^c M + P'$	×	√ (See Theorem 4.2.4) →	√
$L^c L^{ex}* + P'$	×	√ (See Theorem 4.2.5) →	√
$ML^{S}*J* + P'$	× ⟵	× ⟵	× (See Theorem 4.2.6)

Key i   A tick (√) signifies the existence of a choice function $C*(S, \{\tilde{R}_b\})$ satisfying the stipulated conditions and given the stipulated restriction on the extended orderings.

ii   A cross (×) signifies the non-existence of a choice function $C*(S, \{\tilde{R}_b\})$ satisfying the stipulated conditions and given the stipulated restriction on the extended orderings.

iii   The implication arrows (→) indicate which result is implied by another.

Suzumura (1978), Theorem 3), but:

(1) He stipulated the rights system was coherent by construction. He did not have to since Theorem 4.2.3 holds for *any* rights system.

(2) He stipulated that the extended orderings $\{\tilde{R}_b\}$ satisfy the axiom of *complete* identity. This is a much stronger restriction on extended preferences than the axiom of identity which is used here.

(3) He used only $L*M*$ and did not consider using $L*J$ or $L*L^{ex}$ which also gives rise to possibility.[1]

Consider now a summary of my results in this area (see table 1).

---

[1] Suzumura (1982) has more recently produced another paper which makes some generalisations which are similar to my own. In particular, he realises that he did not have to assume the axiom of *complete* identity in Theorem 3 in his 1978 paper, though he still seems to think that a coherent rights assignment is necessary. This more recent paper of Suzumura came to my attention after I had formulated my results in this area.

4.3   Motivation behind rights implementation modification approaches

4.3.1   *Gibbard's L^{GP}* (see p. 48)

Gibbard's motivation behind L^{GP} is given by a particular example of a conflict of interests. What he attempts to show is that his rights implementation rule GPRI is a rule which individuals would voluntarily follow given that they wish to exploit their self-interest in a given situation. Consider Gibbard's motivational example:

Angelina wants to marry Edwin but will settle for the judge, who wants whatever she wants. Edwin wants to remain single, but would rather wed Angelina than see her wed the judge. There are, then, three alternatives:
  w_E: Edwin weds Angelina.
  w_J: The judge weds Angelina and Edwin remains single.
  w_0: Both Edwin and Angelina remain single.
Angelina prefers them in order $w_E w_J w_0$: Edwin, in order $w_0 w_E w_J$.

Here naive considerations of rights and the Pareto principle combine to yield a cycle. First, Angelina has a right to marry the willing judge instead of remaining single, and she prefers w_J to w_0. Hence $w_J P w_0$. Next, Edwin has the right to remain single rather than wed Angelina, and he prefers w_0 to w_E, where the only difference between the two is in whether or not he weds her. Therefore $w_0 P w_E$. Finally, since all prefer w_E to w_J, by the Pareto principle we have $w_e P w_J$. The cycle is complete: $w_J P w_0$, $w_0 P w_E$ and $w_E P w_J$. (Gibbard, 1974, p. 398)

(The relation P in the above extract is defined by Gibbard as $xPy \leftrightarrow y \notin C(S : x \in S, \{R_b\})$, thus rights implementation and the Pareto condition are defined in the same way as in the framework I use in this book.)

Consider how Gibbard considers that this conflict ought to be resolved. Consider again Angelina's and Edwin's preferences:

Angelina (a)	Edwin (e)	
w_E	w_0	
w_J	w_E	descending order of strict
w_0	w_J	preference

The rights assignment is $\{\langle w_J, w_0; a \rangle, \langle w_0, w_E; e \rangle\}$. Angelina will definitely wish to implement her rights, this dismisses her worst alternative, and thus must surely be the rational thing to do. Gibbard's implementation rule GPRI will also enforce her rights since there does not exist a sequence satisfying the stipulated conditions (i) (ii) and (iii) (see p. 48). Consider now Edwin: given we wish to give him the power voluntarily to exercise, or waive his rights, he can if he so wishes dismiss w_E because he wants there to be a better chance that the more preferable w_0 will be chosen. However he should realise (and Gibbard assumes this information is available to him) that Angelina will exercise her rights and thus w_0 will not be chosen. Thus Edwin will see that by exercising his rights he will, in effect, be securing that w_J will be chosen, but Edwin prefers w_E to w_J. If Edwin waives his right then w_E *or* w_J will be chosen. Given this 'it may be to Edwin's advantage to waive his right to w_0 over w_E in favour of the Pareto principle'. Thus Gibbard argues that 'left freely to bargain away their rights, then Edwin and Angelina would agree to the outcome w_E: wedding each other'. (Gibbard (1974), p. 398).

Now Edwin, assessing the situation, will follow Gibbard's rights implementation rule. Edwin notes that there exists a sequence $\Sigma = w_J w_0$ such that

   (i) w_0 is the preferred alternative in his assigned pair

   (ii) w_J is less preferred to w_E

   (iii) $\langle w_J, w_0; a \rangle \in \mathscr{R}$ and $w_J P_a w_0$.

Thus the three aspects that give rise to the existence of a sequence Σ in Gibbard's rights implementation rule are all satisfied with the above example as far as Edwin is concerned, thus $w_0 W_e w_E$ [$\mathscr{R}$], and Edwin's rights will be waived.

It is clear that Gibbard views his rights implementation rule as consistent with 'voluntary rights exercising' and that rights will be waived for a person b only if it is to *his* advantage for them to be waived.

Gibbard's argument, as reproduced above, can be criticised on many grounds.

(1) *Gibbard's motivation behind GPRI is at variance with his motivation behind GRI* Ironically Gibbard's solution to the Sen paradox is arrived at by apparently giving individuals more power to exploit their self interest, a self interest that heavily relies on other people's preferences with respect to their issues. Busybodyness is encouraged.

True, the preferences that would make us agree to it stem from nosiness, but a person's motives, such a libertarian could say, are his own business. There is a strong libertarian tradition of free contract, and on that tradition, a person's rights are his to use or bargain away as he sees fit. (Gibbard, 1974, p. 397)

However, with GRI (see p. 12), the implementation rule which Gibbard uses to resolve his Gibbard paradox, people taking an interest in other people's affairs (in the form of choosing their own issue contingent on other people's issues) is penalised as not conforming to what a libertarian claim should allow (cf. the discussion in Chapter 2).

With GPRI, individuals who do not display unconditional preferences are given some rights, specifically what Gibbard calls '1st order rights', i.e. rights over assigned pairs where the less preferred alternative in an individual pair is the uniquely less preferred alternative for that individual in his ordering over the available set S.

(2) *Ethical interpretation of the resolution procedure* Gibbard's solution relies on individuals pursuing their self-interest as revealed by their actual preferences over the set of alternatives. He does not allow for individuals to withhold or retain rights on 'ethical' grounds. That is, accepting for the moment that Gibbard's rights implemented rule (GPRI) does allow individuals to exploit their self-interest, it does not allow them to exploit their ethical interest.

Sen (1976) has pointed out an alternative set of motives behind the Gibbardian example.

Angelina loves the judge – truly – and would have preferred most to marry him but for her fury at being scorned by the unwillingness of Edwin ('Oh, I hate him!') to marry her ('I *will*, Edwin, just you see!'), and hence her strict order: $w_E w_J w_0$. Edwin hates Angelina's guts ('in so fas as she has any'), and knowing that she will be very happy married to the judge, he would do anything to stop her, even – if need be – himself marrying her ('that will teach her all right'), and hence his strict order $w_0 w_E w_J$. While Gibbard makes arrangements for the wedding of Edwin and Angelina, Edwin can do worse than recite: 'I don't want to wed Angelina and have a right not to – I won't let Gibbard "waive" it; and to stop Angelina from getting happiness married to the judge is none of my bloody business, and my perverse preference on this should not really affect whether they marry or not'. One can, indeed, in such a situation make a case for respecting Edwin's right not to wed Angelina, but not attach great social importance to his views on whether Angelina should marry the judge. (p. 227).

Sen is making the distinction between self-interest, i.e. preferences revealed by an individual, and that individual's moral evaluation of his preference. In the above alternative explanation, Edwin pursuing his self-interest may well waive his rights, but if he judges that 'to stop Angelina from getting happiness married to the judge is none of my bloody business' then Edwin may well decide to exercise his rights. If Gibbard's GRPI is to truly reflect voluntary rights exercising it must reflect both an individual's preferences and his ethical evaluation in the form of allowing individuals to decide whether their self-centred preference *should* count in social choice. Gibbard's GPRI is altogether too inflexible in that he assumes that individuals will always wish to follow their self-interest independent of their sense of morality in a given situation.

(3) *Pragmatic interpretation of the resolution procedure* Let us suppose, for the sake of argument, that individuals will always wish to exploit their self-interest and that their 'ethical' evaluation is consistent with their true preferences. (Thus, Edwin, in Sen's interpretation of motives, will selfishly waive his right despite realising that he is going to on grounds that are none of his business.) I should point out that although to an outsider Edwin's actions here might seem deplorable, on libertarian grounds he *should* be allowed to waive his rights if he so wished. My previous point against Gibbard's GPRI is that it cannot fully reflect an individual's *total* assessment (ethical and self-centred) of a situation.

So, assuming individuals exercise or waive rights dependent on whether it is personally advantageous to do so, does Gibbard's GPRI conform to such action? The answer is a resounding no. There are also many reasons for this.

(a) First, to take a trivial point, Gibbard has an individual b waive his right to dismiss an alternative y from the choice set if and only if for some z, z not equal to y; yR_bz and there exists the stipulated sequence Σ. But since an individual, ending up with an alternative indifferent to y, is not at any disadvantage, why not insist that yP_bz? Gibbard's stipulation of yR_bz and $z \neq y$, rather than having yP_bz is in fact crucial for his possibility result to go through since his 'rights system' is the 'standard rights system' SRS. I discuss this point again in Appendix A of this chapter. It was Kelly (1976b) who first criticised Gibbard on this point, though he did not realise that it was so crucial for Gibbard's result to hold.

(b) Secondly, an individual, having found an alternative at the end of sequence Σ that he likes less than y should make sure that it *is* the alternative he *will* be forced to end up with if he exercises his rights. If not, an individual should consider what will be the alternative.

Consider the following preferences over four alternatives for two individuals:

1	2	
x	y	
w	w	descending order of
y	z	strict preference
z	x	

Let $\langle x, y; 1 \rangle$, $\langle z, x; 2 \rangle \in \mathscr{R}$. Now according to Gibbard's GPRI individual 1 will waive his rights over the pair (x, y). Individual 1 will observe the sequence $\Sigma = zx$, and note that $\langle z, x; 2 \rangle \in \mathscr{R}$ and zP_2x, and given that yP_1z realise that the conditions (i) (ii) and (iii), stated in the condition for rights waiving (see p. 48), are satisfied. He will thus waive his right. But this quite simply ignores the fact that $\Sigma = zx$ is part of an extended sequence of alternatives: wzx. Although person 2's exercising of his rights to z over x eliminates x in favour of z, the Pareto condition eliminates z in favour of w, and we have $wP_1 y$! In effect the sequence $\Sigma' = wz$ repairs the trouble caused by $\Sigma = zx$. Kelly (1976*b*) noted this and argued that individuals, given the information assumed available by Gibbard, should also take note of this. If individual 1 exercises his right in the above case, w will be chosen. If he waives his right, as Gibbard would have him do, w or the less preferred y will be chosen. This is obviously an inferior option.

(c) Thirdly, individuals following GPRI assume that others automatically exercise their rights. However, given that all individuals follow GPRI, this assumption can be erroneous. Kelly (1976*b*) claims that such miscalculations are correctable. Consider his example. There are four alternatives and three individuals. Preferences are:

1	2	3	
y	z	x	descending
x	x	z	order of
w	w	w	strict
z	y	y	preference

Let $\mathscr{R} = \{\langle y, z; 1\rangle, \langle z, x; 2\rangle, \langle x, w; 3\rangle\}$. Person 1 will exercise rights given GPRI. Person 2 will waive his rights to (z, x) on the correct belief that person 1 will exercise his rights. Person 3 will also waive his rights. ($\langle z, x. 2\rangle \in \mathscr{R}$ and $zP_2 x$, $\langle y, z; 1\rangle \in \mathscr{R}$ and $yP_1 z$, and $wP_3 y$, together establish the sequence $\Sigma = yzx$, satisfying the stipulated properties.)

However, the belief that person 2 will exercise his rights is incorrect. Person 2 will waive his rights. According to Kelly this miscalculation is correctable, i.e. person 3 will note that person 2 will waive his rights and therefore *not* include $\Sigma = zx$ in his search for a sequence that could lead him into trouble. Thus person 3 will exercise his rights. Kelly seems to be under the impression that all such miscalucations are correctable. I wish to contest this. Consider the following preferences for two individuals.

1	2	
x	z	
y	w	descending order of
z	x	strict preference
w	y	

Let the rights system be $\mathscr{R} = \{\langle y, z; 1 \rangle, \langle w, x; 2 \rangle\}$. Given Gibbard's GPRI both will waive their rights. This occurs because they each think the other is exercising their rights! But is this miscalulation correctable? If they both see the other not exercising rights, correcting this, will they not both now exercise their rights? However, this action is also a mistake since each would expect the other to keep waiving his right! We have a game problem with no obvious answer.

Concluding on the points made so far: GPRI does not conform to Gibbard's motivation that his rights implementation rule is consistent with voluntary rights exercising because, (a) it does not allow for individuals suppressing their self-interest (as revealed by their preferences) due to an ethical evaluation of the example in question; (b) individuals following the rule, even given correct assumptions about other people's rights waiving, can end up with an inferior consequence than if they did not follow the rule; (c) individuals following GPRI will make mistakes as regards other people's waiving/exercising decisions which are not self-evidently correctable.

This is sufficient to dismiss Gibbard's motivation behind his GPRI as not relevant to the rule he formalised. Kelly (1976b) and Suzumura (1980) have both spent much time considering amendments to Gibbard's GPRI that take account of the failure of GPRI to conform to Gibbard's motivation. Some aspects of their arguments and attempted amendments are discussed in Appendix A of this chapter. They are confined to this appendix on the grounds that the arguments are tedious, and the suggested revised rules that try and conform to voluntary rights exercising (a) are too complicated, (b) often fail to solve the Sen paradox, and (c) always fail to be consistent with voluntary rights exercising. The conclusion of the appendix is that it is not possible to form any rights implementation rule, based on preferences revealed by individuals, that will conform to voluntary rights exercising.

However, Gibbard's GPRI can still be considered as a way to solve the Sen paradox, independent of his original motivation. It can be seen as a mechanical resolution to the Sen paradox and can be judged on other criteria such as information, efficiency etc.

(4) *Gibbard's motivation and his standard rights system* Given that Gibbard retains the standard rights system SRS throughout his 1974 article, it is strange that the Angelina–Edwin–Judge example, chosen to justify his approach, fails to be consistent with his own specification of the rights assignment.

Consider the three alternatives:

w_E = (Angelina marries Edwin, Angelina does not marry the judge)

w_J = (Angelina does not marry Edwin, Angelina marries the judge)

$w_0 =$ (Angelina does not marry Edwin, Angelina does not marry the judge).

The first issue in each alternative seems to be Angelina's marital status as regards Edwin, the second issue is Angelina's marital status as regards the judge. Given that Gibbard assumes that features are technologically separable (i.e. the set X is the cartesian product $M_1 \times M_2 \times \ldots \times M_n$) then we must also consider the possibility of the following alternative

$w_{EJ} =$ (Angelina marries Edwin, Angelina marries the judge)

Let us accept this strange alternative as admissable within the definition of X, the total set of alternatives, and consider the rights assignment. Edwin is given the rights to remain single over marrying Angelina. Thus he is given rights $\langle w_0, w_E; e \rangle \in \mathscr{R}$. In a sense these are j-variants, i.e. Angelina's marital status as regards the judge is the same for both alternatives. However, according to SRS Edwin should also have rights over $\langle w_E, w_0; e \rangle \in \mathscr{R}$, i.e. that he should have *rights* to marry Angelina! Also given the possibility of alternative w_{EJ} Edwin should, given SRS, have rights $\langle w_J, w_{EJ}; e \rangle$ and $\langle w_{EJ}, w_J; e \rangle$.

Consider now Angelina's rights: $\langle w_J, w_0; a \rangle \in \mathscr{R}$. Gibbard gives Angelina rights to marry the judge but this is dependent on the judge being willing. There is nothing in the definition of SRS that says rights should be *assigned* dependent on other people's preferences!

Clearly then the above example does not fit well into Gibbard's issue framework.

(5) *Gibbard's own realisation that GPRI does not conform to voluntary exercising of rights* A final point in this rather long section on Gibbard's motivation behind L^{GP} is that at the end of his article Gibbard seems at pains to show that his rights exercising rule does not waive many rights. In his last section entitled 'The strength of the claim', Gibbard states that rights under his regime 'must be waived only in exceptional circumstances'. He sees 'danger' that rights might be waived too often; but why is he bothered about this? If we accept his motivation and suppose that his rule does conform to his motivation, i.e. that people should 'use or bargain away rights as they see fit' then surely we should not be bothered about the frequency of such rights waiving? It makes more sense analysing the strength of the claim (see Section 4.5 on efficiency later) independently of Gibbard's motivation.

4.3.2   *Gaertner and Krüger's L^{SSP}* (see p. 49)

Gaertner and Krüger (henceforth GK) motivate their approach by arguing that condition L (SRS and SRI) is not prima facie a reasonable libertarian condition. By formulating what they consider to be an appropriate libertarian condition (i.e. L^{SSP}) they find that the Sen paradox is avoided in the process. GK's motivation is based on that of an approach initiated by Blau (1975).

Blau states that if a person 'feels more strongly', in a particular way, about other people's assigned pairs than his own, he should be branded 'meddlesome' and therefore should have his rights taken away. The 'strength' of an individual's preference in Blau's analysis is deduced from an individual's *ordinal* preferences:

Ordinal intensity If a person b prefers x to y, y to z and z to w then his preference for x over w is stronger than his preference for y over z. (Or equivalently his preference for y over z is weaker than his preference for x over w.) Furthermore, this is so even if he is indifferent between x and y or between z and w, but not both.

Meddlesomeness A person b is meddlesome if and only if his preference over two alternatives in his own assigned pair is weaker than his opposition to someone else's preferences over that person's assigned pair.

Blau shows that if at least one person is not meddlesome in each configuration of individual preferences, then in a two person society the Pareto condition and Sen's condition L^S (equivalent to ML^S in this case, see p. 35) cannot lead to impossibility. In the *Lady Chatterley's Lover* illustration (see Chapter 3), both persons are meddlesome, and Blau solves the conflict by modifying the libertarian condition such that it 'invokes the "Golden Rule": persons who do not grossly meddle in the private affairs of others shall have their own respected' (Blau (1975), p. 397). GK extend this idea for use with the standard rights system (SRS). Blau used only SENRS and this is one reason for the limited nature of his possibility result. GK, by relating the idea of meddlesomeness over social alternatives to meddlesomeness over feature alternatives within the social alternative, obtain a possibility result for any number of individuals.

GK illustrates their extension to Blau's idea with the *Lady Chatterley's Lover* example formulated within an issue framework. Let the three alternatives involved in this example be explicitly defined in terms of issues as follows:

$$w = (NR_1, NR_2)$$
$$x = (NR_1, R_2)$$
$$y = (R_1, NR_2)$$

where R_1 and NR_1 are the lascivious reading and not reading the book respectively, R_2 and NR_2 are the prude reading and not reading the book respectively. In line with SRS, issue 1 is assigned to the lascivious and issue 2 is assigned to the prude. Now, the above list, read top to bottom, reflects the prude's preferences. We see that he prefers NR_2 to R_2 when the lascivious's feature is NR_1, but his concern for seeing the lascivious not reading the book (NR_1) is so great that the prude prefers (NR_1, R_2) to (R_1, NR_2). The prude is showing meddlesome behaviour in the sense that opposition to the lascivious reading the book is so great that he is willing to read the book himself to avoid this. We see that the prude 'does not support' his preferences over his personal features in a straight-forward manner. GK applying Blau's 'Golden Rule' thus maintains that the prude's meddlesomeness should be penalised by having his rights taken away. An analogous arrangement holds for the lascivious. GK generalise the 'moral' of this example and state:

This suggests that something is 'wrong' within this system of libertarian protection where the individual

(a) is being granted an absolute protection of a particular preference of his from all social interference, and

(b) is being allowed to deviate from this very preference in other parts of his ordering, parts that he expects no less to be counted in the social choice process.

We shall therefore argue that no individual can have it both ways, namely unconditional social protection of his private sphere *and* maximal gains from collective decisions. (Gaertner and Krüger, 1981, p. 245)

GK thus claim that individuals who stay away from such trade-offs, i.e. who preserve an ordering over their own feature alternatives, in order to secure social protection for their choice between them, should then and only then have their rights respected. It is in this case that individuals have 'self-supporting preferences' (SSP).

Within the framework in which I have formulated GK's SSP we see that a person must preserve his ordering over his feature alternatives (with the possibility of becoming indifferent between them) in his ordering of social alternatives. Thus, for example, given a person b with a set of feature alternatives $M_j = \{x_j, y_j\}$ then given his preferences over social alternatives it must be the case, if he is to have rights over j-variants, that all the alternatives that contain x_j must be at least as preferred, or alternatively at least as worse, as *all* the alternatives which contain y_j.

This then is GK's motivation. The motivation has similarities with Gibbard's motivation behind GRI (p. 20) in that people are being penalised for busybodiness. Though it is obvious that individuals displaying 'unconditional preferences' with respect to their issues need not be displaying 'self-supporting preferences', it should be noted that individuals displaying self-supporting preferences need not be displaying unconditional preferences. To see this, consider the following preferences for individual b who we will assign issue 1:

$$(x_1, y_2, z)\, P_b\, (y_1, y_2, z)\, I_b\, (y_1, x_2, z)\, I_b\, (x_1, x_2, z)$$

where $z = x_3, x_4, \ldots, x_n$, the same for all four alternatives. Here individual b is displaying SSP but not unconditional preferences. Given $(x_1, y_2, z)\, P_b\, (y_1, y_2, z)$ the individual would also have to have the preference $(x_1, x_2, z)\, P_b\, (y_1, x_2, z)$ to display unconditional preference with respect to issue 1.

Note that with GK's definition of SSPRI it is required to look at preferences of individuals over the total set X of alternatives in deducing whether they have SSP. GK define the total set as the set of all 'technologically feasible' alternatives. Given an available set S, a proper subset of X, individuals' rights to assigned pairs in S will thus depend on preferences over alternatives not in fact available. For example, assume the following proper subset of X, $S = \{(x_1, z), (y_1, z)\}$, is available. Assume individual b is assigned issue 1 and has preferences $(x_1, z)\, P_b\, (y_1, z)$. Over this *available* set, individual b satisfies SSP. GK however seek to determine whether individual b satisfies SSP with respect to *all* technologically feasible alternatives in X, including the unavailable ones. Thus potential meddlesome behaviour with respect to feature alternatives in social alternatives which are not in fact available will result in b's rights over the subset S being axed. Individuals must be non-meddlesome to a very high degree to have their rights respected!

For an individual to satisfy SSP, he must 'support' his preference over all feature alternatives in his set M_j before he can have rights to any pair of j-variants. Consider an individual b with a set of feature alternatives $M_j = \{x_j, w_j, y_j\}$. Assume that there are only six technologically feasible alternatives and thus the following preferences for individual b can be assumed to be over the total set X:

$$(w_j, z)\, P_b\, (x_j, z)\, P_b\, (x_j, z')\, P_b\, (y_j, z)\, P_b\, (y_j, z')\, P_b\, (w_j, z')$$

where z and z' are two different vectors of feature alternatives other than for issue j. This individual does not manifest SSP and thus according to L^{SSP} will have no rights over any pairs of j-variants. However, with regard to the alternatives that do not contain w_j, the individual does prefer all the alternatives that contain x_j to all those that contain y_j. His meddlesome behaviour manifests itself because of the alternatives which contain w_j. To take away rights over pairs of j-variants, one of which contains w_j, thus does seem to be consistent with GK's motivation, but should individual b also be penalised over pairs of j-variants neither of which contain w_j? I think this penalty is too severe even within the context of accepting GK's motivation behind this approach. Where an individual b prefers all alternatives which contain his personal feature x_j to all alternatives which contain his personal feature y_j then with respect to all j-variants x and y which respectively include x_j and y_j he should have rights, despite violating SSP, with respect to ordering of alternatives containing other feature alternatives. Consider an individual who is given a large feature set, say $M_j = \{x_j, y_j, z_j, w_j, v_j, s_j\}$. Assume that except for the position of one alternative, say $(s_j, \mathbf{z})$, this individual orders all his alternatives in a manner which satisfies SSP. We could have an ordering over hundreds of alternatives, many of which could be j-variants. However, because the individual places $(s_j, \mathbf{z})$ in his ordering such that his total ordering fails to satisfy SSP, he will have all pairs of j-variants (possibly hundreds of them) axed. Surely this is too severe!

Now I come to my central criticism. GK accept, totally, Blau's 'Golden Rule': persons who do not grossly meddle in the private affairs of others shall have their own respected and only then. However, I would argue that it is not acceptable. Given SRS is the appropriate assignment of rights, I consider SRI to be the appropriate rights implementation rule. However, accepting SRI can lead to conflict cases. Assuming Pareto is more desirable than rights then SRI must be restricted so that (a) rights do not conflict with themselves, and (b) rights are consistent with Pareto. The reasons for restricting SRI here is because we must, to avoid conflict, not because SRI is prima facie inappropriate. GK consider that rights over assigned pairs should be conditional on how 'nosey' people are about other personal issues. We must not forget that the pairs assigned to an individual with SRS differ only with respect to that individual's issue; rights which are implemented are only over these pairs. To make such rights conditional on how nosey the individual is, this being deduced from his ordering over other pairs, seems to me to reduce the concept of a right to a strange notion indeed. Condition L^{SSP} is a protection of rights for self-centred people, but many non-self-centred people would object:

I like to read Economica and believe it to be a personal act deserving protection. There are others who have similar preferences, which I happen to know. Given the choice between I alone reading Economica (and others having been stopped from doing so), and all other hungry souls devouring Economica with I alone being prevented from reading it, I choose the latter (as a good libertarian should) – GK now inform me . . . [that L^{SSP}] will do nothing for my rights to read Economica. I protest, more importantly I protest as a libertarian. (A. K. Sen)[1]

Finally, even supposing we disapprove of individual's meddling behaviour, such that we wish to penalise this individual for such nosiness, why punish by axing rights? The following example taken almost entirely from Sen (1976) shows that, given a conflict between rights and Pareto, GK's solution method basically protects the meddlesome part of individual's behaviour.

Let persons 1 and 2 each have a part-time job, and suppose the possibility arises of a full-time job being available. Each prefers more of a job to less (i.e. 1 to $\frac{1}{2}$ to 0) given the job situation of the other, but prefers that the other

---

[1] This quotation is taken from a communication from A. K. Sen to W. Gaertner concerning Gaertner and Krüger's paper in Economica (1981).

should be jobless (i.e. 0 to $\frac{1}{2}$ to 1 for the other), spoilt as they are by the competitive society in which they live. In fact, they are each 'meddlesome' enough to attach greater importance to the other being jobless than to their own job situation. Consider now four alternative possibilities with the first number standing for person 1's job state and the second for person 2's: $(1, \frac{1}{2})$, $(0, \frac{1}{2})$, $(\frac{1}{2}, 1)$ and $(\frac{1}{2}, 0)$. On grounds of having the right to work if one wishes to, no matter what others want, the choice over $(1, \frac{1}{2})$ and $(0, \frac{1}{2})$ may be assigned to person 1 and that over $(\frac{1}{2}, 1)$ and $(\frac{1}{2}, 0)$ to person 2, since the job of the other person in each case is unaffected. This will lead to either $(1, \frac{1}{2})$ or $(\frac{1}{2}, 1)$ as the solution, eliminating $(0, \frac{1}{2})$ and $(\frac{1}{2}, 0)$ on libertarian grounds.

Let the two persons have the following strict orders, for reasons mentioned above:

Person 1	Person 2
$(\frac{1}{2}, 0)$	$(0, \frac{1}{2})$
$(1, \frac{1}{2})$	$(\frac{1}{2}, 1)$
$(0, \frac{1}{2})$	$(\frac{1}{2}, 0)$
$(\frac{1}{2}, 1)$	$(1, \frac{1}{2})$

Both individuals fail to satisfy SSP and the liberal privilege will be withheld from each. On grounds of the Pareto principle, the choice of $(1, \frac{1}{2})$ or $(\frac{1}{2}, 1)$ should be avoided since both are Pareto inferior, and the choice should be confined to $(0, \frac{1}{2})$ and $(\frac{1}{2}, 0)$. But this amounts precisely to permitting the meddlesome parts of the two persons' preferences to hold sway. Left to himself, person 1 will prefer to work more, i.e. will choose $(1, \frac{1}{2})$ over $(0, \frac{1}{2})$, and left to himself person 2 will prefer to work more also, i.e. will choose $(\frac{1}{2}, 1)$ over $(\frac{1}{2}, 0)$, despite meddling by the other in each case, and GK's solution amounts to eliminating the non-meddlesome part of one's preference and retaining the influence of meddling.

A more appropriate solution would seem to be to respect the self-regarding or the non-meddling parts, namely 1's preference for $(1, \frac{1}{2})$ over $(0, \frac{1}{2})$ and 2's for $(\frac{1}{2}, 1)$ over $(\frac{1}{2}, 0)$, and to ignore the non-self-regarding parts and the Pareto relations based on them.

The same point holds for the *Lady Chatterley's Lover* example. Both the lascivious and the prude fail to satisfy SSP and all rights will be axed. But this leaves the Pareto principle to endorse the meddlesome preferences, i.e. both preferring (NR_1, R_2) to (R_1, NR_2).

I do not wish to say now that in all conflict cases the Pareto principle should be axed rather than rights – this depends on our disapproval of the meddlesome nature of the individual's behaviour. (I will discuss this in Chapter 5 and again in Chapter 6.) What is important here, however, is that if we disapprove of the nosey behaviour then axing rights implies, in cases of conflict with Pareto, that the Pareto condition will endorse the meddlesome (or non-self-centred) parts of the individual's orderings.

4.3.3　*The use of justice principles to constrain rights* (see p. 50)

The motivation behind these approaches that solve the Sen paradox extends the motivation behind the same type of approaches which solve the Gibbard paradox (see Chapter 2). Justice, as revealed by a specific relation over pairs of alternatives, is considered more desirable than rights, so much so that rights, for an individual b, will only be implemented if everybody agrees that b's preferences, in some specific sense, are just preferences. Now with these procedures used in resolving the Gibbard paradox, each individual's evaluation of justice is based on his 'extended ordering'. Each individual ranks alternatives such as (x, b) and (y, a), where (x, b) is state x when putting oneself in the position of b, and (y, a) is state y when putting oneself in a's position. For honest revelation of such preferences each individual must assess the objective circumstances of other individuals, but he is free to impose his own tastes: 'each individual can make comparisons in terms of his own tastes on behalf of himself as well as that of others' (Sen (1970a), p.150).

For the procedures in this context that resolve the Sen paradox, this motivation is extended in that our individual's assessment of an alternative in someone else's position is not just conditional on the more obvious objective circumstances of that individual. It is now argued that:

Placing oneself in the position of the other should involve not merely having the latter's objective circumstances but also identifying oneself with the other in terms of his subjective features. (Sen, (1970a), p. 150)

'Subjective features' means, in particular, 'tastes'. Thus the axiom of identity (I^A) is imposed such that each individual b placing himself in the position of a person c takes on the tastes and preferences of person c.

On ethical grounds the axiom of identity can be considered as an important part of the exercise of 'extended sympathy'. This extended sympathy is based on the so-called golden rule of the Gospel: 'Do unto others as ye would that others do unto you'. This is amusingly illustrated by the celebrated epitaph of Martin Engelbrodde, which Arrow (1963) quoted as an example of this approach of 'extended sympathy':

> Here lies Martin Engelbrodde,
> 　Ha'e mercy on my soul, Lord God,
> As I would do were I Lord God,
> 　And Thou wert Martin Engelbrodde.

My main objections to the approaches developed in Section 4.2.3 are based on:

(1) The notion that justice should always outrank rights.

(2) That the specific formulation of the libertarian conditions require a *unanimous* 'positive' agreement that any rights implemented must be just.

(3) The imposition of the axiom of identity domain restriction.

(1) Taking justice now in general terms, it must surely be accepted, in line with Berlin's statement (quoted in Chapter 2, p. 23), that 'the extent of a man's liberty must be weighed against the claims of many other values of which . . . justice . . . [is one of the] . . . most obvious examples'. What is not suggested is that justice should always outrank rights. Dependent on the notion of justice that is introduced, and the case in question, then maybe rights in some cases should be axed on the basis of violation of justice, but never always. There must be many cases where individual rights should outrank justice, and in these cases these approaches to solving the Sen paradox (or the Gibbard paradox) will not be a morally appropriate solution.

(2) For me, even more objectionable, is that rights for an individual b can only be implemented with these approaches if there is unanimous agreement that individual b's preferences are just. Take first the set of approaches where each individual is allocated a transitive and asymmetric justice relation (e.g. J_b, M_b^A, L_b^{Lex}) which we can call P_b^J (see p. 52). With these approaches, before rights can be implemented by an individual b for an alternative x over a y, it must be the case that $\forall b : xP_b^J y$. Such required unanimous agreement is too severe. It may be the case that each individual is 'neutral' with regard to some person's assigned pair in the sense that $\forall b : \{$not $xP_b^J y$ and not $yP_b^J x\}$ (note that P_b^J is not necessarily complete). In a significant sense the exercise of rights here will not positively violate justice, but rights will be axed in such cases. Also everybody but one individual could agree that $xP_b^J y$, but an individual's rights for x over y will be axed. Thus even if it was accepted that justice should always outrank rights, it surely cannot be agreed that they should be outranked in this way.

Take now the procedures which further constrain the rights implementation rule of a libertarian condition which is not vulnerable to the Gibbard paradox, e.g. $L^c M$ and $L^c L^{ex}*$ (see p. 52). Each individual with these approaches is allocated a complete, transitive and reflexive justice relation R_b^J (e.g. $L_b^{ex}*$, M_b). It now can not be the case that $\forall b : \{$not $xR_b^J y$ and not $yR_b^J x\}$. However, there might still be objections to cases where an individual's rights to x over y are axed because just *one* individual b reveals $\{$not $xR_b^J y\}$, others revealing $xR_b^J y$.

Given this motivational criticism one natural question to ask is: can the libertarian conditions be respecified such that it is not necessary to have a unanimous positive agreement that an individual's rights to an x over y are just, but require something weaker? Some such weakenings are considered in the second appendix of this chapter (Appendix B). It is seen that such respecifications fail to resolve the Sen paradox.

(3) The key assumption that ensures that resolutions to the Gibbard paradox will also resolve the Sen paradox is the imposition of the axiom of identity. Given the motivation underlying these approaches it would indeed be desirable that individuals' preferences do satisfy this axiom and thus exhibit extended sympathy − it would be desirable anyway. However, accepting this desirability of having individuals satisfy this axiom, does not overcome the problem that is a domain restriction. If individuals do not reveal preferences that are consistent with I^A, which they are presumably free to do, then what should be done? I find 'domain restriction' as a method of solving paradoxes of social choice very objectionable since such approaches say nothing of what to do when the restrictions are not satisfied.

4.4   Informational requirements

The informational requirements for the procedures discussed in Section 4.2 will now be stated. These 'costs' must be weighed against the other features of these procedures discussed in the other sections (e.g. the discussion on motivation in the previous section).

4.4.1   *Gibbard's L^{GP}* (see Section 4.2.1, p. 48)

Under Gibbard's motivational interpretation, i.e. that individuals follow the rights implementation rule 'voluntarily' in pursuit of their self-interest, there is no role for an 'authority' or 'moral arbitrator'. Each individual assesses for himself the decision to 'exercise' or 'waive' his rights. According to Gibbard each individual would use the implementation rule GPRI for this assessment. Individuals are thus assumed to have much information: apart from knowledge of their own assigned pairs they must know all other individuals' assigned pairs and they each must know everybody's preferences over the available set of alternatives. As well as being assumed to have this information they must be able to use it such that they can, consistent with GPRI, exercise or waive their rights.

However, as shown in Section 4.3.1 and in Appendix A of this chapter, Gibbard's GPRI does *not* conform to his motivation, and thus should be best seen as a resolution procedure for the Sen paradox independently of the original motivation leading to its construction. Thus we can now view the operation of this rule as follows. Each individual reveals his preferences over the available set. These are reported to a moral arbitrator who armed with Gibbard's rights implementation rule will decide who should be allowed to exercise their rights.

4.4.2 Gaertner and Krüger's L^{SSP} (see Section 4.2.2, p. 49)

With this approach each individual is required to reveal their preferences over the total 'technologically feasible' set X. The question of defining X is thus immensely difficult. The moral arbitrator is again needed to assess, given the set of preferences, who satisfies self-supporting preferences and thus who can have rights.

4.4.3 Procedures that use extended utility information (see Section 4.2.3, p. 50)

These approaches obviously demand much utility information. Each individual is assumed to be able honestly to reveal an 'extended ordering' over the available set. Thus each individual, in order to be able to reveal such preferences must have information regarding the objective circumstances of other individuals in society. Further, if individuals wish to satisfy the axiom of identity (they will not necessarily want to) they must also know information about the subjective features of other individuals, in particular their tastes. Again the moral arbitrator steps in to deduce which rights should be implemented.

4.4.4 Conclusion on informational requirements

All approaches share the following informational requirements.
(1) Individuals are required to reveal honest preferences and are assumed to have sufficient information about the alternatives to be able to reveal such preferences.
(2) The existence of some moral arbitrator to use the information available in order to assess which rights should (must) be implemented. Alternatively it could be assumed that the individuals themselves have knowledge of the rights implementation rule operating and thus themselves will follow it without the intervention of a moral arbitrator. There is still a problem of enforcement of these rights implementation rules, i.e. making sure that individuals will behave consistently with them.

On information grounds Gibbard's L^{GP} requires the least information. Individuals are required only to reveal their respective preferences over the available set of alternatives. The other procedures require more information. L^{SSP} requires for each individual their preferences over the total set X. The procedures that constrain rights with justice require individuals' extended orderings, thus implying that on top of knowing the nature of the available alternatives they must know much about the position of other people in society.

On balance, behind L^{GP} I would rank, in order of least information required, L^{SSP}, and then the procedures that require extra utility information.

4.5   Efficiency

Given the rights system, and given that SRI is accepted to be prima facie desirable then modifications to SRI should only occur because (1) the Gibbard paradox must be avoided, and (2) there exists a yet *more* desirable social criterion which conflicts with rights implementation in social choice.

In this chapter we are considering rights modification procedures that resolve the Sen paradox. With these procedures there is thus an implicit ranking of the Pareto condition over and above rights. Pareto must in these procedures be taken to be more desirable than rights implementation given by some Pareto inconsistent libertarian condition.

Assuming that the Pareto condition is the only more desirable social criterion than rights implementation, and given that SRI is still desirable given the rights system, then 'efficiency' comparisons of these procedures become relevant. A procedure would be chosen to constrain rights such that (1) the Gibbard paradox is avoided and (2) is consistent with the Pareto condition, but preserves rights in a fair way as much as possible.

Given the original motivation behind the procedures discussed in Section 4.2 then efficiency is not relevant, rights are being axed because they should not because they must. However, I have strongly criticised the motivations underlying all these procedures, and thus think they are best seen as methods of resolving the Sen paradox independently of the original motivation leading to their construction. Given the motivation consistent with the opening paragraph of this section, then 'efficiency' comparisons *are* relevant, just as they were in Chapter 2.

4.5.1 L^{GP} versus L^{SSP} (see pp. 49, 50)

A straight-forward comparison of the rights implementation rules of these two conditions is not possible using the relations $>_E$ or $\geqslant_E$ defined in Chapter 2 (see p. 26). This can be illustrated from the following examples taken from Krüger and Gaertner (1983). They use Gibbard's wall colour case (Gibbard (1974), p. 394), where Mr Parker (P) and Mr Gibbard (G) choose the colour of their bedroom walls (w and y stand for white colour and yellow colour respectively; wy for example will denote a state where everything else the same, G will have white walls and P yellow walls).

Situation 1

G: $wyP_g yyP_g wwP_g yw$

P: $wyP_p wwP_p yyP_p yw$

According to L^{SSP} both G and P forfeit their rights. With L^{GP} no rights are waived.

Situation 2

> G: $wwP_g ywI_g wyP_g yy$
> P: $yyP_p ywI_p wyP_p ww$

With L^{SSP} both will have their rights implemented. With L^{GP} Mr G's rights to ww over yw, and Mr P's right to yy over yw are waived.

Thus, obviously the two conditions cannot be compared directly with our efficiency relations.

However, given a simple restriction on individual orderings, we can make an efficiency comparison:

Theorem 4.5.1[1] *If individuals' preferences $\{R_b\}$ are all 'strict' (i.e. no individual is indifferent between any two alternatives) then GPRI $>_E$ SSPRI.*

Proof: Consider any individual b. Without loss of generality assign him issue i and let $\langle (x_i, z), (y_i, z) ; b \rangle \in \mathcal{R}$ with $(x_i, z) P_b (y_i, z)$. Assume individual b's preferences satisfy SSP and thus his rights over $\langle (x_i, z), (y_i, z) ; b \rangle \in \mathcal{R}$ will be implemented by SSPRI. The first stages of this proof will show that individual b will also have rights implemented for $\langle (x_i, z) (y_i, z) ; b \rangle \in \mathcal{R}$ given GPRI.

Suppose the opposite, i.e. that GPRI will waive individual b's right to (x_i, z) over (y_i, z). For this to be the case there must exist an alternative w such that $(y_i, z) P_b w$ and there must exist a sequence $\Sigma = y^1, y^2 \ldots y^\lambda$ such that,

(i) $y^i = w$
(ii) $y^\lambda = (x_i, z)$
(iii) $\forall i = 1, 2, \ldots, 1 - \lambda$, at least one of the following holds

    (a) $\forall c : y^i P_c y^{i+1}$

    (b) $\exists c : (c \neq b) : [\langle y^i, y^{i+1} ; c \rangle \in \mathcal{R}$ and $y^i P_c y^{i+1}]$

(see Section 4.2.1, p. 48).

Case 1 Assume that x_i and y_i are the only two feature alternatives in individual b's set M_i. Consider now the link between $y^{\lambda-1}$ and y^λ. If the link is caused by (iii)(a) then $y^{\lambda-1} P_b y^\lambda$ and $y^{\lambda-1}$ must contain x_i, otherwise indivi-

---

[1] Alan Gibbard in correspondence with Gaertner conjectured that L^{GP} was more efficient than L^{SSP}. Krüger and Gaertner (1983) showed, as I have done, that this is not so. Krüger and Gaertner go on to say that 'whenever there is a cycle under the mixed libertarian approach, leading to an alienation of some individual's right, property SSP is violated'. Their 'mixed libertarian approach' is outlined in the section entitled 'Second modification' in Appendix A of this chapter. Theorem 4.5.1 was inspired by this statement.

dual b would fail to satisfy SSP. If the link is caused by (iii)(b) then $y^{\lambda-1}$ and y^λ must be j-variants for some other person's issue j ($j \neq i$). Thus $y^{\lambda-1}$ must contain x_i and, to be consistent with SSP, $y^{\lambda-1} P_b$ (y_i, z). Similarly all the alternatives in the sequence $\Sigma = y^1, \ldots, y^{\lambda-2}$ must contain x_i and for each $y^i, y^i P_b$ (y_i, z). But y^1 (= w) cannot contain x_i since this would violate SSP.

Case 2 Assume now there are three alternatives, x_i, y_i and v_i, in individual b's set M_i. Now there is the possibility that some element of the sequence contains v_i. Let y^s be an alternative in Σ which contains v_i such that y^{s+1} contains x_i. y^λ contains x_i so y^{s+1} could be y^λ. The link between y^s and y^{s+1} must be due to (iii)(a), otherwise y^s would contain x_i. Thus $y^s P_b y^{s+1} P_b$ (y_i, z), otherwise SSP would be violated. Consider now y^{s-1}. If the link between y^{s-1} and y^s is caused by Pareto then y^{s-1} must contain v_i, otherwise SSP would be violated. If the link is due to (iii)(b) then it must contain v_i since y^{s-1} must be a j-variant of y^s such that $j \neq i$. Similarly all the alternatives $y^{s-2}, y^{s-3}, \ldots, y^1$ must contain v_i. But y^1 cannot contain v_i since $y^s P_b$ (y_i, z) and individual b satisfies SSP.

Other cases Cases for sets of feature alternatives for individual b which exceed three can be dealt with in a similar manner. As soon as an alternative enters the sequence Σ which includes a feature alternative t_i not equal to x_i then it must continue in the sequence unless replaced by yet another feature alternative different from t_i or x_i. This must continue in the sequence unless replaced by a still different feature for individual b. No element of the sequence can be less preferred to (y_i, z) because this would violate SSP.

(x_i, z) and (y_i, z) are arbitrary i-variants. The above thus holds for all of individual b's i-variants. Thus if the individual satisfies SSP and thus will have his rights implemented by L^{SSP} (through SSPRI), then his rights would also be implemented by L^{GP} (through GPRI). Thus, GPRI $\geqslant_E$ SSPRI.

To show that GPRI $>_E$ SSPRI, it is only necessary to give an example, already given earlier in this section, where we have two individuals and four alternatives $\{wy, yy, yw, ww\}$ and preferences:

Individual 1: $wyP_1 yyP_1 wwP_1 yw$

Individual 2: $wyP_2 wwP_2 yyP_2 yw$

Individual 1 is assigned issue 1, individual 2 is assigned issue 2. GPRI will implement rights and SSPRI will not. Thus we can now state GPRI $>_E$ SSPRI.

A significant feature of Gibbard's L^{GP} is that it will always preserve what Gibbard calls '1st order rights' for an individual. Gibbard shows that if an individual is assigned the right to x over y, then, at the very least, if y is his sole last choice from among the available alternatives, then no matter what others may prefer, the individual's right to x over y will be implemented (see Gibbard (1974), Theorem 5). Gaertner and Krüger's L^{SSP}, or for that matter Gibbard's L^{G} or conditions $L*L^{\text{ex}}$, $L*M*$ and $L*J$, do not share this property. However, it should be noted that this property holds because of the rights system, SRS. If two individuals were assigned the same pair $\{x, y\}$ and these were the only two alternatives available then obviously both cannot have 'first order' rights to this pair.

4.5.2   *Justice constrained rights implementation rules*

Conditions $L*L^{\text{ex}}$, $L*M*$ and $L*J$ resolve the Sen paradox given that the axiom of identity is satisfied (see p. 50). In Chapter 2 it was shown that:

(1) $\text{SRI*} (L^{\text{ex}}) >_{\text{E}} \text{SRI*} (J)$

(2) $\text{SRI*} (L^{\text{ex}}) >_{\text{E}} \text{SRI*} (M*)$

This still holds with the axiom of identity, or even the axiom of complete identity. Thus $L*L^{\text{ex}}$ is the most efficient of these three libertarian conditions.

Conditions $L^{\text{c}}M$ and $L^{\text{c}}L^{\text{ex}}*$ resolve the Sen paradox given the axiom of identity (see p. 53). Now, $\{\text{not } yL_b^{\text{ex}}x\} \rightarrow xM_b y$, for every possible extended ordering R_b. The implication does not hold the other way round even if $\tilde{R}_b$ satisfies the axiom of complete identity. Thus $L^{\text{c}}M \rightarrow L^{\text{c}}L^{\text{ex}}*$ given L^{c} (which is further constrained by justice) is the same for both. Again, even under the axiom of complete identity the implication does not hold the other way round. Thus $L^{\text{c}}M$ allows more rights to be implemented than $L^{\text{c}}L^{\text{ex}}*$ given the same L^{c} for both.

Now $xL_b^{\text{ex}}y \rightarrow xM_b y$. Thus $\text{SRI*}(M) >_{\text{E}} \text{SRI*}(L^{\text{ex}})$. However, $\text{SRI*}(M)$ when combined with an incoherent rights system (like SRS) will not solve the Gibbard paradox. A further constraint will be needed on the rights implementation rule $\text{SRI*}(M)$ which will make it less efficient relatively to $\text{SRI*}(L^{\text{ex}})$. However, given a 'coherent' rights system then combining $\text{SRI*}(M)$ with it will produce a more efficient rights implementation rule than combining it with $\text{SRI*}(L^{\text{ex}})$. Given the axiom of identity in this situation, then $\text{SRI*}(M)$ will be more efficient than $\text{SRI*}(L^{\text{ex}})$ and will resolve the Sen paradox.

4.5.3   *Other comparisons*

Comparisons between SSPRI (or GPRI) and any of the justice constrained rights implementation rules is not possible using the relations $\geqslant_{\text{E}}$ or $>_{\text{E}}$. Given a particular $\{\tilde{R}_b\}$ (of which $\{R_b\}$ is contained) and a particular $S \subseteq X$ then an efficiency comparison may be made. However, when considering all

$S \subseteq X$ and all possible $\{\tilde{R}_b\}$, even restricted to conform to the axiom of complete identity, no general conclusions may be made.

4.5.4   *Conditional rights implementation rules*

In order to maximise the 'efficiency' of a procedure it might well be asked: why not make the resolution procedures operable *only* when conflict situations arise? That is, use SRI (or SRI*) in all cases except those which would lead to an empty choice set over the available set of alternatives. Doing this would raise the efficiency of all these procedures but the strict ranking under the efficiency relation will still hold.

Obviously, as stated in Chapter 2, doing such a thing relies on the total acceptance of SRI as a prima facie desirable rights implementation rule given the rights system. It will also imply a violation of the condition of independence of irrelevant alternatives which will be defined again in the next section.

4.6   **Rationality, minimal rights and independence**

Consider again the following:

Contraction consistency α

$$\forall x : x \in S^1 \subseteq S^2 \subseteq X \to [x \in C(S^2, \{R_b\}) \to x \in C(S^1, \{R_b\})]$$

Minimal rights (MR) If the available set is $\{x, y\}$ and $\langle x, y ; b \rangle \in \mathscr{R}$, then if $xP_b y$, then $y \notin C(\{x, y\}, \{R_b\})$.

These two conditions can easily be rewritten for the extended framework of Section 4.2.3. As stated in Chapter 2 these conditions, given a rights system, are quite appealing.

Theorem 4.6.1 *For any choice function $C(S, \{R_b\})$ satisfying the Pareto condition and a libertarian condition which has a rights system consistent with SENRS^M, condition MR or condition α must be violated.*

Proof: Given that the rights system is consistent with SENRS^M there must exist some subset S^0 of X and a set of preferences such that for some $x, y \in S^0$: $\langle x, y ; b \rangle \in \mathscr{R}$, $xP_b y$ and $\{y\} = C(S^0, \{R_b\})$. Such a situation exists since the choice set cannot be empty in cases where, given some rights system consistent with SENRS^M, SRI would imply an empty choice set in conjunction with the Pareto condition. If MR is satisfied then $y \notin C(\{x, y\}, \{R_b\})$. However, this implies that α is violated since y is the choice set over S^0. If α is satisfied then y should not be dismissed from the set $\{x, y\}$. This violates MR.

Consider now a weaker version of minimal rights.

Potential minimal rights (PMR) If $\langle x, y ; b \rangle \in \mathscr{R}$ and $xP_b y$ then for any $\{R_b\}$ satisfying some specific restrictions on rankings over pairs of alternatives other than $\{x, y\}$, $y \notin C(\{x, y\}, \{R_b\})$.

Consider again the following condition:

Independence of irrelevant alternatives (I)

$$\forall b : (\forall x, y \in S : xR_b y \leftrightarrow xR'_b y)$$

$$\rightarrow C(S, \{R_b\}) = C(S, \{R'_b\})$$

Theorem 4.6.2[1] *Given any rights system, any choice function which satisfies PMR, but not MR, implies that the choice function does not satisfy condition I.*

Proof: Given condition I, *MR* if and only if *PMR*.

4.6.1 *Gibbard's condition L*^{GP}

A choice function satisfying condition P and condition L^{GP} will satisfy *MR* but will violate α. This is because the sequence Σ in Gibbard's condition for rights waiving is taken over the available set not the total set X. If the alternatives in the sequence were taken over the total, universal set X, then the choice function could satisfy α but *MR* will be violated. However, in this case each individual will still have *PMR*, thus by Theorem 4.6.2, condition I will be violated.

Karni (1978) made similar points to the above with reference to his condition INOA (see p. 39); Gibbard's procedure will violate INOA but can be made consistent with it, at the expense of violating condition I, by changing the condition for rights waiving such that Σ can contain any alternatives from the universal set X.[2]

---

[1] This result has strong implications for resolution procedures which resolve the Gibbard paradox. Gibbard's condition L^G (see Chapter 2) violates *MR* but satisfies *PMR*. Thus any choice function satisfying L^G must violate condition I.

[2] Karni (1978) makes these points around a 'proposition' that has strong similarities with Sen's 'Paretian epidemic' result formulated within a non-binary framework (see Section 3.3). Consider Karni's 'proposition 1' reconstructed with my notation:

Let $C(S, \{R_b\})$ satisfy P, INOA and I. If an individual b has his rights implemented by Gibbard's GPRI, for a pair $\{x, y\}$, then no other individual can have any rights implemented by GPRI.

INOA, which implies α and δ, together with condition I strengthens GPRI into SRI. Thus by the Paretian epidemic result, given an individual has full rights both ways over a pair, no other individual can have such rights over any ordered pair whatsoever.

4.6.2 *Gaertner and Krüger's condition L^{SSP}*

A choice function satisfying condition P and condition L^{SSP} can satisfy α but will violate MR. This is because an individual who fails to satisfy SSP will not have minimal rights. However, PMR is satisfied since, consistent with any strict preference over his assigned pair, an individual can have a particular preference over other alternatives such that he satisfies SSP. Thus by Theorem 4.6.2 condition I will be violated with Gaertner and Krüger's procedure.

4.6.3 *Justice constrained libertarian conditions*

All the procedures that were discussed in Section 4.2.3 imply violation of MR in social choice. This is because information only from the extended orderings over an assigned pair $\{x, y\}$ is used in deciding whether rights should be implemented for this pair. Potential minimal rights, reformalised for use with this extended informational framework, are also violated with these procedures. Given a set of preferences $\{\tilde{R}_b\}$ *only* over an assigned pair $\{x, y\}$, if rights are not implemented they will continue not to be implemented whatever changes occur with preferences $\{\tilde{R}_b\}$ with respect to *other* alternatives.

4.7   Conclusion

Three different types of 'rights implementation modification' methods of resolving the Sen paradox have been discussed and evaluated under different criteria. The motivation leading to the construction of each is quite different. Gibbard's procedure was motivated by seeking to allow individuals to exercise or waive their rights 'voluntarily' in accordance with their self interest. Gaertner and Krüger's self-supporting preference approach was motivated by Blau's 'Golden Rule' that 'persons who do not grossly meddle in the private affairs of others shall have their own respected'. The set of procedures which used libertarian conditions constrained by justice sought to preserve rights only when all individuals agreed that a person's preference over his assigned pair was in some specific sense 'just', and this only referring to cases where the individual's preferences satisfied the axiom of identity.

Of the three procedures I have discussed, I think Gibbard's is the best out of a bad bunch. It does not require preferences over unavailable alternatives which Gaertner and Krüger's procedure requires, and does not require the utility information necessary to formulate justice constrained rights implementation rules. It grants each individual at least first order rights, and in the case of individuals revealing strict preference is more efficient than Gaertner and Krüger's approach. It also preserves independence and minimal rights. It does however violate the rationality condition α. This I feel is a necessary sacrifice given the desirability of rights. By changing the definition of rights waiving such that alternatives in the sequence Σ can be taken over unavailable alternatives in the total set X, then rationality can be preserved but, apart from violating minimal rights, the independence condition would be violated, more information would be needed (i.e. preferences over the unavailable set) and the 'efficiency' of the procedure would be reduced. Where Gibbard's approach is weak is that the rights implementation rule is rather arbitrary. As I have stated it is not consistent with voluntary rights exercising and thus it lacks motivational justification. However, given we are comparing only the three methods of this chapter the other procedures do not have appropriate motivation either, and they have many more disadvantages with respect to other criteria. My main objections to Gaertner and Krüger's procedure, apart from the motivation leading to its construction is that it requires too much information, it violates independence and minimal rights, and in many cases is less efficient than Gibbard's procedure. Now Gaertner and Krüger's specification of their rights implementation rule could be changed such that SSP need only be satisfied with respect to the available set. Then, as with Gibbard's approach, minimal rights will be preserved, as would independence, and the informational requirement would be reduced. However, the procedure would still not grant '1st order rights' and given strict preferences would still be less efficient than Gibbard's. Given that I find the rule lacking in appropriate motivation, just as with Gibbard's I would mark down this version of Gaertner and Krüger's approach on efficiency grounds.

My main objections to the use of justice constrained libertarian conditions is that such procedures require too much information, violate minimal rights, only resolve the conflict given that the individuals satisfy the axiom of identity, and only allow the implementation of rights if *every* individual considers such rights just. Given a choice amongst the sets of justice constrained rules I would choose $L*L^{ex}$ in cases where the rights are conflicting with themselves as well as Pareto, and choose $L*M$ in cases where rights are only in conflict with Pareto. This is on efficiency grounds.

Finally, I stress that my arguments above have been formulated given that Pareto is sacred and should not be modified. There are many procedures that preserve more rights and constrain the Pareto condition. These will be discussed in the next chapter.

Appendix A: Towards a voluntary rights exercising rule?

As stated in Section 4.3.1 (a) (p. 61), Kelly (1976*b*) and Suzumura (1980) have considered in some detail the possibility of amending Gibbard's rights implementation rule (GPRI) with the objective of formulating implementation rules consistent with voluntary rights exercising. The purpose of this appendix is to review some of these rules (and others) with the aim of showing that they all fail in this objective and that any such attempts will be doomed to failure. However, one of the rights implementation rules, though not conforming to voluntary rights exercising, does solve the Sen paradox and is thus interesting in itself, independently of the motivation that initiated its invention.

4.A.1   *First modification*

The first modification, initiated by Kelly (1976b), has to do with the first, rather technical and minor, objection raised in Section 4.3.1. With Gibbard's GPRI a person b's rights to x over y will be waived if there exists some $z, z \neq y$, such that $yI_b z$ and Gibbard's stipulated sequence Σ exists. Kelly (1976b) argued:

b doesn't seem to have gotten into trouble if he is forced in the end to take a z where he is indifferent between z and y. Waiving might be appropriate for a cautious exerciser if $yP_b z$ for some Σ, but not if only $yR_b z$ [as in the definition Gibbard supplies].

To meet this objection, Kelly formulated the following rights implementation rule.

Kelly's first amended rights exercising rule (KPRI–1) If $\langle x, y, b \rangle \in \mathscr{R}$, b will exercise that right if $xP_b y$ and b's right is not waived. b's right is waived if there exists a finite sequence of available alternatives $\Sigma = y^1, y^2, \ldots, y^\lambda$ such that:

(i) $y^\lambda = x$

(ii) $yP_b y^1$ (rather than Gibbard's alternative requirement that:

$yR_b y^1$ $(y \neq y^1)$)

(iii) For every $i = 1, 2, \ldots, \lambda + 1$

either (a) $\forall e : y^i P_e y^{i+1}$

or (b) $\exists e\, (e \neq b$ and $\langle y^i, y^{i+1}; e \rangle \in \mathscr{R}$ and $y^i P_e y^{i+1})$

Unfortunately, contrary to Kelly's opinion, this does not solve the Sen paradox, or even the Gibbard paradox when combined with the standard rights system.

Condition L^{kl} SRS and KPRI–1 respectively exist and operate in society.

Theorem 4.A.1 (see Suzumura (1980), Theorem 2) *There does not exist a choice function $C(S, \{R_b\})$ satisfying condition L^{kl}.*

Proof: Let there be two individuals, 1 and 2. Define four alternatives as

$$xy = (x_1, y_2, x_3, \ldots, x_n)$$

$$xx = (x_1, x_2, x_3, \ldots, x_n)$$

$$yx = (y_1, x_2, x_3, \ldots, x_n)$$

$$yy = (y_1, y_2, x_3, \ldots, x_n)$$

Let the preferences of individual 1, who is assigned issue 1 be

$$xxP_1 yyP_1 xyI_1 yx$$

Let the preferences of individual 2, who is assigned issue 2 be

$$yxP_2 xyP_2 xxI_2 yy$$

It is easily checked that with L^{k1} all rights will be exercised and thus the choice set over $\{xx, yy, xy, yx\}$ will be empty.

4.A.2   *Second modification*

If, in addition to the other requirements in Kelly's first amended rights exercising rule, we required that individuals displayed 'unconditional preferences' with respect to their issues before rights could be exercised, then possibility will be restored in the context of the standard rights system. This result was first formulated by Krüger and Gaertner (1983):

Krüger and Gaertner's amended rights exercising rule (KGPRI) If $\langle x, y ; b \rangle \in \mathscr{R}$, b will exercise that right if $xP_b y$, and b's rights are not waived. b's rights are waived if:

(1)   There exists a finite sequence of available alternatives

$$\Sigma = y^1, y^2, \ldots, y^\lambda \text{ such that}$$

(i) $y^\lambda = x$

(ii) $yP_b y^1$

(iii) For every $i = 1, 2, \ldots, \lambda + 1$

either (a) $\forall e : y^i P_e y^{i+1}$

or (b) $\exists e \ [e \neq b \text{ and } \langle y^i, y^{i+1} ; e \rangle \in \mathscr{R} \text{ and } y^i P_e y^{i+1}]$

and (2)   Person b does not have 'unconditional preferences' with respect to his personal issue i (see Chapter 2, p. 12).

Condition L^{Kg} (Krüger and Gaertner's 'mixed libertarian' condition, see Krüger and Gaertner (1983)). SRS and KGPRI respectively exist and operate in society.

Theorem 4.A.2 *There exists a choice function* $C(S, \{R_b\})$ *satisfying conditions* L^{Kg} *and P.*

Proof: See Krüger and Gaertner (1983), Theorem 3.

Though a reproduction of the above proof would be laborious and unnecessary here, their approach to the proof provides some useful insights into what is going on. In particular their proof explicitly shows that, given Kelly's condition L^{kl} does not create impossibility by itself, then it is consistent with the Pareto condition in social choice. Thus the only purpose of insisting that individuals exhibit unconditional preferences in KGPRI is to ensure that the Gibbard paradox does not arise. Thus instead of requiring that individuals display unconditional preferences before they can exercise rights according to KPRI–1, we could alternatively make use of the other libertarian conditions, formulated in Chapter 2, that solve the Gibbard paradox.

For example, by replacing SRS with SENRS (or SENRS^M) (see pp. 10, 35), then the libertarian conditions defined as the combination of SENRS (or SENRS^M) and KPRI–1 will produce possibility. This is because with this alternative rights system we are free to choose a 'coherent rights system' thus ensuring that the implementation of rights cannot by itself produce impossibility. Given this we then know by Krüger and Gaertner's proof that this libertarian condition will also be consistent with the Pareto condition in social choice. This also reveals why Kelly made his mistake. In his 1976 article Kelly did not use SRS, but SENRS^M. SENRS^M and KPRI–1 will yield possibility, but Kelly is wrong to imply that this result would carry over to the case when SRS is used. Kelly makes explicit use of SRS in his later book (Kelly (1978), p. 141), and fails to note that replacing SENRS^M with SRS will yield impossibility.

One final point on this second modification. Though KGPRI takes us away from the notion of voluntary rights exercising, it does, in conjunction with SRS, provide a libertarian condition that solves the Sen paradox. Interestingly Krüger and Gaertner (1983) state that L^{Kg} is more efficient than their other libertarian condition L^{SSP}, i.e. it will, for each $\{R_b\}$ and available set S, never axe more rights than L^{SSP} and may axe less rights.

4.A.3   *Third modification*

A more important objection to GPRI is the second point (b) raised in Section 4.3.1 (3). That is, for voluntary rights exercising, if a person finds an alternative at the end of the sequence Σ that he likes less than y he should make sure that is the alternative he will end up with if he did exercise his rights. In Section 4.3.1 (3), an example was shown where using GPRI (or for that matter KGPRI) made an individual waive his right when it was not sensible for him to do so (see p. 59). Kelly (1976b), in an effort to formulate a rule that solved this difficulty, formulated his second amended rights implementations rule.

Kelly's second amended rights exercising rule (KPRI–2) If $\langle x, y ; b \rangle \in \mathscr{R}$, b will then exercise that right if $xP_b y$ and if b does not waive that right. b waives $\langle x, y ; b \rangle \in \mathscr{R}$ if there is a finite sequence of available alternatives $\Sigma = y^1, y^2, \ldots, y^\lambda$ such that:

(1) $y^\lambda = x$

(2) $yP_b y^1$

(3) For every $i = 1, 2, \ldots, \lambda - 1$

either (a) $\forall e : y^i P_e y^i P_e y^{i+1}$

   or (b) $\exists e : [(e \neq b)$ and $\langle y^i, y^{i+1} ; e \rangle \in \mathscr{R}$ and $y^i P_e y^{i+1}]$

(4) For every finite sequence of available alternatives

$\Sigma' = z^1, z^2, \ldots, z^{\lambda'}$ such that

(a) $z^{\lambda'} = y^1$

(b) $z^1 P_b y$

(c) For every $i = 1, 2, \ldots, \lambda' - 1$

either (i) $\forall e : z^i P_e z^{i+1}$

   or (ii) $\exists e : [\langle z^i, z^{i+1} ; e \rangle \in \mathscr{R}$ and $z^i P_e z^{i+1}]$

There is a sequence $\Sigma'' = \omega^1, \omega^2, \ldots, \omega^{\lambda''}$ of available alternatives such that

(d) $\omega^{\lambda''} = z^1$

(d) $yP_b \omega^1$

(f) For every $i = 1, 2, \ldots, \lambda'' - 1$

either (i) $\forall e \, \omega^i P_e \omega^{i+1}$

   or (ii) $\exists e \, [e \neq b, \langle \omega^i, \omega^{i+1} ; e \rangle \in \mathscr{R}$ and $\omega^i P_e \omega^{i+1}]$

In this rule part (4) says that any extending sequence Σ' that repairs Σ in the eyes of b can enter some other out of control sequence Σ'' resulting in an alternative worse than y.

Given the result in Theorem 4.A.2, it is not surprising that the above implementation rule, when combined with SRS, yields impossibility. The proof is exactly the same since KPRI–1 will always exercise rights when KPRI–2 does (Suzumura (1980), Theorem 3).

The question remains: does imposing unconditional preferences in an analogous way to our second modification regain possibility in this case?

4.A.4   *Fourth modification*

Fourth amended rights exercising rule (FPRI) If $\langle x, y ; b \rangle \in \mathcal{R}$, b will exercise that right if $xP_b y$ and if b's rights are not waived. b's rights are waived if (1) there exist sequences Σ, Σ' and Σ'' as in KPRI–2, and (2) person b does not exhibit 'unconditional preferences' with respect to his issue.

Condition L^{Fk} SRS and FPRI respectively exist and operate in society.

Theorem 4.A.3 *If the number of individuals exceeds three then there does not exist a choice function $C(S, \{R_b\})$ satisfying condition P and condition L^{Fk}.*

Proof: Let us define eight alternatives as

$$x^1 = (y, w, w, w)$$
$$x^2 = (w, w, w, w)$$
1-variants assigned to individual 1

$$x^3 = (y, y, y, y)$$
$$x^4 = (y, y, w, y)$$
3-variants assigned to individual 3

$$x^5 = (y, w, y, w)$$
$$x^6 = (y, y, y, w)$$
2-variants assigned to individual 2

$$x^7 = (w, y, w, y)$$
$$x^8 = (w, y, w, w)$$
4-variants assigned to individual 4

Let preferences of four individuals over this subset of eight alternatives be

Individuals 1 and 2		Individuals 3 and 4	
x^8	x^4	x^2	x^6
x^1	x^5	x^3	x^7
x^2	x^6	x^4	x^8
x^3	x^7	x^5	x^1

(Alternatives on the same line are in the same indifference class. This list goes down in descending order of strict preference.)

It is easily checked that all the alternatives will be dismissed by the operation of the libertarian and Pareto conditions.

Note that the number of individuals exceeding three is a *sufficient* condition. We could have just two individuals say individual 1 and individual 3 and let individual 1 be decisive over issues 1 and 2 and let individual 3 be decisive over issues 3 and 4. The proof goes through with this case. Note also that the above proof holds for a choice function satisfying a libertarian condition defined as the combination of SENRS and FPRI, and Pareto. This is a very negative result for Kelly's second revised rule.

Suzumura (1980) attempted to rescue Kelly's second amended revised rule with other modifications. He failed on all attempts, producing many other impossibility results. Thus attempts that have been made to resolve these problems of individuals waiving rights when it is not sensible for them to do so have failed. Note that this objection is independent to the objections raised before, i.e. that

(1) GPRI fails to reflect an individual's ethical judgement of the situation (see p. 58)
(2) GPRI implies people make mistakes with regard to the rights exercising of others — mistakes which are not self-evidently correctable (see p. 60)

4.A.5   *The impossibility of a voluntary rights exercising rule*

At this point it is worth returning to the preference structure of the example used to illustrate Gibbard's motivation (see p. 55):

1	2	
x	z	
y	x	descending scale of
z	y	preference

$$\{\langle y, z ; 1\rangle, \langle z, x ; 2\rangle\} = \mathscr{R}$$

Now person 2 waives his right because he sees person 1 exercising over $\langle y, z ; 1\rangle$ which would result in y being chosen if he did not waive his right, an alternative worse than x. However, it seems clear from Gibbard's exercising rule that the person 1 will realise that the Pareto condition will also hold, i.e. there is a principle attached to the choice function that will ensure that mutually beneficial bargaining will be allowed to occur (see Gibbard's rights waiving condition, part (iii) p. 48). Thus, he should also realise that y will also be dismissed from the choice set by this condition. A person conforming to Gibbard's motivation must look at the consequences of exercising his right and compare this with the consequences of waiving his right. Now in the above example, if person 2 exercises his right the choice set will be empty. If he waives his right then x will be chosen. How can he compare these two situations? One way we could avoid the problem is that the authorities could impose stiff penalties for an individual if his exercising leads to impossibility, i.e. force him to have an alternative much less preferred to *all* the available alternatives $\{x, y, z\}$. In this situation, *both* individuals will waive their rights.

This is not the only problem. Consider the following:

1	2	
y	x	
x	z	descending order of
w	w	strict preference
z	y	

Let $\{\langle y, z ; 1\rangle, \langle x, w ; 2\rangle\} = \mathscr{R}$

If person 2 exercises his rights then x or y will be chosen (case 1).
If person 2 waives his rights then x, w or y will be chosen (case 2).

All rights exercising rules discussed will have person 2 retain his rights and it is not based on miscalculation. However, is this sensible? If we assume a person does not know anything about the choice function that will operate apart from the fact that it is consistent with the Pareto principle and will grant him rights over his assigned pair if he so wished, how will he decide?

Suppose that in case 1 he thinks it is equally likely that x or y will be chosen. Suppose that in case 2 he thinks it is equally likely that x, w or y will be chosen. Suppose further that person 2 only mildly prefers x to z, and only mildly prefers z to w. This is totally consistent with the above ordinal preference. With this example, individual 2 will not have to be very risk averse to waive his rights!

It is not my contention that this will be the case, only that it is a possibility, and that exercising rules cannot be consistent, in every case, with a person wishing to exercise his rights when they are based only on ordinal preferences.

Appendix B: Alternative specifications of justice constrained rights implementation rules

One objection I raised against the use of justice constrained rights implementation rules to resolve the Sen paradox was that an individual's rights to a pair of alternatives will be implemented *if and only if* all individuals unanimously agree that such a right is just according to their respective justice relations. Can we weaken such a strong 'justice' requirement for rights and retain possibility?

Consider, for example, the following rights implementation rule which makes use of the Rawlsian maximin relation M_b (see p. 17).

SRI*WM* If $\langle x, y ; b \rangle \in \mathscr{R}$ then if $(x, b) \tilde{P}_b (y, b)$ and $\{$not $(\forall a : y M_a x)\}$ then $y \notin C^*(S : x \in S, \{\tilde{R}_b\})$.

Condition L*WM* SRS and SRI*WM* respectively exist and operate in society.

Obviously $\{\forall a :$ not $y M_a x\} \rightarrow \{$not $(\forall a : y M_a x)\}$ but not, in general, vice versa. Thus $L*WM* \rightarrow L*M*$ and not in general vice versa (see p. 18). We are weakening the condition that constrains the axing of rights, thus strengthening the libertarian condition.

Given the axiom of complete identity I^C (see p. 50), then $L*M* \leftrightarrow L*WM*$. All individuals share the same extended ordering. Thus given I^C the Sen paradox could be resolved with the use of condition $L*WM*$ − trivially. But the motivation behind $L*WM*$ is that one wishes to weaken the condition that constrains rights. Unfortunately, relaxing the requirement of I^C to I^A results in condition $L*WM*$ failing to resolve the Sen paradox, or even the Gibbard paradox.

Theorem 4.B.1 *There does not exist a choice function $C^*(S, \{R_b\})$ satisfying condition $L*WM*$, even when individual's preferences satisfy the axiom of identity I^A.*

Proof: Let individual 1 be assigned issue 1 where he has two features x_1, y_1. Let individual 2 be assigned issue 2 where he has two features x_2, y_2. Let preferences be given as follows. They satisfy the axiom of identity.

1	2 and others	
$(xy, 2)$	$(yy, 1)$	
$(xx, 2)$	$(xy, 2)$	
$(yx, 2)$	$(xx, 2)$	
$(yy, 1)$	$(yx, 2)$	descending order of
$(yy, 2)$	$(xy, 1)$	strict preference
$(xy, 1)$	$(xx, 1)$	
$(xx, 1)$	$(yx, 1)$	
$(yx, 1)$	$(yy, 2)$	

where $xy = (x_1, y_2, z)$
       $xx = (x_1, x_2, z)$
       $yx = (y_1, x_2, z)$
       $yy = (y_1, y_2, z)$ (z being a particular list of other features).

Call this set S'. All other alternatives are deemed indifferent to $(xy, 2)$ for individual 1, and are deemed indifferent to $(yy, 1)$ for individual 2 and others. Now $(yy, 1) \tilde{P}_1 (xy, 1)$ and $\langle yy, xy ; 1 \rangle \in \mathscr{R}$.

(1) $\{(xy, 1) \tilde{R}_1 (yy, 2)$ and $(xy, 2) \tilde{R}_1 (yy, 2)\}$ does not hold.

(2) $\{(xy, 1) \tilde{R}_1 (yy, 1)$ and $(xy, 2) \tilde{R}_1 (yy, 1)\}$ does not hold.

Therefore $\{$not $xyM_1yy\}$ and thus $\{$not $(\forall b : xyM_byy)\}$
Therefore $xy \notin C^*(S', \{\tilde{R}_b\})$
Analogously it is easily checked that
$xx \notin C^*(S', \{R_b\})$
$yx \notin C^*(S', \{R_b\})$
$yy \notin C^*(S', \{R_b\})$
Thus the choice set over $S' = \{xx, yx, xy, yy\}$ is empty.

I have tried many other weakenings of the conditions that constrain rights implementation, and these using many different types of justice relations. They all fail to resolve the Sen paradox even given the axiom of identity. Thus attempting to modify the libertarian conditions with weaker constraints on rights implementation, in order to overcome the motivational criticisms I have given, does not seem possible.

Also, modifying many of the implementation rules of the Gibbard paradox resolving libertarian conditions (L^c) (see p. 52) with such weaker constraints on rights implementation does not succeed in solving the Sen paradox given the axiom of identity. (Imposing the axiom of complete identity invariably nullifies such weakenings.) To illustrate this consider the following condition.

*Condition ML^{S}WM** SENRS^M and SRI*WM* respectively exist and operate in society.

SRS is now being replaced by SENRS^M (see p. 35). We are now free to choose a coherent rights system to ensure the Gibbard paradox cannot arise. However we have the following result.

Theorem 4.B.2 *There does not exist a choice function $C^*(S, \{R_b\})$ satisfying condition ML^{S}WM* and the Pareto condition P', even if individual's preferences satisfy the axiom of identity, I^A.*

Proof: According to SENRS^M let individual 1 be assigned the pair $\{x, y\}$, and let individual 2 be assigned the pair $\{w, z\}$.
There are three possibilities:
(1) $\{x, y\}$ and $\{w, z\}$ are the same pair.

(2) $\{x, y\}$ and $\{w, z\}$ have one element in common.

(3) $\{x, y\}$ and $\{w, z\}$ have no elements in common.

Note that in cases 2 and 3 the rights system is coherent and the Gibbard paradox can not arise.

Case 1 $w = x, y = z$. Let preferences be:

Individual 1:

$$(x, 1)\,\tilde{P}_1\,(y, 2)\,\tilde{P}_1\,(x, 2)\,\tilde{P}_1\,(y_1 1)$$

with all other alternatives (e.g. $(x, 3), (y, 3)$ etc.) being deemed indifferent to $(x, 1)$ according to individual 1.

Individual 2 (and others):

$$(y, 2)\,\tilde{P}_2\,(x, 1)\,\tilde{P}_2\,(y, 1)\,\tilde{P}_2\,(x, 2)$$

with all other alternatives being deemed indifferent to $(y, 2)$ for individual 2.

These preferences satisfy the axiom of identity I^A.

It is easily checked that both individuals' rights will be implemented with $ML^S WM^*$. Thus impossibility for $S = \{x, y\}$

Case 2 $y = w$. Let preferences (which satisfy the axiom of identity) be:

Individual 1:

$$(y, 2)\,\tilde{P}_1\,(z, 2)\,\tilde{P}_1 (x, 2)\,\tilde{P}_1\,(z, 1)\,\tilde{I}_1\,(z, a : \forall a = 3, m)\,\tilde{P}_1\,(x, 1)\,\tilde{I}_1$$
$$(x, a : \forall a = 3, m)\,\tilde{P}_1\,(y, 1)$$

with all other alternatives being deemed indifferent to $(y, 2)$ by individual 1. (m = number of individuals).

Individual 2 and others:

$$(z, 1)\,\tilde{P}_2\,(x, 1)\,\tilde{P}_2\,(y, 1)\,\tilde{P}_2\,(y, 2)\,\tilde{P}_2\,(z, 2)\,\tilde{I}_2\,(z, a : \forall a = 3, m)$$
$$\tilde{P}_2\,(x, 2)\,\tilde{I}_2\,(x, a : \forall a = 3, m)$$

with all other alternatives being deemed indifferent to $(z, 1)$ for individual 2 (and others) (m = number of individuals).

It is easily checked that individual 1 and 2 will have their rights implemented $ML^S WM^*$. Thus alternatives y and z will be dismissed from the choice set. Now for all individuals, z is preferred to x, i.e. $\forall b : (z, b)\,\tilde{P}_b\,(x, b)$. Thus by condition P', x will be dismissed from the choice set. Thus the choice set will be empty over $S = \{x, y, z\}$.

Case 3 All four alternatives $\{x, y, z, w\}$ are distinct.

Let preferences be (which satisfy the axiom of identity)

Individual 1:

$$(w, 1) \tilde{I}_1 (w, a : \forall a = 3, m) \tilde{P}_1 (y, 2) \tilde{P}_1 (z, 2) \tilde{P}_1 (w, 2) \tilde{P}_1 (x, 2)$$

$$\tilde{P}_1 (x, 1) \tilde{I}_1 (x, a : \forall a = 3, m) \quad \tilde{P}_1 (y, 1) \tilde{I}_1 (y, a : \forall a = 3, m)$$

$$\tilde{P}_1 (z, 1) \tilde{I}_1 (z, a : \forall a = 3, m)$$

(where m = number of individuals).
Individual 2 (and others):

$$(y, 2) \tilde{I}_2 (y, a : \forall a = 3, m) \tilde{P}_2 (w, 1) \tilde{P}_2 (x, 1) \tilde{P}_2 (y, 1) \tilde{P}_2 (z, 1)$$

$$\tilde{P}_2 (z, 2) \tilde{I}_2 (z, a : \forall a = 3, m) \tilde{P}_2 (w, 2) \tilde{I}_2 (w, a : \forall a = 3, m)$$

$$\tilde{P}_2 (x, 2) \tilde{I}_2 (x, a : \forall a = 3, m)$$

(where m = number of individuals)
It is easily checked that both individuals' rights will be implemented given $ML^S WM^*$, thus y and w will be dismissed from the choice set over $\{x, y, w, z\}$. The Pareto condition P' implies that z and x will be dismissed. Thus the choice set over $\{x, y, w, z\}$ will be empty.

The above two theorems illustrate that the resolutions to the paradoxes which involve constraining rights to conform to justice are not robust to mild weakenings of the strong justice requirements used.

CHAPTER 5

Pareto modification approaches to resolving the Sen paradox

5.1 Introduction

In this chapter methods of resolving the Sen paradox which modify the Pareto condition will be reviewed. Some of these Pareto modifications are consistent with any libertarian condition which is not vulnerable to the Gibbard paradox, while others must be used in conjunction with a particular libertarian condition. This will be made clear during the course of the exposition.

In the following 'methods' section four different types of Pareto modification approaches to resolving the Sen paradox will be outlined. Discussion of the motivation leading to their construction, efficiency and informational requirements will be left to the subsequent sections.

5.2 Methods

5.2.1 *Sen's 'conditional Pareto condition'* (See Sen (1976))

Let R_b^* be a subrelation of individual b's preference R_b reflecting the parts of his preference ordering that he wants to count in social choice. P_b^* and I_b^* are the asymmetric and symmetric factors of R_b^* respectively.

Condition PC (Conditional weak Pareto condition) For any x, y in X if xP_b^*y for all b, then $y \notin C(S : x \in S, \{R_b\})$.

Respecting rights (Being 'liberal') A person b 'respects the rights of others' (or, is a 'liberal') if and only if for each m-tuple of individual preference orderings $\{R_b\}$, person b wants a subrelation R_b^* of his preference ordering R_b to count, such that there exists an ordering T_b of which R_b^* is a subrelation and so is each other individual's preference over each of his assigned pairs.

Theorem 5.2.1 *There exists a choice function $C(S, \{R_b\})$ satisfying condition PC and condition L^S if there exists at least one person in the community who respects rights of others.*

Proof: See Sen (1976), p. 244.

Sen explicitly states in his original theorem (Sen (1976), theorem 9) that the conditional Pareto condition can be used in conjunction with any libertarian condition which combines SRI with a 'coherent' rights system.

Suzumura (1978) has shown that Sen's conditional Pareto condition can be used in conjunction with Gibbard's libertarian condition L^G if there exists at least one 'liberal' individual who claims only those parts of his preferences to count which are compatible with others' unconditional preferences over their assigned pairs. Trivial redefining of the concept of respecting rights would enable Sen's conditional Pareto condition to be used in conjunction with any Gibbard paradox resolving libertarian condition in the context of Theorem 5.2.1.

5.2.2   Austen-Smiths 'restricted Pareto condition' (See Austen-Smith (1982))

Let $A(S) = \{y \mid y \in S$ and $\not\exists\, b$ such that for some alternative x in S, $\langle x, y ; b \rangle \in \mathscr{R}$ and $xP_b y\}$

Condition RCWP (Rights constrained weak Pareto condition)

$$\forall x, y \in X, \ [x \in A(S) \text{ and } \forall b : xP_b y] \rightarrow y \notin C(S : x \in S, \{R_b\})$$

Theorem 5.2.2 *There exists a choice function $C(S, \{R_b\})$ satisfying condition RCWP and condition ML^S.*

Proof: See Austen-Smith (1982) Theorem 3.

Condition *RCWP* can be used in conjunction with any libertarian condition which resolves the Gibbard paradox when the set $A(S)$ is suitably redefined to include elements of the available set S not vetoed by any individual implementing his rights, given the rights implementation rule.

5.2.3   Hammond's 'private Pareto condition' (See Hammond (1980))

Within the issue framework an alternative is seen to be made up of n feature alternatives $x = (x_1, x_2, \ldots, x_n)$, one for each of the n issues i. In Chapter 2 it was mentioned that some issues may be personal to some individual while others may be non-personal, 'public' issues. Hammond defines social alternatives so as to differentiate explicitly between 'personal' feature alternatives and 'public' feature alternatives, and further assumes that each individual b has one and only one personal issue.

The typical social alternative is now represented as

$$x = (x_1, x_2, \ldots, x_m, z_{m+1}, z_{m+2}, \ldots, z_n)$$

where x_i for $i = 1, 2, \ldots, m$ are the personal features for the m individuals, and z_i for $i = m + 1, m + 2, \ldots, n$ are the $n - m$ 'public' feature alternatives. In a more abbreviated form the typical social alternative can be presented as $x = (x_1, x_2, \ldots, x_m, x_N)$ where x_N is a vector of the public feature alternatives in x. Let M_N denote the cartesian product $M_{m+1} \times M_{m+2} \times \ldots \times M_n$.

Privately oriented preferences $\hat{P}_b$ $\hat{P}_b$ is a privately oriented strict preference relation for individual b if there exists a strict relation $\hat{P}_b^0$ on the product space $M_i \times M_N$, where issue i is b's personal issue, such that for every $x, y \in X$

$$x\hat{P}_b y \leftrightarrow (x_i, x_N) \hat{P}_b^0 (y_i, y_N)$$

So $\hat{P}_b$ is privately oriented if it ignores the private issues of individuals other than b, and is equivalent to a strict preference relation $\hat{P}_b^0$ on just the product space $M_i \times M_N$. We must define the relation $\hat{P}_b^0$:

The strict preference relation $\hat{P}_b^0$ For any preference ordering R_b for individual b, define the irreflexive and transitive strict preference relation $\hat{P}_b^0$ on $M_i \times M_N$, where i is person b's issue as

$$(x_i, x_N) \hat{P}_b^0 (y_i, y_N) \leftrightarrow [\text{For } \textit{all } u, w \in X \text{ satisfying}: u_j = w_j \text{ for all } j \in H - \{i\}, (u_i, u_N) = (x_i, x_N) \text{ and } (w_i, w_N) = (y_i, y_N), \text{ we have } uP_bw]$$

It might be helpful to note that if there was only one set of 'public' feature alternatives, the same for all social alternatives in X, then for all $x, y \in X$: $x\hat{P}_b y$ if and only if $x_i P_b^u y_i$ for x_i in x and y_i in y such that $x_i, y_i \in M_i$ with issue i assigned to individual b. Remember that $x_i P_b^u y_i$ if and only if person b reveals a strict unconditional preference for his feature alternative x_i over y_i. This relation was used in the formulation of Gibbard's libertarian condition L^G (see Chapter 2, p. 12). In fact, it is this libertarian condition which Hammond uses for his possibility theorem.

Condition PP (Private Pareto condition)

$$\forall x, y \in X, \forall b : x\hat{P}_b y \rightarrow y \notin C(S: x \in S, \{R_b\})$$

Theorem 5.2.3 *There exists a choice function $C(S, \{R_b\})$ satisfying condition PP and condition L^G.*

Proof: See Hammond (1980) Theorem 4.3.

5.2.4   *Generalised justice constrained Pareto condition* (See Wriglesworth (1982b))

The utility framework is extended in the same way as in Chapter 2, Section 2.3.2.3 and Chapter 4, Section 4.2.3.

Let P_b^J be any justice relation for individual b. The relations J_b, M_b and L_b^{ex} defined before are examples of such a relation. Each individual will be assigned one such relation but, for an individual b, his P_b^J might be a different justice relation to P_c^J the justice relation of another individual c (for example for individual b: $P_b^J = L_b^{ex}$ but for individual c: $P_c^J = M_c$).

A general justice constrained libertarian condition will be defined as the combination of the standard rights system (SRS) and the following rights implementation rule.

Generalised justice constrained rights implementation rule $(\bar{P}^J RI)$ If $\langle x, y; b \rangle \in \mathcal{R}$, then if $(x, b) \tilde{P}_b (y, b)$ and $\{\forall b : xP_b^J y\}$, then $y \notin C^*(S : x \in S, \{\tilde{R}_b\})$.

Condition LP^J (Generalised justice-constrained libertarian condition) SRS and $\bar{P}^J RI$ respectively exist and operate in society.

For example, if $\{\forall b : P_b^J = M_b\}$ then $LP^J = L^*M$. If $\{\forall b : P_b^J = J_b\}$ then $LP^J = L^*J$. If $\{\forall b : P_b^J = L_b^{ex}\}$ then $LP^J = L^*L^{ex}$.

Each P_b^J used to constrain the libertarian condition can now be used to constrain the Pareto condition.

Condition PP^J (Generalised justice-constrained Pareto condition)

$$\forall x, y \in X, [\forall b : \{(x, b) \tilde{P}_b (y, b) \text{ and } xP_b^J y\}]$$
$$\to y \notin C^*(S : x \in S, \{\tilde{R}_b\})$$

Theorem 5.2.4 *There exists a choice function* $C^*(S, \{\tilde{R}_b\})$ *satisfying condition* PP^J *and condition* LP^J *if, for one individual, his justice relation* P_b^J *is transitive and asymmetric.*

Proof: If the conditions PP^J and LP^J are to dismiss all the alternatives from any subset $S = (x^1, x^2, x^3, \ldots, x^h)$, then there must exist a cycle of the form

$$\forall b : x^1 P_b^J x^2 P_b^J x^3 \ldots x^h P_b^J x^1$$

This is impossible due to the transitivity and asymmetry of the justice relation P_b^J for one individual.

The rights implementation rule $\bar{P}^J RI$ can be used in conjunction with any rights system in Theorem 5.2.4.

5.3 Motivation

5.3.1 *Sen's conditional Pareto condition* (see p. 91)

The basis of Sen's approach lies in the belief that revealed individual preferences without knowledge of the motivation underlying them is an inadequate basis for social judgement involving issues such as liberty.

Consider Sen's reasoning as regards his *Lady Chatterley's Lover* example (see p. 35). Sen takes on the role of the 'prude' and the reader is asked to take on the role of the 'lascivious'. Sen's original labelling of alternatives is different and I have changed this to be consistent with my own.

I would rather not read the stuff myself (i.e. I prefer w to x), and I would rather you would not (i.e. I prefer w to y), but I decide to 'respect' your tastes on what I agree is your benighted business (while wondering whether 'respect' is quite the word), conceding that my preference for w over y be ignored. My dislike of your gloating over 'muck' was so strong that I would have preferred to read the work myself to stop you from falling into this (i.e. I preferred x to y), but being a consistent kind of man, I notice that, if I insist that my preference for w over x should count as well as my preference for x over y, then there is not much point in my 'renouncing' my preference for w over y. So I may decide not to want my preference for x over y to count, even though the choice over the pair $\{x, y\}$ is not exclusively your business.

On a similar ground, you might not want your preference for x over y to count, since you do wish your preference for y over w to count and decide not to want that your preference for x over w should count (since it is my business). But the Pareto preference for x over y is built on counting my preference and yours for x over y, and if neither of us wants our respective preferences over this pair to count, there can hardly be much force in the Pareto ranking in this case. If on these grounds the Pareto preference is overridden, this is not done by virtue of any 'outside observer denying a unanimous choice', but on the basis of our own denial that our preferences for x over y should 'count' in deciding what is socially better.

This notion of counting suggests a *conditional* version of the Pareto principle. (Sen, 1976, p. 236)

In the above example, both individuals are 'respecting rights of others' and thus rights implementation will be consistent with the conditional Pareto condition in social choice by Theorem 5.2.1.

In this case the resolution comes about by 'voluntary' restrictions of preferences by the individuals themselves. Suzumura (1978), following a suggestion by Hammond, claimed that an individual could be a 'passive liberal' in the sense that he knows he wants to respect the rights of others but only knows his own preference ordering. Thus a 'well informed umpire' will step in to do the job of restricting his preferences for him.

Sen repeatedly stresses that the Pareto condition left in its original form enforces the 'meddling' aspects of individuals' preferences in conflict cases (see the discussion in Chapter 4, Section 4.3.2). He wishes to allow the individuals, through allowing them to reveal a subrelation of their respective orderings, to judge whether these preferences should count in social choice.

However, Sen does not allow individuals to judge whether their 'non-meddling' preferences over their respective assigned pairs should or should not count in social choice. An individual b's right to a pair $\{x, y\}$ is implemented for x over y if xP_by, independently of whether in fact the individual reveals xP_b^*y. The subrelation R_b^* is defined as that part of individual b's preference that he wishes to see count in *social choice* but Sen only uses this relation R_b^* in formulating the conditional Pareto condition. There is thus an explicit bias in Sen's resolution procedure against the Pareto condition. Individuals can veto the Pareto principle over a pair by revealing a particular subrelation of preferences they wish to see count in social choice, but are not given the same power of veto as regards their preferences over their own assigned pairs.

Thus far, Sen's procedure is not a complete resolution to the Sen Paradox. Nothing has been said about cases of conflict when no individual wishes to respect rights of others. Sen suggests an 'outsider may try and judge what should be done and may decide that certain parts of a person's preferences *should not* count in the choice in question'. If the outsider thinks that the Pareto principle should be revoked over a pair of alternatives in a conflict case, he need not judge that somebody else's preference should not count over this pair. He can consider his own preferences, in the same way as anybody else, and thus can veto the Pareto condition over the particular pair of alternatives by a suitable revelation of a subrelation of his preferences which he wants to see count in social choice. If on the other hand the outsider thinks that a person's rights over an assigned pair should be revoked to resolve the conflict, then the resolution will be achieved independently of the guidelines of the Sen procedure; the well informed outsider may as well choose the choice set directly, i.e. in essence he is being given the power of a dictator (not in the Arrovian sense), albeit hopefully a just one! The problem of how such a moral dictator is chosen is a deep one and Sen does not consider this problem despite explicitly acknowledging that in some cases 'the motivations . . . might point the finger at the libertarian condition' (Sen (1976), p. 237).

It is clear, however, that given that at least one individual respects the rights of others (he may be a well informed moral individual who does not have rights himself in the case in question) there is no need for an 'outsider' to morally arbitrate, the resolution will be achieved by the individuals themselves, through their revelation of R_b^* in conjunction with the choice function, satisfying the stipulated requirements. In such cases, which alternative is eventually chosen will depend upon, to some extent, (1) who is respecting rights, and (2) in what way.

Austen-Smith (1982) sees this as a fundamental problem with the Sen approach. Consider the example which Austen-Smith uses to illustrate this:

Take $S = \{x, y, w, z\}$. Let $\langle x, y ; b \rangle \in \mathscr{R}$ and $\langle z, w ; c \rangle \in \mathscr{R}$. Let preferences of individuals be

$$b: \ wP_b xP_b yP_b z$$

$$c: \ yP_c zP_c wP_c x$$

$$k: \ wP_k xP_k yP_k z$$

$$\forall h \neq c, b, k: yP_h wP_h xP_h z$$

Given the standard rights implementation rule (SRI) and the Pareto condition P the choice set will be empty in this example.

Austen-Smith first considers b as the only individual who wishes to respect rights, the others wish *all* their preferences to count in social choice. Individual b reveals $xP_b^* yP_b^* z$. Given this, the choice set is $\{x\}$. Austen-Smith then considers that instead of individual b, the individual k may wish to respect rights. Despite having the same preferences as b, individual k might reveal $wP_k^* xP_k^* y$. In this case the choice set will be $\{z\}$. If both individuals b and k were 'liberal' in this way then either x or z will be chosen. Austen-Smith claims this feature of the Sen procedure is very 'unappealing'.

In contrast to Austen-Smith, I find that this flexibility of the Sen approach a strong point in its favour. Sen stresses that ethical solutions to the liberal paradox depend on the motives behind preferences. Thus, dependent on the nature and motives behind the above abstract example, there could be a case where $\{x\}$ should be chosen or there could be another case (with different motives and possibly alternatives of a different nature) where $\{z\}$ should be chosen. The difficulties in incorporating motives formally into the analysis are obviously great. However, I think that the Sen approach is a step in the right direction since there seems to be a strong likelihood that liberals, by varying the subrelation of their preferences that they want to count (depending on the nature and motivations behind the particular case in question), will help secure ethical solutions to the paradox in each case.

Will unethical Pareto links be vetoed with the Sen scheme? That is, will there exist at least one individual who will withdraw his or her preferences over the undesirable link? Sen (1979) stresses that a person voluntarily refusing to enforce a Pareto link, does so 'because he is libertarian enough to see no *moral* gain'. The liberal individual, that is, realises that his true preferences in a particular situation are nosey and unethical and thus should not count. Note also that it takes only one person to disapprove of an unethical Pareto link for it to be vetoed. In large societies (and most are) which would contain at least some virtuous and impartial observers, it would be exceedingly surprising to see all individuals supporting an undesirable Pareto link. If, in fact, all members of the society do fully endorse a particular Pareto link then it seems to suggest that it should be preserved; in essence all of society is making a moral decision for it to count. Thus the Sen scheme has the advantages of having undesirable Pareto links vetoed and preserving Pareto links that are desirable.

This leaves the possibility of some ethical Pareto links being vetoed in addition to the undesirable ones. Consider again the preferences in the Austen-Smith example. Assume that in a particular case the preferences over $\{z, y\}$ are unethical and, say, individual k is liberal enough to see this and thus would want $wP_k^* x P_k^* y$ to count in social choice. Thus z will be chosen. Now assume that individual b is an immoral, selfish individual who is very much in the know and does not want his least preferred alternative to be chosen. He could then react to this by declaring himself to be liberal and revealing $xP_b^* y P_b^* z$ as the preferences that he wants to count. Thus with both individuals being liberal, both Pareto links will be vetoed and either $\{x\}$ or $\{z\}$ will be chosen, a situation that the selfish b might find advantageous.[1] The question is: does this negative aspect of the Sen approach outweigh the advantages discussed previously? I do not think so. Note that the selfish individual cannot stop z being chosen. All he can do is open up the possible set of alternatives that can be chosen such that *in addition* x can be chosen. This does not mean x *will* be chosen. The decision between z and x is left to the choice function as the final moral arbitrator. Thus, despite individual b's veto, a well constructed, ethical choice function will override his veto and endorse the Pareto link over (w, x) after all.

I do not claim that the Sen approach is perfect, in that ethical solutions will always result, but I do think that the flexible approach, in that liberals can choose how to be liberal, is a step in the right direction. It would defin-

---

[1] It is clear that individuals can choose to reveal an R_b^* 'strategically'. It is important that while R_b^* can be chosen by an individual because he wants, in some senses, to manipulate the social choice in his favour, we do not allow him to reveal his preference R_b for this reason. Throughout this thesis it is assumed that R_b is person b's honest preferences. Thus any R_b^* that an individual might reveal must be a subrelation of his true preference R_b.

itely not be desirable to have a rigid, inflexible rule that will automatically axe a Pareto link invariant to motives and the nature of the example in question.[1]

5.3.2 *Austen-Smith's restricted Pareto condition* (see p. 92)

At the heart of Austen-Smith's approach is what he calls 'the important notion of an ethical hierarchy'. In his view libertarianism should be preserved as having 'a higher order value relative to Paretianism'. He does not say that the Pareto condition is prima facie undesirable, only that rights implementation should be considered as more desirable. This view can be inferred from the following example which Austen-Smith presents to illustrate the 'costs of taking on board $RCWP$' in terms of unnecessary vetoing of the Pareto condition.

Let $S = \{x, y, z\}$ and for some $b \in H$ let $\langle x, y ; b \rangle \in \mathscr{R}$. Let preferences be

$$b: xP_b yP_b z$$

$$\forall c \, (\neq b): yP_c z$$

In this case, given condition P and standard rights implementation, $\{x\}$ will be the choice set over S. However, instead of condition P, if condition $RCWP$ was used, the Pareto link over the pair (y, z) would be axed. Austen-Smith accepts this as an unnecessary 'cost' with his procedure, i.e. it is 'inefficient' in the sense that it does not preserve the Pareto condition when application of it will not yield a conflict with rights. However, he defends his approach on grounds that 'the social decision making process' is not 'critically dependent upon which subset of individuals choose to be liberal' in the way the Sen approach is.

As I have argued in the previous subsection, this aspect of the Sen approach is (to me at least) a very attractive feature in its favour. With condition $RCWP$ this flexibility is destroyed. In the above example the Pareto link will be axed independent of the motivation behind individuals' preferences and independent of the nature of the alternatives involved. This inflexibility is a disadvantage of this approach. To 'minimise' the costs of having the Pareto condition violated in too many unnecessary cases, Austen-Smith suggests that his condition $RCWP$ should be used only in conflict cases, otherwise retaining condition P. This does not, however, overcome my criticism of inflexibility (though the procedure would become more 'efficient').

Consider the following example of a conflict situation.
Let $S = \{x, y, w, z\}$
Let $\langle x, y : b \rangle \in \mathscr{R}$ and $\langle z, w : c \rangle \in \mathscr{R}$.

---

[1] See additional note at end of chapter.

Let preferences be

$$b: wP_b xP_b yP_b z$$

$$c: yP_b zP_b wP_b x$$

$$\forall h \neq c, b: yP_b z \text{ and } wP_b x$$

Given *RCWP* the Pareto links over the pairs $\{w, x\}$ and $\{y, z\}$ will both be axed and this will be independent of motivations behind the preference and independent of the nature of the alternatives. With Sen's more flexible approach, this would not necessarily be the case. Which Pareto link(s) will be vetoed will depend on who and how individuals ethically judge what preferences should count in social choice. This shows clearly why Austen-Smith is wrong to conclude:

... if the [Sen] approach is considered attractive (and no constraints are imposed upon who is liberal), then our new principle shall likewise be acceptable.

In summary then, my main criticism of Austen-Smith's procedure is that (1) it is insensitive to motivation behind preferences and the nature of the example in question, (2) it ignores the possibility that rights should be axed in some cases, (3) it axes Pareto links with an arbitrary rule, in many cases unnecessarily, and without justification other than that rights are more desirable than Pareto.

5.3.3   *Hammond's private Pareto condition* (see p. 92)

According to Hammond, his resolution scheme, 'is an attempt to establish fairly generally exactly what sort of rights can be respected by the social rule, and how far the Pareto criterion can be followed without violating individual's rights' (Hammond, 1980). Hammond, within the issue framework, uses Gibbard's libertarian condition L^G. That this libertarian condition establishes 'fairly generally what sort of rights can be respected by the social choice rule' is questionable to say the least. L^G gives a particular resolution to the Gibbard paradox which has many drawbacks (as discussed in Chapter 2). Hammond does not consider alternative ways of resolving the Gibbard paradox.

To resolve the Sen paradox, which in this context is the potential conflict between condition L^G and condition P, Hammond formulates his private Pareto condition *PP*. This, in *his* view, meets the objective of seeking to find 'how far the Pareto criteria can be followed without violating individuals' rights'. He asserts that to avoid a conflict of rights with the Pareto condition 'this principle has to be modified so that it is *only* applied when individuals' preferences are privately oriented' [the emphasis is my own].

Hammond further asserts:

It may be thought desirable to heed an individual's rights even though his preferences are privately conditional, or to heed an individual's preferences in applying the Pareto principle even though his preferences are not privately oriented. But then something else has to give; somebody's rights may have to be violated even though their preferences are unconditional; or somebody's preferences may have to be ignored in applying the Pareto principle, even though their preferences are privately oriented. Neither is satisfactory.

It is thus clear that Hammond views his condition PP as a necessary weakening of condition P to facilitate a resolution to the Sen paradox given condition L^G ('then something else has to give'). This is simply not true! Within a significantly broad class of 'available' subsets of X, Hammond's condition PP when combined with condition L^G gives no additional guidance in social choice whatsoever. This class of subsets of X are all subsets for which the public features are the same for each social alternative, and which are 'technologically complete'. I must define what I mean by 'technologically complete'.

Let $\bar{M}_i(S)$ be the issue set, the elements of which are the feature alternatives for issue i in an available set $S \subseteq X$.

Technologically complete sets Given any set $S \subseteq X$ and given $\bar{M}_i(S)$ for all $i = 1, 2, \ldots, n$ the set S will be said to be 'technologically complete' if and only if S is equal to the cartesian product $\bar{M}_1(S) \times \bar{M}_2(S) \times \ldots \times \bar{M}_n(S)$.

Theorem 5.3.1 *Given that there is more than one individual, then for all subsets S of X which are 'technologically complete' and for which the public feature alternatives are the same for each alternative in S, the private Pareto condition PP does not dismiss any alternative from the choice set which would not otherwise be dismissed by condition L^G, in the context of a choice function $C(S, \{R_b\})$.*

Proof: Assume, for two alternatives x and y in a technologically complete set S' such that the public features are the same for each social alternative in this set, $\forall b : x\hat{P}_b y$. Thus by condition PP, $y \notin C(S', \{R_b\})$. It remains to prove that alternative y would be dismissed anyway by rights implementation for some individual b, given condition L^G.

Given the public features are the same for each alternative in S', then for individual b, for all $w, z \in S'$ such that w_i is in w, z_i in z, $w\hat{P}_b z$ if and only if $wP_b^u z$, issue i being his personal issue, and P_b^u being the unconditional preference relation over features defined in Chapter 2, p. 12.

If for individual b's issue i, some feature alternative $w_i \in M_i$ is the ith feature in both x and y then for this individual it cannot be the case that $x\hat{P}_b y$ for this would require the individual to have strict unconditional preference

$w_i P_b^u w_i$ which is impossible. Analogously, for another individual c assigned an issue j no one feature x_j can be in both x and y.

Thus $x = (x_i, w)$ and $y = (y_i, w')$ where for issue i was assigned to individual b, $x_i \neq y_i$, and w the vector of other feature alternatives in x is not equal to the analogous vector w' in y. (The feature for a second individual must be different.)

For the individual b it must be the case that $x_i P_b^u y_i$ (since $x \hat{P}_b y$) thus he must also have preference $(x_i, w') P_b (y_i, w')$. (x_i, w') is available due to S' being technologically complete. Now by the standard rights system, $\langle (x_i, w'), (y_i, w'); \rangle b \in \mathscr{R}$ and thus by condition L^G, $y = (y_i, w') \notin C(S', \{R_b\})$.

The devolution example presented in Chapter 2 and Gibbard's wall colour example both involve a set S which is technologically complete and which has public features the same for all social alternatives. Thus the limited power of condition PP as an independent source of social comparison is quite significant.

To illustrate further some aspects of condition PP consider the following example. Consider the set of four alternatives $\{(b_1, b_2), (a_1, a_2), (b_1, a_2), (a_1, b_2)\}$, where for individuals 1 and 2, $a_1, b_1 \in M_1$ and $a_2, b_2 \in M_2$. Consider the following preferences

$$\forall b : (b_1, b_2) P_b (a_1, b_2) P_b (a_1, a_2) P_b (b_1, a_2)$$

There is unanimous preference over all the alternatives in this set. The weak Pareto condition imposed on the choice function $C(S, \{R_b\})$ would by itself dictate that the alternative (b_1, b_2) should be chosen. However, condition PP will not dismiss any alternative from the choice set. No privately oriented preferences can be constructed for individual 1.

Can this total axing of the Pareto principle be defended in this case? The Pareto principle and rights are totally consistent with each other in this example thus no defence can be put forward on grounds that a conflict must be resolved. Maybe the Pareto principle applied to this example would be unethical? Though one may think of some motivations behind the individuals' preferences that would lead to the conclusion, it may simply be the case that all individuals other than individual 2 want very much to agree with the respectable, moral individual 2. Individual 2's preferences are very self-oriented, they clearly satisfy Gaertner and Krüger's SSP and are thus not obviously 'meddlesome'. It is hard to think why, in such a case, individuals' wishes should not be respected. In any case, there is clearly no flexibility which allows the motivations behind preferences and the *nature* of the alternatives in the example to be considered as relevant in deciding whether the Pareto principle should count or not.

Another major drawback with Hammond's procedure is that each individual is assigned only one issue. The reason Hammond assumes this is clear from the following example. Let individual 1 now be allocated both issues in the above example. Let his preferences now be

$$(a_1, a_2) P_1 (a_1, b_2) P_1 (b_1, a_2) P_1 (b_1, b_2)$$

If we determine his privately oriented preferences on the basis of issue 1 we would have

$$(a_1, a_2) \hat{P}_1 (b_1, a_2); (a_1, a_2) \hat{P}_1 (b_1, b_2)$$

$$(a_1, b_2) \hat{P}_1 (b_1, a_2); (a_1, a_2) \hat{P}_1 (b_1, b_2)$$

Note that despite the individual exhibiting Gaertner and Krüger's SSP, in this case his privately oriented preferences do not reproduce his total true preferences. If we determine individual 1's privately oriented preferences on the basis of issue 2 we would have

$$(a_1, a_2) \hat{P}_1 (a_1, b_2); (a_1, a_2) \hat{P}_1 (b_1, b_2)$$

$$(b_1, a_2) \hat{P}_1 (a_1, b_2); (a_1, a_2) \hat{P}_1 (b_1, b_2)$$

Consider now the privately oriented preference for the pair $\{(a_1, b_2), (b_1, a_2)\}$ If we construct a privately oriented preference with respect to issue 1 we have $(a_1, b_2) \hat{P}_1 (b_1, a_2)$ but if we construct them with respect to issue 2 we get $(b_1, a_2) \hat{P}_1 (a_1, b_2)$. This shows clearly that privately oriented preference need not be a subrelation of an individual's true preferences. Given two possible privately oriented orderings for these two alternatives, which should be used as regards the Pareto condition, if any?

One issue could be chosen from the two assigned to individual b and this could be used to construct his privately oriented preferences, but as is clear from the above example, social judgement, which in part could be dictated by condition PP, could depend crucially on which issue we choose for this purpose. The moral justification for choosing one issue over another for individual b would be hard to find.

In summary, we see there are several unattractive features of condition PP.

(1) Over a significantly broad class of subsets, independent of which preference might be revealed, condition PP offers no social judgement over and above condition L^G.

(2) In cases of unanimous agreement in the orderings of alternatives, and thus no possible conflict between rights and Pareto, condition PP can be seen to axe all Pareto comparisons purely because for *one* individual b the relation $\hat{P}_b^0$ is void and this is without moral justification based on motivation behind individual preferences and the nature of the alternatives in question.

(3) Individuals can only be allocated one private issue if we wish to avoid the possibility of having two (or more) different profiles of privately oriented preferences for one individual.

Given that Hammond's objective (motivation) was to see 'how far the Pareto criterion can be followed without violating individual rights' the above criticisms are a damning indictment of Hammond's approach.

5.3.4   *Justice constrained Pareto condition* (see p. 95)

The motivation behind this approach is that 'justice' is a very important criterion for social choice, so much so that both rights *and* the application of the Pareto principle should only occur when everybody considers it 'just' according to their respective justice relations P_b^J. By constraining the Pareto condition as well as rights with the justice relations we obtain two advantages over the resolution procedures presented in Chapter 4, Section 4.2.3.

First, we can dispense with the axiom of identity as a restriction on the choice function. My objection to the axiom of identity was discussed in Chapter 4, Section 4.3.3 under point 3 (p. 70). By constraining the Pareto condition in addition to rights, we can produce a possibility result for all logically possible extended orderings $\{\tilde{R}_b\}$, not just a subset of them. The present type of procedure is thus a more complete resolution to the Sen paradox.

Secondly, the possibility results in Chapter 4, Section 4.2, were proved because we used specific justice relations which, under the axiom of identity, were implied by the Pareto relation $\bar{\bar{P}}$. This obviously limits the scope of the types of justice relations we can allocate to individuals. With the present approach each individual can be allocated any justice relation P_b^J so long as for at least one individual P_b^J is transitive and asymmetric.

The above points are what I would consider as two 'motivational' gains over the previous approaches which use justice relations to constrain rights only; but what of the 'costs' of these gains? Now the Pareto condition is in addition modified by justice. Pareto can only be enforced in social choice if *everybody* considers it just. Given unanimous preference for an alternative x over y, Pareto will be axed over this pair if just one individual fails to reveal a strict preference for x over y with his justice relation P_b^J — this can be considered too severe. In some cases even though justice conflicts with the Pareto principle it might nevertheless be morally right to endorse the Pareto preference — it again depends on the motivation underlying the extended preference and the nature of the alternatives in question.

Having said this, it should be noted that if one individual's preference satisfies the axiom of identity, and for this one person $P_b^J = M_b^A, L_b^{ex}$ or J_b then condition P if and only if condition PP^J, i.e. the Pareto condition will not be constrained in such a case.

In essence, the main motivational criticism of this approach is that justice is given a universal primary weight in social choice over rights and Pareto, and in such a way as to constrain the rights implementation over a pair for some individual, or to constrain the Pareto judgement over a pair for which there is unanimous strict preference, even if just one individual thinks the opposite preference is 'just'.

5.4 Informational requirements

The informational requirements for the procedures discussed in Section 5.2 will now be stated. These 'costs' must be weighed against the other features of these procedures discussed in the other sections.

5.4.1 *Sen's conditional Pareto condition*

In addition to preferences over the available set, the m-list of relations R_b^*, over the available set, of preferences which individuals want to see count in social choice is required. In the case where there is a conflict between rights and the conditional Pareto condition then Sen suggests the need for a well informed 'outsider' to morally arbitrate. Such an outsider will require much information as regards individuals' motivation, nature of the alternatives, intensity of preference etc. Such information will not be very easily available.

5.4.2 *Austen-Smith's restricted Pareto condition*

Informationally this procedure is very efficient. Individuals are just required to reveal preferences over the available set of alternatives in question.

5.4.3 *Hammond's private Pareto condition*

To formulate an individual's privately oriented preferences it is necessary to look at his preference over the total set X in question, rather than the subset S available. Hammond defines his choice function, as I do, such that it yields non-empty choice sets for every non-empty subset S of X. However, privately oriented preferences are constructed on the basis of preferences over the total set X and thus are invariant to the subset S available in the case in question (see the definitions in Section 5.2.3, p. 93). The universal set X is not really practically definable, and to insist on information on unavailable alternatives in a resolution procedure demands far too much information, including a satisfactory statement of what the total set includes. The total set X is used in the definition of a choice function to stipulate that given any available set of alternatives, choice must be made. To this end it need not be defined precisely. To construct a modification of the Pareto condition assuming that we have information on what the total set X consists of, is operationally impractical — it would need an impossible amount of information.

5.4.4   Justice constrained Pareto condition

This procedure also demands much information. The informational requirements are exactly the same as for the procedures discussed in Chapter 2 (see Section 2.4.2.3). It should be noted that because the axiom of identity is not used, less information is needed than for the resolution procedures of Chapter 4, Section 4.2.3 (see also Chapter 4, Section 4.4.3). If individuals wish to satisfy the axiom of identity they must, as well as knowledge of other people's objective circumstances (which must be known in the present case), know about other people's subjective circumstances, e.g. tastes. The information requirements of this procedure are still, of course, very severe.

5.5   Efficiency

Up to this point in the book 'efficiency' has been discussed with respect to rights implementation. A rights implementation rule was deemed more efficient than another if it preserved more rights. A 'Pareto-efficiency' measure which can compare different modified Pareto conditions in terms of the degree to which they preserve Pareto judgements in social choice will now be defined.

Let $\mu^P(S, \{R_b\})$ be the number of pairs of alternatives $\{x, y\}$ for which, given $S \subseteq X$ and a particular $\{R_b\}$, we have $\forall b : xP_by$. Let $\mu^{Pm}(S, \{R_b\})$ be the number of pairs of alternatives $\{x, y\}$ for which, given $S \subseteq X$ and a particular $\{R_b\}$, we have (a) $\forall b : xP_by$, and (b) the modified Pareto condition Pm dictates that $y \notin C(S : x \in S, \{R_b\})$.

Given an available set S, and an m-list of preferences $\{R_b\}$, the 'Pareto-efficiency' of a modified Pareto condition Pm can be defined as

$$\Pi^{Pm}(S, \{R_b\}) = \frac{\mu^{Pm}(S, \{R_b\})}{\mu^P(S, \{R_b\})} \quad \text{if } \mu^P(S, \{R_b\}) \neq 0$$

$$= 1 \quad \text{otherwise}$$

For all possible sets of preferences, $\{R_b\}$, and all possible available sets S

$$1 \geqslant \Pi^{Pm}(S, \{R_b\}) \geqslant 0$$

If $\Pi^{Pm}(S, \{R_b\}) = 1$, then the modified Pareto condition Pm is implementing all the Pareto judgements, given S and $\{R_b\}$, as would condition P. If $\Pi^{Pm}(S, \{R_b\}) = 0$, then no Pareto judgements are being implemented by Pm despite there being unanimous preference for some pair in S.

If a modified Pareto condition P' is *at least as efficient* as another P'', we will write $P' \geqslant_{PE} P''$. This is defined as

$$P' \geqslant_{PE} P'' \leftrightarrow [\forall S \subseteq X, \forall \{R_b\}: \Pi^{P'}(S, \{R_b\}) \geqslant \Pi^{P''}(S, \{R_b\})]$$

If a modified Pareto condition P' is *strictly more efficient* than another P'', we will write $P' >_{PE} P''$. This is defined as $P' >_{PE} P$

$$P' >_{PE} P'' \leftrightarrow [P' \geqslant_{PE} P'' \text{ and for some } S \subseteq X \text{ and } \{R_b\}: \Pi^{P'}(S, \{R_b\}) > \Pi^{P''}(S, \{R_b\})]$$

$\geqslant_{PE}$ is reflexive and transitive. $>_{PE}$ is transitive and asymmetric. Neither is necessarily complete.

With rights implementation methods for resolving the Sen paradox discussed in Chapter 4, the Pareto condition is not modified, thus obviously Pareto efficiency is at a maximum for all such procedures. In comparing the total efficiency of different procedures it was only necessary to consider the efficiency of the rights implementation rules used.

In the context of Pareto modification, a comparison of two different procedures, given that for each the rights system and the rights implementation rule are the same, can be discussed in terms of Pareto efficiency. However, if it was required to compare the efficiency of a resolution procedure which uses the justice constrained Pareto condition with that of Hammond's private Pareto procedure, then Pareto efficiency might not be the only efficiency criterion that should be used. Hammond's private Pareto condition is designed ro be consistent with condition L^G whereas the justice constrained Pareto condition is designed to be consistent with the justice constrained libertarian condition. An overall efficiency comparison must then be based on the rights efficiency and the Pareto efficiency of the resolution procedures.

As stressed in Chapter 2 and again in Chapter 4, efficiency is only one criterion for assessing different resolution methods. The importance of a Pareto-efficiency comparison depends upon why the Pareto condition is modified, i.e. the motivation behind the modification. If Pareto is being modified because it should, on ethical grounds, then efficiency is not so relevant. If, on the other hand, the Pareto modification is motivated by the need to resolve the conflict between Pareto and rights, it otherwise being a desirable condition, then efficiency is more relevant — one would not want to axe Pareto judgements unnecessarily. It should be noted that the modified Pareto conditions discussed in Section 2 can be seen as a way to resolve the Sen paradox independently of the motivation that led to their construction. Thus efficiency can be viewed as being important despite in some cases the original motivation suggesting it is not.

In the following four sections, the efficiency of the different Pareto-modification procedures of this chapter will be discussed. It will be seen that the relations $\geqslant_{PE}$ and $>_{PE}$ are of limited use, the modified Pareto conditions not being comparable with such relations. However, the definitions leading to the formulations of $\geqslant_{PE}$ and $>_{PE}$ make explicit what is meant by efficiency and thus are important to stop any ambiguity.

5.5.1 *Sen's conditional Pareto condition*

Sen's resolution procedure, as stated in Section 2, can be assessed given any libertarian condition which is not vulnerable to the Gibbard paradox. (Some trivial redefining of what is meant by 'respecting rights' is necessary.)

The efficiency of the conditional Pareto condition depends not only upon the subset of alternatives available and the preferences, but on which individuals respect rights and how they respect rights. If all individuals decide they do not want any of their preferences to count in social choice, then the conditional Pareto condition would be grossly inefficient. On the other hand it could be the case that individuals only reveal their respective R_b^* as different to their respective R_b in conflict cases, and then only one Pareto judgement may be axed (see the discussion on the motivation in Section 5.3.1). Here the conditional Pareto condition would be very efficient. This flexibility, which elsewhere I have judged to be an aspect of this approach which is good, makes any formal efficiency comparisons with the other modified Pareto conditions impossible. However, 'potentially' the conditional Pareto condition can be seen as the most efficient of all the modified Pareto conditions – but then it is quite possible that it will be inconsistent with the libertarian condition! The price of high efficiency might be that the conditional Pareto condition will not help resolve the paradox (nobody decides to respect rights) – in such cases the efficiency will depend on what Sen's outsider does and he is in no way bound to modify the Pareto condition.

5.5.2 *Austen-Smith's restricted Pareto condition*

Austen-Smith's restricted Pareto condition axes all Pareto judgements over a pair if the most preferred alternative of this pair is dismissed by rights implementation. Austen-Smith himself admits that this is not an 'efficient' way of modifying the Pareto condition, see his example presented at the beginning of Section 5.3.2. Consider another example: let all individuals have the following preferences $\forall b : xP_byP_bzP_bw$. Assume that for an individual d, $\langle y, z ; d \rangle \in \mathscr{R}$ and his rights are implemented (this is consistent with all libertarian conditions here). Despite unanimous preference the choice function could choose alternative w and be totally consistent with Austen-Smith's Pareto condition.

5.5.3 *Hammond's private Pareto condition*

Hammond's procedure is motivated by 'efficiency' considerations:

The present paper . . . is an attempt to establish fairly generally exactly what sort of rights can be respected by the social choice rule, and how far the Pareto criterion can be followed without violating individuals' rights. (Hammond, 1980)

However, for a significantly large class of subsets of X Hammond's private Pareto condition PP, when combined with condition L^G, gives no additional guidance in social choice whatsoever – see Theorem 5.3.1, p. 101.

Also condition L^G is not the most efficient of all the libertarian conditions not vulnerable to the Gibbard paradox, as has been discussed in Chapter 2.

5.5.4 *Justice constrained Pareto condition*

The efficiency of condition PP^J (as with the rights implementation rule of condition LP^J) depends upon what justice relations are being used by individuals.

Given that

(1) $xJ_b y \rightarrow xL_b^{ex} y, \forall x, y \in X$

(2) $xM_b^A y \rightarrow xL_b^{ex} y, \forall x, y \in X$

then

(1) PP^J (where $\forall b : P_b^J = L_b^{ex}) >_{PE} PP^J$ (where $\forall b : P_b^J = J_b$)

(2) PP^J (where $\forall b : P_b^J = L_b^{ex}) >_{PE} PP^J$ (where $\forall b : P_b^J = M_b^A$)

Thus with rights and Pareto being constrained with leximin for all individuals, a more efficient resolution, than if constrained by Suppes or strict ranking maximin, is produced.

It has not been possible to make any general efficiency comparisons. Which modified Pareto condition is the more efficient will depend on the preferences of the individuals in those cases in question. Basically all that can be said is that all the modified Pareto conditions, with the possible exception of Sen's, are inefficient. The efficiency of all the procedures would be increased if the standard Pareto condition was modified (by the respective modifications discussed) *only when* a conflict between it and the rights occurs.

5.6 Rationality, independence and minimal Pareto

Consider the following definitions, some of which we have seen before.

Contraction consistency (α)

$$\forall x : x \in S^1 \subseteq S^2 \subseteq X \to [x \in C(S^2, \{R_b\}) \to x \in C(S^1, \{R_b\})]$$

Independence of irrelevant alternatives (I)

$$\forall b : \{\forall x, y \in S : x \, R_b \, y \leftrightarrow x R'_b y\}$$
$$\to C(S, \{R_b\}) = C(S, \{R'_b\})$$

Minimal Pareto (MP)

$$\forall x, y \in X, \forall b : x P_b y \to y \notin C(\{x, y\}, \{R_b\})$$

Minimal Pareto says that if the available set is just two alternatives, and everybody strictly prefers one to the other then the least preferred alternative should not be chosen from this set.

5.6.1   *Sen's conditional Pareto condition*

If some individual 'respects rights' then there exists a choice function satisfying ML^S and PC. The existence of an individual respecting the rights of others could be seen as a domain restriction on the type of preferences $\{R_b^*\}$ that individuals wish to see count in social choice — if any possible $\{R_b^*\}$ were allowed then condition PC can conflict with rights in a very similar way to condition P. The existence of an individual 'respecting rights' is only one form of a restriction on $\{R_b^*\}$ that will secure possibility, other restrictions can be imagined, e.g. R_b^* being void for each individual b (this, of course would be very Pareto inefficient).

Theorem 5.6.1 *Any domain restriction on $\{R_b^*\}$, which is sufficient to ensure that there exists a choice function $C(S, \{R_b\})$ satisfying condition ML^S and condition PC, implies that condition α and condition MP can not both also be satisfied in social choice.*

Proof: Let two individuals, 1 and 2, be assigned the pairs (x, y) and (w, z) respectively. If the two pairs are the same then there will not exist a choice function satisfying ML^S.

Suppose the pairs have one alternative in common, say $y = w$. Let preferences be

1	2	Others (if any)	
z	y = w	y	descending order
x	z	z	of strict
y	x	x	preference

Assume that there exists a choice function satisfying ML^S and PC. Thus by ML^S, y and z will be dismissed from the choice set implying that x will be chosen. If x is chosen from the smaller set $\{z, x\}$ then minimal Pareto will be violated. If x is dismissed from the smaller set $\{z, x\}$ then condition α will be violated.

Assume now the pairs are totally distinct. Let preferences be

1	2	Others (if any)	
z	y	y	descending order
x	w	w	of strict
y	z	z	preference
w	x	x	

Assume there exists a choice function satisfying ML^S and PC. Thus by ML^S, y and z will be dismissed from the choice set. Thus w or x must be chosen. If w is chosen and is also chosen given the set $\{y, w\}$ then minimal Pareto will be violated. If w is chosen but is not chosen from the set $\{y, w\}$, a smaller set, then condition α will be violated. If x is chosen from the set of four alternatives and is also chosen from the set $\{z, x\}$ then MP will be violated. If x is chosen from the larger set but not chosen from the set $\{z, x\}$ then α will be violated.

Thus, given that there exists a choice function satisfying ML^S and PC, condition α and condition MP cannot also be satisfied.

It can be seen that if minimal Pareto is to be satisfied with Sen's procedure, then the individuals' revelation of the preferences that they want to see count in social choice must depend on the available set – this implies that the rationality requirement α will be violated. If the individuals revealed $\{R_b^*\}$ are independent of the available set, like their preferences $\{R_b\}$ then condition α will not be violated but minimal Pareto will.

Given that there are no constraints on how individuals restrict their true preferences to the ones they want to see count in social choice, condition I will be violated given this procedure:

Consider the following two sets of preferences over six alternatives for two individuals:

A		B		
1	2	1	2	
u	u	w	y	
w	y	x	z	descending order
x	z	u	u	of strict
y	w	v	v	preference
z	x	y	z	
v	v	z	w	

Let $\langle x, y \,;\, 1 \rangle \in \mathscr{R}$ and $\langle z, w \,;\, 2 \rangle \in \mathscr{R}$. Assume there exists a choice function satisfying ML^S and PC. Now preferences over the alternatives $\{w, x, y, z\}$ are the same in both case A and case B. By independence of irrelevant alternatives $C(\{w, x, y, z\}, \{R_b^A\}) = C(\{w, x, y, z\}, \{R_b^B\})$. However, Sen's procedure uses extra 'non-utility' information in the form of $\{R_b^*\}$. In case A individual 1 might reveal $R_1^* = R_1$ and individual 2 might reveal $zP_2^*wP_2^*x$. Thus z will be chosen from the set $\{w, z, x, y\}$. In case B, individual 2 might reveal $R_2^* = R_2$ and individual 1 reveal $xP_1^*yP_1^*z$. Thus x will be chosen.

In both case A and B the preferences over the set $\{w, z, x, y\}$ are the same yet with the Sen procedure choice can be different thus violating independence. I have previously defended this form of flexibility of Sen's approach and consider the above illustration more of a criticism of the condition of independence of irrelevant alternatives, than a criticism of this flexibility. Independence basically excludes the possibility of using the *extra* information obtained by $\{R_b^*\}$.

5.6.2   *Austen-Smith's restricted Pareto condition*

Theorem 5.6.2 *There does not exist a choice function $C(S, \{R_b\})$ satisfying ML^S, $RCWP$ and α.*

Proof: In a case of conflict between rights and Pareto, Austen-Smith resolves the conflict by a curtailment of the power of Pareto. Thus there exist cases where an alternative x will be chosen despite all people preferring another alternative y which is available. However, if given these preferences, the available set was only $\{x, y\}$, x would be dismissed by $RCWP$, thus violating α.

Rationality is violated since the set $A(S)$ in the set of alternatives not vetoed by individual rights, is defined with respect to the available set only. This allows Austen-Smith's $RCWP$ to be totally consistent with minimal Pareto.

5.6.3   *Hammond's private Pareto condition*

Consider the following set of alternatives

$$xx = (x_1, x_2, z) \qquad yy = (y_1, y_2, z)$$
$$xy = (x_1, y_2, z) \qquad yx = (y_1, x_2, z)$$

where $z = x_3, x_4, \ldots, x_n$ are the same for all four alternatives. Let $x_1, y_1 \in M_1$ and let individual 1 be assigned issue 1. Let $x_2, y_2 \in M_2$ and let individual 2 be assigned issue 2.

Consider the following two sets of preferences for the two individuals:

A		B		
1	2	1	2	
xx	yy	yy	xx	descending order
yx	yx	yx	yx	of strict
xy	xy	xy	xy	preference
yy	xx	xx	yy	

Now consider choice over $\{yx, xy\}$. Given condition PP in case A, xy will be chosen, but in case B, yx will be chosen. Since preference over the *pair* are the same in both cases (A and B), independence is violated. Also in case A, minimal Pareto is violated.

The reason for this is that privately oriented preferences are defined with respect to preferences over the total set X. When looking at the choice over the pair $\{yx, xy\}$ the social judgement given by condition PP depends on how individuals order *other* pairs.

5.6.4 *Justice constrained Pareto conditions*

Given that $\forall b : (x, b) \widetilde{P}_b (y, b)$ then the standard weak Pareto condition within the extended informational framework will dismiss y from the choice set given that x is available. Condition PP^J will only dismiss y from the choice set if in addition $\forall b : xP_b^J y$. Whether this extra stipulation is satisfied depends on the extended preferences over the pair $\{x, y\}$ – it is not dependent on any preferences over pairs other than $\{x, y\}$. There is thus no immediate conflict between condition PP^J and condition α as with Austen-Smith's $RCWP$ – if $\forall b : (x, b) \widetilde{P}_b (y, b)$ and $\forall bxP_b^J y$ then, given condition PP^J, y will be dismissed from the choice set over any available set which contains x.

The implications for minimal Pareto and independence depend in part on the specific justice relations used. It is quite possible that given $\forall b : (x, b) \widetilde{P}_b$ (y, b) one could have $\forall b : xP_b^J y$ or $\forall b : yP_b^J x$.

Suppose we formulated a choice function via the following social preference relation.

$$xRy \leftrightarrow \text{not} (\forall b : yP_b^J x)$$

$$C^*(S, \{\widetilde{R}_b\}) = \{x : x \in S \text{ and } (\forall y) [y \in S \to xRy]\}$$

This choice function satisfies LP^J and PP^J by construction. Assume that $\forall b (x, b) \widetilde{P}_b (y, b)$ and $\forall b : yP_b^J x$. Thus given the above choice function $\{y\} = C^*(\{x, y\}, \{R_b\})$ and minimal Pareto will be violated. It is also possible that $\forall b : (x, b) P_b (y, b)$ and $\forall b : xP_b^J y$. In this case $\{x\} = C^*(\{x, y\}, \{R_b\})$. Thus independence can be violated. For each individual, his preferences over alternative x and y 'in his own shoes' are the same in each case.

5.7   Conclusion

Four types of Pareto modification procedures have been presented and evaluated. A common aspect of all these approaches is that the Pareto condition *should* be modified to resolve the Sen paradox. However, the procedures have not all been motivated in the same way.

Sen motivated his approach by arguing that the Pareto condition which is based purely on preferences is not always morally justified. Sen allows the individuals a 'veto' over Pareto via their extra revelation of a subrelation of the respective preferences they want to see count in social choice. The modification of Pareto here is more on ethical grounds than because modification is necessary to resolve a conflict with rights — indeed one of my main criticisms of this approach is that the conditional Pareto condition can still conflict with rights and Sen is vague on how this conflict should be resolved.

Austen-Smith and Hammond both motivate their respective modification by stressing the need to resolve the conflict. They accept the Pareto condition as universally desirable, but less so than rights, thus they sought a modification which was consistent with rights yet efficient.

The justice constrained Pareto condition was motivated by stressing the importance of 'justice' in Pareto comparisons. Pareto judgement over a pair must be fully endorsed by a unanimous 'justice' judgement over this pair.

An important aspect of any Pareto modification is that it should be sensitive to the motivation behind preferences. Sen's conditional Pareto condition is unique amongst the modified Pareto conditions considered, in that it is sensitive to a 'moral' judgement of individuals not solely based on utility information. In the *Lady Chatterley's Lover* case (see Section 5.3.1, p. 95) it is clear that the individuals themselves, through a moral evaluation of the circumstances, can resolve the conflict through voluntary restrictions of their preferences. Such an approach can imply that, given the same set of preferences over the same set of alternatives, the social outcome will not always be the same, it depends on who and how people restrict their preferences. This flexibility towards the motivation underlying the preferences is advantageous despite the possibility of violating the condition of independence. In my view, however, it does not go far enough; only Pareto judgements are dependent on the way people reveal their respective R_b^*. Rights are still automatically implemented according to preferences (albeit not straightforwardly in some cases so as to avoid the Gibbard paradox). Though I believe rights are always desirable, in conflict cases it may sometimes be the case that they are *less* desirable than Pareto. Consider now an example of a conflict case where I think there are good grounds to axe rights rather than Pareto. This can be contrasted to the 'workshop case' (Chapter 4, Section 4.3.2, p. 67), and Sen's version of the Angelina–Edwin–Judge example (Chapter 4, Section 4.3.1, p. 58), where motivations supported the dropping of the Pareto condition.

There are two individuals who each own a house on the side of a beautiful valley. Individual 1 owns the adjoining fence between their two properties. At present the fence has fallen down due to rotten wood and bad weather. He has planning permission to build a new fence. He has two sets of plans (both of which are approved by the planning authorities) one for a low fence and the other for a high fence. Individual 2 has planning permission to build an oil rig on his land! He has strong reasons to believe that there is sufficient oil under his land to make this financially worthwhile for him.

There are four possible alternative states which can occur:

(HF, NR) = (individual 1 builds a high fence, individual 2 does not build the rig)

(LF, NR) = (individual 1 builds a low fence, individual 2 does not build the rig)

(HF, R) = (individual 1 builds a high fence, individual 2 builds the oil rig)

(LF, R) = (individual 1 builds a low fence, individual 2 builds the oil rig)

Now consider the individuals' preferences:

Individual 1: $(HF, NR) P_1 (LF, NR) P_1 (HF, R) P_1 (LF, R)$
Individual 2: $(LF, R) P_2 (LF, NR) P_2 (HF, R) P_2 (HF, NR)$

Individual 1 wants to build a high fence rather than build a low fence but is much more concerned about the presence of an oil rig next door. The oil rig in his opinion will destroy the beautiful setting of his old house. Both the alternatives which involve this rig being built will be *greatly* less preferred to the other two by individual 1.

Individual 2 wants to build the oil rig rather than not but is much more concerned about the possible presence of a high fence between his and individual 1's property. This fence will destroy his view of the valley completely. (It is all right for individual 1, his view will not be affected!) Both the alternatives which involve the high fence being built are vastly less preferred by individual 2 to the other two.

Implementation of rights, given the standard rights system, will secure the option (HF, R). But this is Pareto inferior to (LF, NR), both individuals *greatly* preferring the alternative (LF, NR) to (HF, R). (Note that both individuals display unconditional preferences, thus rights implementation will secure (HF, R) given Gibbard's libertarian condition L^G in the same way that condition L would.)

Hammond's resolution to this conflict, as with Austen-Smith's will axe the Pareto preference and secure (HF, R) as the chosen alternative. But is this the best choice? (HF, R) is *much* less attractive to both individuals than alternative (LF, NR). Given the above motivations of the individuals and the nature of the example there is a very strong case that the Pareto condition should respect this unanimous preference, and that (LF, NR) should be chosen. This will imply the violation of rights for both individuals but both individuals might well accept this on ethical grounds.

Both individuals are very concerned about the beauty of the valley. However, individual 1 considers the oil rig as the biggest threat to this beauty and individual 2 considers it is individual 1's high fence. Both individuals might concede that the beauty of the valley should be kept for both of them despite individual 1 giving up a little privacy and individual 2 giving up his oil rights. Both will be very much concerned about the possibility of having the alternative (HF, R) chosen and thus will both agree that (LF, NR) is a reasonable and fair compromise. Note that the Pareto preference is not really 'meddlesome' in this case, both individuals are showing a desire to conserve the beauty of the valley, something which is of course of concern to both of them.

I think this example shows clearly that in some conflict cases the Pareto condition should be preserved and that rights (or at least some of them) should be waived. Again, I stress that resolution procedures which invariably axe rights or invariably axe Pareto, without any consideration of motives behind preference and the nature of the choice in question, will be guilty of an inflexibility which is very necessary to secure a 'best' solution to the conflict.

Some of the Pareto modification procedures require an excessive amount of information. For Hammond's procedures a total (universal) set X must be defined, preferences over this obtained, and each individual's privately oriented preferences deduced. For the operation of the justice constrained Pareto and libertarian conditions individuals are required to make interpersonal comparisons. Austen-Smith's restricted Pareto condition does not involve such extensive information, but at a cost of being inefficient and inflexible to the motivation behind preferences. Sen allows individuals to reveal a subrelation of their preferences which they want to see count in social choice. This does involve more information gathering, but the gains in the form of a sensitivity to the moral circumstances of a particular case justify this extra informational cost.

If one accepts that Pareto is desirable, yet less so than rights, then Pareto efficiency is relevant for assessing the procedures. General comparisons of efficiency are impossible but it is clear that the modified Pareto conditions in many cases axe Pareto unnecessarily. The possible exception is Sen's conditional Pareto condition where particular restrictions of preferences can result in an efficient modification of Pareto but this is not guaranteed.

All the procedures are inconsistent with either minimal Pareto, independence or rationality. Dependent on why the Pareto condition is being modified, violation of the above conditions could well be justified. If the unanimous preference for x over y is morally bad, then it might well be immoral independently of other alternatives that might be available — thus violation of minimal Pareto will be justified. Different motivations underlying the same set of preferences over the same set of alternatives might suggest that different social outcomes should be chosen for each case — thus violation of independence might well be justified. If in a conflict case Pareto is desirable, but less so than rights, then despite, say, x being unanimously preferred to y, y might still be chosen to avoid violation of rights. In this case, given that Pareto is desirable, then if the available set changes and consists of only x and y, minimal Pareto should be preserved and x should be chosen. This can justify a violation of the rationality condition α.

Pareto modification can well be justified despite not conflicting with any other desirable condition, it depends on the motivation behind the preferences. However, there exist cases where there is conflict and Pareto is desirable. In such cases *if* rights are deemed more important, then Pareto *must* be modified, but efficiently. However, I stress that sometimes rights should be constrained instead. Further discussion of the appropriateness of Pareto as a social condition and its importance relative to rights, will be pursued in the next chapter.

Additional note (see p. 99)
Another problem Austen-Smith finds with the Sen approach is that given the *strong* version of the conditional Pareto condition ($\forall b : xR^*_by$ and $\exists b : xP^*_by \rightarrow y \notin C^*(S : x \in S, \{R_b\})$) the procedure violates 'anonymity'. However, Austen-Smith does not consider the standard condition of anonymity (condition A, defined in Chapter 3, Section 3.1) as the appropriate condition to use in this case. With the standard anonymity condition the social decision is required to be invariant with respect to permutations of individual preferences. Austen-Smith claims that 'in the present case' the assignment of rights should also be permuted, along with preferences, and then wishes the social decision to be unaffected. However, Austen-Smith claims that the way individuals desire to be 'liberal' (i.e. the way they respect rights) should *not* be permuted along with assigned pairs and preferences in this exercise:

> It is not the name of an individual, or that individual's preference order, that makes the individual a liberal — it is some aspect (psychological or moral) of individuals external to the model which fulfils this function.

Because the individuals' desires to be liberal are not permuted along with preferences and rights it is not surprising that the Sen scheme violates Austen-Smith's condition of anonymity called condition A^*. The motivation behind the definition of condition A^* is strange. On the same grounds that Austen-Smith insists that desires to be liberal should not be permuted, surely rights should *not* be permuted? Rights are allocated on moral considerations, independently of individuals' preferences. Surely the rights assignment is also external to the model and thus, like individuals' desires to be liberal, should not be permuted along with preferences. In this case we are back with the original, standard, condition of anonymity. That this condition is violated by the Sen approach is obvious; but any choice function satisfying a libertarian condition will violate anonymity — the decision to allocate rights could be seen to imply that one does not *wish* anonymity to apply to social choice! If, on the other hand, one does wish to permute rights along with preferences ('in the present case') then one should, on the same grounds, also permute individuals' desires to be liberal. In this case the Sen social decision *will* be invariant to such permutations.

CHAPTER 6

Liberty versus Pareto?

6.1 Introduction

Given the standard rights system (SRS) the implementation of rights (through the standard rights implementation rule, SRI) can result in an apparently irreconcilable conflict (the Gibbard paradox). For all rights systems which assign to at least two individuals a pair of alternatives each, the implementation of rights (through SRI) can conflict with the Pareto principle in social choice (the Sen paradox), again there is a seemingly irreconcilable conflict of interests.

How should these 'paradoxes' best be resolved? In Chapters 2, 4 and 5, several resolution procedures have been discussed and evaluated. It is time now to take stock. In the next two sections a couple of important issues will be considered.

First, I wish to justify the 'unrestricted domain' assumption, as regards individuals' preferences, which is incorporated into the definition of the choice function $C(S, \{R_b\})$: choice, given any subset of alternatives, must be made for *any* given logically possible set of individual orderings $\{R_b\}$.

Secondly, given that the paradoxes arise, what type of resolution procedure should be employed? I will discuss what I feel to be the important properties a resolution procedure should satisfy, and the consequential implications for the weakening of the conditions imposed on social choice.

6.2 Do the paradoxes exist?

Is it reasonable to insist that choice must be made for all logically possible individual orderings $\{R_b\}$? Maybe the configurations of preferences which result in the paradoxes, though 'analytically' possible, will never actually arise in the real world, and as such, choice need not be made for such cases.

The paradoxes only arise for a very small proportion of the total logically possible set of preference configurations $\{R_b\}$. For example, Blau (1975, p. 398) has worked out that a conflict between Sen's condition L^S and the Pareto condition, given two individuals and four alternatives, will only occur for four of the possible 75^2 configurations of individual preferences. Assuming that all orderings are equally likely for every individual, then the probability of the paradoxes arising are extremely small. However, they can, given

118

this equi-probability assumption, still exist and as such a fair resolution to such conflicts should still be sought, albeit for these rare cases.

The assumption of 'equi-probability' has, however, been heavily criticised by Sen:

Depending on people's values and their personal and group interests there would be a fair amount of link up between individuals' preferences: individual preferences are not determined by turning a roulette wheel over all possible alternatives, but by certain specific social, economic, political and cultural forces. (Sen, 1970a, p. 165).

It could be the case that society's 'specific, social, economic, political and cultural forces' are such that the configuration of preferences which result in the paradoxes will *never* be revealed. After all, we discount the possibility of individuals revealing intransitive preferences. There may well be other types of preferences (consistent with them being orderings) which should be ignored on grounds that they can never arise. Blau (1975), pursuing this reasoning, points out that, in the two person case, the conflict between the Pareto principle and Sen's condition L^S arises if both persons are 'meddlesome' in the sense of having stronger preferences *against* the other on the other's assigned pair than on his own assigned pair.

That one of them might exhibit such a preference is remarkable enough, but that both should do so seems to border on the socially pathological. (Blau, 1975, p. 396)

If the preference configurations that lead to the paradoxes never arise then they should not be admitted into the domain of the choice function. Fine (1975) and Breyer (1977) have both sought to resolve the potential conflict between rights and Pareto by restricting the domain of admissable individual preference orderings $\{R_b\}$. This approach resolves the paradoxes by simply assuming they will never occur!

However, if it is established that they can occur, then restricting the domain of admissible preferences can no longer be considered an appropriate way out of the problem. Such an approach is purely one of defeat, not saying anything about what should happen when the paradoxes do exist.

This book has given many examples of conflict cases, albeit some of them in a trivial setting. Are all these cases, and the supplied motivation, simply impossible? Consider Sen's workshop case (Sen (1976), see Chapter 4, p. 66). There the impossibility arises because both individuals prefer having a full-time job to a half-time job, either of these to being unemployed, given the job situation of the other; but, spoilt as they are by the competitive society in which they live, each prefers that the other should be jobless. Indeed, each is so hatefully jealous of the other that he gets more fulfilment out of the job-lessness of the other than from his own job.

Though such preferences can be considered undesirable, are they impossible? Surely cases can be seen where two individuals can hate each other so much that each will wish to make a personal sacrifice (own job) to seek the suffering of the other (his unemployment). People have died for less!

Note that in this example, if one individual has such an adverse opinion of the other to make him want to reveal such 'meddlesome' preferences this would surely increase the chance that the other individual will have an analogous adverse opinion of him, and as such will reveal analogous 'meddlesome' preferences. This point is in contention with Blau's assertion above. Hate breeds hate!

I conclude, in total agreement with Sen (1976, p. 233), 'if meddlesomeness is a disease, it is certainly not a rare disease'.

It thus seems clear (to me at least) that the paradoxes *can* arise. Given they do, then a resolution to the problem must be made through a weakening of the imposed conditions on choice that lead to such possible conflicts. The problem is how should such weakenings be specified, and with what justification?

6.3   In search of a resolution

There are three different reasons for modifying an imposed condition of social choice:

Reason (a) The condition is not in itself socially appealing for all cases.

Reason (b) The condition under some possible circumstances is impossible to satisfy.

Reason (c) The condition can be satisfied by a social choice function $C(S, \{R_b\})$, but can conflict with a yet more desirable social condition.

It has been argued in Chapters 2 and 4 that, given the appropriate rights system, the implementation of rights by the standard rights implementation rule (SRI) *is* socially desirable. The decision to specify a rights system is, in itself, a declaration that there is a social value that choice over assigned pairs should be based on the respective individual's preferences. This social value is independent of the motivation underlying an individual's preference over his assigned pair — the pair differs with respect to his own business and the reasons for his preference are his business. Thus the libertarian condition (as specified by an appropriate rights system in conjunction with SRI) should not be modified for reason (a) above.

However, for some appealing rights systems (e.g. SRS), for certain cases the implementation of rights through SRI can lead to an empty choice set. To achieve choice for all possible cases the libertarian condition must be modified. Such a modification should be fair and should not waive individual rights unnecessarily. Reason (b) is thus a possible justification for modifying a libertarian condition such as condition L.

Rights, even when assigned coherently, can conflict with other social criteria, and in particular the Pareto principle. I have argued that for some cases rights, though desirable, will be less desirable than the Pareto condition (see the discussion in Section 5.7). Thus for some circumstances rights should be modified for reason (c) above.

Turning now to the Pareto condition, we must ask what grounds there are for modification of this condition in social choice. Sen (1976, 1979) has forcibly argued that the desirability of implementing this condition is dependent on the motivations underlying the unanimous preference, especially in situations involving liberty. (Note that the Pareto condition is potentially relevant for any pair of alternatives which may be available.) Sen's interpretation of the *Lady Chatterley's Lover* example, see Chapter 5, p. 95, clearly illustrates a case where Pareto should be modified on these grounds. There, Sen's argument for axing the Pareto condition is not because it *must* so as to resolve the conflict, but because it *should* on moral grounds; the individuals, given Sen's interpretation of their motives, will *want* the curtailment of this condition in this case. For the most part it might well be the case that if an alternative x is unanimously preferred to another, y, then the Pareto condition should apply, but not in all possible cases. Reason (a) above is thus a possible reason for modifying the Pareto condition. Such a modification should be based on the motivations underlying the preferences in the case in question, i.e. more information is needed.

For all logically possible types of configurations of individuals' preferences the Pareto condition can be satisfied by many choice functions $C(S, \{R_b\})$. Reason (b) is thus not a possible reason for the modification of this condition.

In some cases the Pareto condition, applied to some unanimous preference over a pair of alternatives, might well be desirable but, given the rest of the individuals' preferences, will conflict with rights. If in such a case rights are deemed more desirable than Pareto, then the Pareto condition should be modified in order to achieve a resolution. Reason (c) is thus a reason for modifying the Pareto condition.

The above discussion has strong implications for achieving a fair and just resolution to the paradoxes.

Firstly, the Pareto condition should be modified to take account of the motivations underlying the preferences of individuals. This is very difficult to do within a social choice framework but Sen's modification of the Pareto condition to his 'conditional Pareto condition' (condition *PC*) is a step in the right direction. The conditional Pareto condition *PC* will only endorse unanimous preference over a pair of alternatives, as the standard Pareto condition would, if these preferences were endorsed by everyone wanting these preferences to count in social choice. Individuals can judge, dependent on their own motivation and nature of the case in question, whether their preferences over certain pairs should count in social choice. Given the motivation Sen supplies for his *Lady Chatterley's Lover* example, it is clear that the Pareto condition for this case will not apply, the individuals themselves will renounce it on ethical grounds.

However, this modification of the Pareto condition will not resolve all conflict cases. Firstly, the libertarian condition by itself could result in an empty choice set. Thus, as suggested earlier, the condition *must* be modified to achieve a resolution. Secondly, rights, even when assigned coherently, may conflict with the conditional Pareto condition. Here again some modification is necessary to achieve a resolution. But which condition should be modified? This, as I have argued, depends on the case in question. Sen has made a similar conclusion:

The set of individual orderings in general provides too little information for deciding what to do ... the same set of individual orderings under one interpretation of the motivations underlying the preferences might suggest the dropping of the Pareto principle, while under another interpretation of the motivations, it might point the finger at [the libertarian condition]. (Sen, 1976, p. 237)

Given this conclusion, it is surprising that most of the resolutions of the Sen paradox, discussed in Chapters 4 and 5, have at the outset chosen *one* of the conditions as the prime candidate for modification for all possible cases.

A best resolution to these conflicts must be more pragmatic, taking into account the nature of the alternatives and the motivations underlying the preference structure. As such, a proper resolution to these paradoxes cannot be appropriately specified as some fixed rule which can be formally incorporated into a social framework but rather it must be a set of broad and general guidelines which, once all the relevant information has been obtained, can be used to assess which social condition or conditions should be modified (and in what way), for the unique case in question. Obtaining such information might well be difficult but if a best resolution is to be achieved such informational costs are a necessary requirement.

CHAPTER 7

Group rights

7.1   Introduction

So far in this book only individuals have been assigned rights in society. The scope of the analysis is now extended to permit groups rather than only individuals to be decisive agents in social choice. This very important extension has been relatively ignored in the existing literature and deserves much more attention. Most societies decentralise their decision-making process with 'states' or 'local authorities' having rights to certain choices as regards their internal affairs. Will these independent group decisions, as regards their respective internal affairs, always be consistent with more global objectives of society as a whole? The results in this chapter go some way towards answering this question.

In the next section a formal framework for analysis is developed for incorporation of group rights into a social choice framework. Section 7.3 investigates how far group rights can be respected in the context of a social choice function satisfying the Pareto condition. The chapter concludes with a discussion on the significance of the results. The proofs of the Theorems, which are mostly quite long and laborious, are confined to the Appendix to this chapter.

7.2   A framework for analysis

The following framework draws heavily from that of Stevens and Foster (1978).

Social alternatives Let X be the total set of social alternatives, available and unavailable. Let S be a finite subset of alternatives which we can consider as the available set $S \subseteq X$. A typical alternative $x \in X$ can be viewed as a full description of a social option that society faces.

Individual preferences These will be represented in exactly the same way as before.

Group structure Let T denote a collection of $t \geq 2$ non-empty groups of individuals, $T = \{G^1, G^2, \ldots, G^t\}$, subject to the condition that each group

G^i of T is distinct from every other group G^j, i.e. for all $i, j = 1, 2, \ldots, t$, if $i \neq j$ then $G^i \neq G^j$. Note the distinctiveness of group permits G^i to be a proper subset (or superset) of G^j. Let the collection T be termed 'group structure'.

Group preferences Let R^i denote the group preference of G^i as determined by a group voting rule F^i, where $R^i = F^i(\{R_b\}: b \in G^i)$. Let P^i and I^i represent the asymmetric and symmetric factors of R^i respectively. No regularity restrictions are placed upon group preference R^i, e.g. R^i may be intransitive, incomplete etc. Note that there is a separability characteristic, over groups, implicit in the function F^i.

Social choice function This will be defined in exactly the same way as before, retaining the notation $C(S, \{R_b\})$.

We can now formally incorporate group rights into this framework in an analogous way to that for individual rights. The 'rights system' first defined is the one that follows most naturally from Sen's SENRS, first given in Chapter 2, p. 10.

Group rights system 1 (GRS–1) For each group G^i there is at least one pair of social alternatives x and y such that $\langle x, y ; G^i \rangle$ and $\langle y, x ; G^i \rangle$ are in $\mathscr{R}$.

Analogously to the standard rights implementation rule (SRI) for individuals we have:

Standard group rights implementation rule (SGRI) If $\langle x, y ; G^i \rangle \in \mathscr{R}$ and xP^iy then $y \notin C(S: x \in S, \{R_b\})$

Condition L^{GR1} GRS–1 and SGRI respectively exist and operate in society.

So far nothing specific has been said about the type of group voting rules used by groups to determine their group preference. In the present context we will look at two broad classes of group voting rules.

Pareto inclusive group voting rule A group voting rule $F^i(\{R_b\}: b \in G^i)$ will be said to be Pareto inclusive if and only if

$$\forall x, y \in X : \{\forall b \in G^i : xP_b y\} \to xP^i y$$

Majoritian inclusive group voting rule A group voting rule $F^i(\{R_b\}: b \in G^i)$ will be said to be majoritian inclusive if and only if

$$\forall x, y \in X : \{N^i(xPy) > N^i(yPx)\} \to xP^i y$$

where $N^i(xPy)$ denotes the number of individuals in G^i who strictly prefer x to y.

All majoritian inclusive group voting rules are Pareto inclusive but not in general vice versa.

7.3 Pareto versus group rights

This section explores how far group rights can be respected in the context of a choice function satisfying the Pareto condition P. In particular we shall be interested in conditions on the group structure of society which are necessary and sufficient to assure the existence of a choice function $C(S, \{R_b\})$ satisfying condition L^{GR1} and condition P, given some stipulations about the group voting rules each group uses to generate their respective group preference.

Theorem 7.3.1 *Given that group preference for each group must be determined by a Pareto-inclusive group voting rule, the condition that the group structure T is such that $\cap G^i \neq \{\emptyset\}$ is both necessary and sufficient to assure that there will exist a choice function $C(S, \{R_b\})$ which satisfies condition L^{GR1} and condition P.*

Proof: See the Appendix to this chapter.

The necessity part of the previous theorem was first established by Batra and Pattanaik (1972). They showed that if any two groups were disjoint from each other, then conflicts between these two groups' rights and the Pareto principle can follow in an analogous way to Sen's 'Impossibility of a Paretian Liberal' (Sen, 1970b). Theorem 7.3.1 extends this result and tells us that the existence of at least one individual who is a member of all decisive groups is sufficient to establish that there will exist a choice function $C(S, \{R_b\})$ satisfying conditions L^{GR1} and P, for some set of Pareto inclusive group voting rules and some rights systems consistent with GRS–1.

To insist that group voting rules are Pareto inclusive is not a very severe stipulation. For example, a group voting rule which reveals a strict group preference for an alternative x over another y if and only if all members of the group prefer x to y is Pareto inclusive. This rule may be considered inappropriate if it is required to give a group rights over a pair of alternatives, despite some dissent from a minority of its members. As such we might wish group voting rules not only to be Pareto inclusive but also majoritian inclusive.

The next two theorems give the analogous result to Theorem 7.3.1 for the case where the group voting rules used by groups must be majoritian-inclusive. Before stating these, some more notation and definitions will prove useful.

Let, without loss of generality, the groups be indexed according to size such that $N(G^1) \geqslant N(G^2) \geqslant \ldots \geqslant N(G^t)$ where $N(K)$ is the number of individuals in subset K of society. Next, let the number of individuals common to all groups be denoted by $m = N(\cap G^i)$.

Definition: 'two set' group structure (see Stevens and Foster (1978), p. 403) A group structure T is termed a 'two-set' if and only if $m = 1, N(G^t) \leqslant 2$ and for $i = 1, \ldots, t - 1, N(G^i) = 2$.

Theorems 7.3.2 and 7.3.3 are based on Theorems 1 and 2 in Stevens and Foster (1978) respectively. However, Stevens and Foster's Theorem 2 is in error and Theorem 7.3.3 below is a corrected version as given by Wriglesworth (1982*a*).

Theorem 7.3.2 (see Stevens and Foster (1978), Theorem 1) *Given that the group structure T is made up of three or more groups, and given that group preference for each group must be determined by a majoritian inclusive group voting rule, the condition that the group structure T is a 'two set' is necessary and sufficient to assure there will exist a choice function $C(S, \{R_b\})$ which satisfies condition L^{GR1} and condition P.*

Proof: See Stevens and Foster (1978), Theorem 1.

Theorem 7.3.3 (see Wriglesworth (1982*a*), Theorem 2) *Given that the group structure T is made up of exactly two groups and given that group preferences for each group must be determined by a majoritian inclusive group voting rule, the condition that the group structure T is such that:*

(1) $N(G^1) = m + 1$, *where m is odd*
and (2) $N(G^2) = m + 2$ *and* $G^2 \subseteq G^1$ *where m is even,*
is necessary and sufficient to assure there will exist a choice function $C(S, \{R_b\})$ which satisfies condition L^{GR1} and condition P.

Proof: See the Appendix to this chapter.

To insist that group voting rules used by groups are not only Pareto inclusive but majoritian inclusive means that the group structure must become very heavily restricted to assure possibility. This will be discussed further in the next section.

To prove the sufficiency part of the previous three theorems, any rights system can be chosen such that each group has at least one assigned pair (i.e. any rights system consistent with GRS–1). However, is the assignment of rights a 'variable' which should be chosen to secure possibility? A potential problem is that even if the stipulated conditions on group structure are satisfied for a particular case, possibility may only be guaranteed if the rights system is of a particular type.

Now, if a government was forming a constitution it could assign rights to groups deliberately to secure possibility (assuming the group voting rules and group structure meet the stipulated conditions). However, should the assignment of rights be based on such considerations? One could argue that the assignment of rights should be based solely on the nature of the social options available, by giving consideration to whether alternatives differ from each other with respect to some particular group's business. As such, the assignment of rights should be considered as part of the prior choice data, in much the same way as the set of available social options.

The following theorems will go some way towards overcoming this problem. First, it turns out that so long as we only insist that group voting rules must be Pareto inclusive, the condition that the group structure T is such that $\cap G^i \neq \{\emptyset\}$ is necessary and sufficient to assure possibility *independent* of the rights system in existence.

Theorem 7.3.4 *Given that group preference for each group must be determined by a Pareto inclusive group voting rule, then for any logically conceivable rights system taken over any finite set of available alternatives, the condition that the group structure T is such that $\cap G^i \neq \{\emptyset\}$ is both necessary and sufficient to assure that there exists a choice function $C(S, \{R_b\})$ which satisfies condition L^{GR1} and condition P.*

Proof: See the Appendix to this chapter.

The above theorem is more powerful than Theorem 7.3.1 and comes at no extra cost in terms of stipulated conditions on group structure. (Theorem 7.3.1 is obviously implied by Theorem 7.3.4.)

For the case where group voting rules are required to be majoritian inclusive, the necessary and sufficient restrictions on group structure which assure possibility do depend on the type of rights system in existence, as will be seen by the results of the following theorems. First, the meaning of a 'coherent' rights system is defined in the context of group rights.

Coherent group rights system For a given set of group voting rules, group rights will be said to be assigned coherently if and only if for all possible group structures T there exists a choice function $C(S, \{R_b\})$ satisfying condition L^{GR1}.

For the special case where each group comprises of one individual, each group's preference being determined by that group's individual preference, this definition is equivalent to that given in Chapter 2, p. 10. It is important to note that a group rights system which is coherent for one set of group voting rules need not be coherent for another set.

Theorem 7.3.5 (see Wriglesworth (1982a), p. 46) *Given that group preference for each group must be determined by a majoritian inclusive group voting rule, the condition that the group structure T is a 'two-set' is necessary and sufficient to assure that for every logically possible coherent rights assignment taken over any finite set of available alternatives, there exists a choice function $C(S, \{R_b\})$ satisfying condition L^{GR1} and condition P.*

Proof: See the Appendix to this chapter.

The restrictions on group structure are exactly the same as those given in Theorem 7.3.3. Thus for the cases where there are three or more groups we are paying no penalty for a richer result. Given that the group structure is a 'two-set' each group can be assigned any number of pairs of alternatives and, so long as the rights system is coherent, possibility is guaranteed. However, for the case of exactly two groups, the restriction is more severe than that given in Theorem 7.3.2, that result being critically dependent on the freedom to choose a particular rights assignment (consistent with GRS–1) for the purpose of proving sufficiency.

What about rights system which are not coherent? In cases of individual rights we saw in previous chapters many examples where rights were assigned incoherently. In particular the incoherent "Standard Rights System" (SRS) which assigns rights according to issues, was shown in many cases to be the most obviously appropriate rights system. Assigning rights with respect to issues can also be quite appropriate for group rights. Indeed, the Scottish/Welsh devolution example presented in Chapter 2 is an especially fitting example for group rights. Returning to an issue framework for defining social alternatives (see definition on p. 5) we can define the analogue of SRS for groups' rights assignments.

Group rights system 2 (GRS–2) For each group G^j of group structure T there is an issue j such that for every pair of j-variants x and y, $\langle x, y ; G^j \rangle \in \mathscr{R}$.

Condition L^{GR2} GRS–2 and SGRI respectively exist and operate in society.

Given disjoint groups and the stipulation that the group voting rules must be Pareto inclusive for each group, the Gibbard paradox can arise with the imposition of condition L^{GR2} on a social choice function in an analogous way to that for condition L (see p. 7).

From Theorem 7.3.4 we see that given that each group must determine their group preference by a Pareto inclusive group voting rule, the condition that $\cap G^i \neq \{\emptyset\}$ is both necessary and sufficient to assure the existence of a choice function satisfying condition L^{GR2} and condition P. This is because the rights system GRS–2 is just one of many consistent with GRS–1.

But what about cases where group preference for each group must be determined by a majoritian inclusive group voting rule?

Theorem 7.3.6 *Given that group preference for each group must be determined by a majoritian inclusive group voting rule, a necessary and sufficient condition for a choice function $C(S, \{R_b\})$ to exist which satisfies condition L^{GR2} (or condition L^{GR2} and condition P) is that the group structure T is such that there exists only two groups and $N(G^1) = 2$, $N(G^2) = 1$ and $G^2 \subseteq G^1$.*

Proof: See the Appendix to this chapter.

Given the extremely restrictive nature of this condition on group structure, it should not be too surprising to find the following result holds.

Theorem 7.3.7 *Given that group preference for each group must be determined by a majoritian inclusive group voting rule, a necessary and sufficient condition for a choice function $C(S, \{R_b\})$ to exist which satisfies condition L^{GR1} (or condition L^{GR1} and condition P), for every conceivable rights assignment, taken over any finite set of alternatives, is that there exist only two groups and $N(G^1) = 2$, $N(G^2) = 1$ and $G^2 \subseteq G^1$.*

Proof: See the Appendix to this chapter.

7.4   Conclusion

In this concluding section the importance and implications of all the above results will be discussed.

The libertarian condition L^{GR1} is formally very similar to Sen's libertarian condition L^S (see Chapter 2, p. 10); but the significance of allowing different groups in society to have rights over certain private choices is even more far reaching than allowing just individuals' rights.

To reject $[L^{GR1}]$ would amount to saying that not even an extremely limited amount of autonomy is to be given over any area of decision making to various social groups defined in terms of language, religion, race, colour, economic interest or any other property. Denial of condition $[L^{GR1}]$ will thus rule out every conceivable form of federal structure (using the term in the broadest sense possible). Sen [1970a, b] introduced a stronger version of $[L^{GR1}]$ [i.e. the libertarian condition L^S]. . .

We find even this stronger condition of Sen perfectly acceptable. However, even if one rejects $[L^S]$ one may still find $[L^{GR1}]$ acceptable in so far as the recognition of some amount of autonomy over at least some spheres of decision making, for various social groups (which exist in practically every society) may constitute a basic precondition for these social groups to agree to be part of the same society at all. (Batra and Pattanaik, 1972, p. 7)[1]

In the light of this lucid justification for incorporating group rights into a social choice framework, the relevance and implications of the theorems in the preceding section will now be considered.

Firstly, consider the stipulation that group voting rules for each group must be Pareto inclusive. It is hard to think of any group of individuals not wishing to formulate their decisions via such a rule. In this context the group voting rules are only used to determine each group's respective preference over their respective assigned pairs. If, for a group there is no strict unanimous preference with respect to an assigned pair of alternatives there is no stipulation as regards the way the group orders the two alternatives. Indeed, in such a case, a group need not order its assigned pair at all. To insist that group voting rules are Pareto inclusive is thus a very mild restriction indeed. The main result concerning the stipulation that group voting rules are Pareto inclusive is Theorem 7.3.4. The implications of this theorem can be separated into two parts. Firstly there are the implications that follow from the necessity aspect of the theorem and secondly those that follow from the sufficiency aspect.

As I have said before, the necessity part of the proof of Theorem 7.3.4 was first established by Batra and Pattanaik (1972). The main implication of this is rather negative, in that, if there exist just two groups which are disjoint from each other, there cannot exist any set of Pareto inclusive group voting rules which can assure the existence of a choice function $C(S, \{R_b\})$ satisfying condition L^{GR1} and condition P. This impossibility is totally analogous to Sen's impossibility of a 'Paretian Liberal' (Sen 1970b), where the groups are individuals and thus necessarily disjoint. To avoid impossibility, given that some groups are disjoint from each other, the force of either the Pareto condition or the group libertarian condition must be weakened. The various suggested amendments to libertarian conditions and the Pareto conditions discussed in the previous chapters can be relevant here, given suitable (and trivial) adaptation of the procedures to take explicit account of the fact that rights are determined by group preference, not necessarily individual preference.

However, unique to cases of group rights, as opposed to only individual rights, is the possibility that groups are not disjoint, i.e. there exist individuals who are members of more than one 'interest' group. This leads us to the implications of the sufficiency aspect of Theorem 7.3.4. The main implication is a little more positive: if there exists at least one individual who is a

[1] Batra and Pattanaik used different notation to that used in this book. The square brackets indicate where I have substituted their notation for my own.

member of all decisive groups then there will exist a set of Pareto inclusive group voting rules which will guarantee that there will exist a choice function satisfying condition L^{GR1} and condition P, and this will be true for *any* conceivable assignment of rights taken over *any* finite set of available alternatives. If the stipulation that the group voting rules are Pareto inclusive is all we require then, for cases where no pair of groups are disjoint from each other, group rights and the Pareto principle will never be in conflict with each other.

As stated earlier, the stipulation that group voting rules are Pareto inclusive is very mild, and unfortunately, strengthening the stipulation as regards group voting rules basically invalidates the more positive implications of Theorem 7.3.4. The results of Theorems 7.3.2, 7.3.3, 7.3.5, 7.3.6 and 7.3.7, where we insist that group voting rules for each group be not only Pareto inclusive but also majoritian inclusive, show that the necessary and sufficient conditions on group structure which assure possibility are so restrictive as to be hardly of any practical relevance for the real world. In fact the restrictions on group structure given in Theorems 7.3.2, 7.3.5, 7.3.6 and 7.3.7 are so severe that the stipulated *one* individual, who must be a member of all decisive groups, has the effective power to veto any strict group preference as regards *any* assigned pair of alternatives.

Despite the severity of the restrictions given in these theorems the results are important. As a consequence of these theorems we know that, in practically all cases, a choice function $C(S, \{R_b\})$ can only satisfy group rights (as determined by majoritian inclusive group voting rules) and the Pareto principle if one of these conditions is further weakened, i.e. resolutions to the potential conflict between group rights and Pareto must proceed along the lines of the resolutions discussed in earlier chapters. Which condition (group rights or Pareto) should be modified will depend on the nature of the case in question and the motivations underlying individual and group preferences. The discussion in Chapter 6 is also very relevant to libertarian conflicts involving group rights.

I have only been considering two general categories of group voting rules, Pareto inclusive and majoritian inclusive. There are a multitude of other stipulations that can be made. For example, we could insist that group voting rules used by groups are strong Pareto inclusive, i.e.

$$\forall x, y \in X : [\{\forall b \in G^i : xR_by \text{ and } \exists b \in G^i : xP_by\} \to xP^iy]$$

Alternatively, we could insist that all group voting rules satisfy

$$\forall x, y \in X : [\{N^i(xPy) > \tfrac{1}{2}\} \to xP^iy]$$

To provide all the theorems and proofs that take account of such amendments would clutter up the pages of this chapter and would not serve to add any useful points. The general point is that the conditions on group structure are very sensitive to the stipulations as regards the group voting rules used by groups. Strong stipulations (e.g. insisting voting rules are majoritian inclusive) will, in the context of previous theorems, be associated with more restrictive conditions on group structure than those associated with weaker stipulations (e.g. insisting voting rules are Pareto inclusive).

Also, the restrictions on group structure will generally, given a stipulation about the group voting rules, be more severe if the weak Pareto condition P was replaced by the strong Pareto condition P^* (see Chapter 3, p. 34). Again, stating all the relevant theorems and proofs would not serve much useful purpose.

The concept of group rights, as opposed to individual rights greatly expands the scope and relevance of the liberal paradoxes to practically any form of decentralised decision-making process. Any form of society which allows different members states' rights to choose between certain options may find the implementation of these rights will lead to a Pareto inefficient outcome. Whether we have the United Kingdom allowing Wales and Scotland rights with respect to the issue of devolution, or the Common Market seeking to formulate a common economic policy while having to respect the rights of member nations, the potential conflict between group rights and the Pareto principle can arise.

Appendix: Proofs of Theorems

Proof of Theorem 7.3.1 See proof of Theorem 7.3.4.

Proof of Theorem 7.3.3

(1) *Necessity*

Let G^1 be assigned (x^1, y^1) and let G^2 be assigned (x^2, y^2). Assume that group preference for each group is determined by a majoritian inclusive group voting rule and assume there exists a choice function $C(S, \{R_b\})$ satisfying condition P and condition L^{GR1}.

(a)   Assume that the set $\{x^1, x^2, y^1, y^2\}$ contains four totally distinct social alternatives. Let individual preferences be:

$G^1 - G^2$	$G^2 - G^1$	$G^1 \cap G^2$		Others	
		S^1	S^2		
y^2	y^1	y^1	y^2	y^1	descending order
x^1	x^2	x^2	x^1	x^2	of strict
y^1	y^2	y^2	y^1	y^2	preference
x^2	x^1	x^1	x^2	x^1	

Where S^1 and S^2 partition $G^1 \cap G^2$ into two sets of individuals. $G^1 - G^2$, $G^2 - G^1$, $G^1 \cap G^2$ and 'others' partition the total set of individuals into four sets.

(i) If $m \; (= N(G^1 \cap G^2)) = 0$ then the two groups are disjoint. Condition L^{GR1} dismisses alternatives y^1 and y^2. Condition P dismisses alternatives x^1 and x^2. Thus we have impossibility.

(ii) If $m \neq 0$, m is odd and $N(G^1) \neq m + 1$, then by distinctiveness of groups and the assumed indexing, $N(G^1) \geqslant m + 2$. Let S^1 have $(m + 1)/2$ members and S^2 have $(m - 1)/2$ members. Impossibility now follows as in (i) above.

(iii) If $m \neq 0$, m is even and either $G^2 \nsubseteq G^1$ or $N(G^1) > m + 2$, then impossibility will follow:
   (a) if $G^2 \nsubseteq G^1$, then letting S^1 and S^2 have $m/2$ members each impossibility follows as in (i).
   (b) if $N(G^1) > m + 2$, then let S^1 have $(m + 2)/2$ members and let S^2 have $(m - 2)/2$ members. Impossibility will again follow as in (i).

(b)   Let the pairs (x^1, y^1) and (x^2, y^2) have one social alternative in common, say $y^1 = y^2 = y$. Let individual preferences be:

$G^1 - G^2$	$G^2 - G^1$	$G^1 \cap G^2$		Others	
		S^1	S^2		
x^2	y	y	x^2	y	descending order
x^1	x^2	x^2	x^1	x^2	of strict
y	x^1	x^1	y	x^2	preference

(i) If $m = 0$ impossibility follows: condition L^{GR1} will dismiss alternatives y and x^2, condition P will dismiss alternative x^1.

(ii) If $m \neq 0$, m is odd and $N(G^1) \neq m + 1$ then by distinctiveness of groups and the assumed indexing, $N(G^1) \geqslant m + 2$. Let S^1 have $(m + 1)/2$ members and S^2 have $(m - 1)/2$ members. Impossibility now follows as in (i) above.

(iii) If $m \neq 0$, m is even and either $G^2 \nsubseteq G^1$ or $N(G^1) > m + 2$ then impossibility will follow:
   (a) if $G^2 \nsubseteq G^1$, then letting S^1 and S^2 have m/2 members each impossibility follows as in (i).
   (b) if $N(G^1) > m + 2$, then let S^1 have $(m + 2)/2$ members and let S^2 have $(m - 2)/2$ members. Impossiblity will again follow as in (i).

Analogous results can be constructed for the cases, $x^1 = x^2$, $x^1 = y^2$ and $x^2 = y^1$ respectively.

(c)   Let the pair (x^1, y^1) be the same pair as (x^2, y^2). Say this pair is (x, y). Impossibilities follow analogously to the above given the preferences:

$G^1 - G^2$	$G^2 - G^1$	$G^1 \cap G^2$ $S^1 \quad S^2$	Others	
x	y	y $\quad x$	x	descending order of
y	x	x $\quad y$	y	strict preference

(2) *Sufficiency*

Let each group be assigned *one* pair of alternatives each. Let these pairs be totally distinct from each other. Let group preference, for both groups, be determined by the following majoritian inclusive group voting rule:

$$[\{N^i(xPy) > N^i(yPx)\} \to xP^i y]$$

and

$$[\{N^i(yPx) > N^i(xPy)\} \leftrightarrow yP^i x]$$

Define a social preference relation as

$$xPy \leftrightarrow \{ xQ_1 y \text{ or } xQ_2 y\}$$

$$xRy \leftrightarrow \{\text{not } yPx\}$$

where $xQ_1 y \leftrightarrow \{\langle x, y ; G^i\rangle \in \mathscr{R} \text{ and } xP^i y\}$, and $xQ_2 y \leftrightarrow \{\forall b : xP_b y\}$.

Define a choice rule as

$$C = [x|x \in S \text{ and } (\forall y) \, [y \in S \to xRy]]$$

This rule satisfies conditions L^{GR1} and P by construction. The proof that C is in fact a choice function $C(S, \{R_b\})$ follows by proving that R is complete, reflexive and acyclic for all possible $\{R_b\}$ (see Sen (1970a), Lemma 1*l, p.16).

R is reflexive and complete by observation. It remains to prove that R is acyclic, i.e. cycles of the form $z^1 Pz^2 P \ldots Pz^h Pz^1$ over any set $S = \{z^1, z^2, z^3, \ldots z^h\}$ cannot occur given the necessary conditions on group structure.

Assume such a cycle exists. In fact, if there is to be such a cycle it must be the case that for some four alternatives: $z^1 Pz^2 Pz^3 Pz^4 Pz^1$:

(a)   A cycle involving three alternatives could not be caused by the two groups' decisiveness over their assigned pairs since this would involve four alternatives (assigned pairs do not overlap). Thus such a cycle would have to be caused by Pareto in conjunction with one group's decisiveness. But this implies that those members in the majority of the group are displaying intransitive preferences.

(b)   A cycle of five or more alternatives can always be reduced to a cycle of four. Only two links in the cycle can be caused by group decisiveness, hence a cycle of five or more implies Pareto is operating over three or more links. The Pareto relationship is transitive and we can easily ignore all but two of the links in the cycle.

The cycle over four alternatives $z^1Pz^2Pz^3Pz^4Pz^1$ must have Pareto in conjunction with *both* groups' decisiveness forcing the links; assigned pairs do not overlap, so groups' decisiveness cannot cause a cycle alone. Pareto in conjunction with one group's decisiveness cannot cause a cycle, since this would imply intransitive preferences for the majority of the group.

Without loss of generality, let G^1 be decisive over (z^1, z^2) and let G^2 be decisive over (z^3, z^4). Then, for the cycle to exist, Pareto must be forcing the links (z^2, z^3) and (z^4, z^1). This implies that the majority of G^2 have preferences $z^2Pz^3Rz^4Pz^1$. The strict preference links are because of Pareto; and z^3Rz^4, since if not, and the majority strictly prefer z^4 to z^3, we have a contradiction with the above assumption that $z^3P^2z^4$. Thus the majority of G^2 strictly prefer z^2 to z^1.

Case 1 Assume m is odd and $N(G^1) = m + 1$.
If $N(G^2) = m + 1$, thus $N(G^2)$ is even, then $N^2(z^2Pz^1) = N^2(z^1Pz^2) \geqslant 2$. Despite the one member of G^2 that is not a member of G^1 there is still a majority of at least one in $G^1 \cap G^2$ that favours z^2 over z^1. Thus G^1 cannot force z^1Pz^2.

If $N(G^2) = m$, then $N^2(z^2Pz^1) - N^2(z^1Pz^2) \geqslant 1$. But there only exists one member of G^1 that is not a member of G^2, hence we cannot have z^1Pz^2 by G^1's decisiveness and we cannot have a cycle of social preference.

Case 2 Assume m is even, $G^2 \subseteq G^1$ and $N(G^1) \leqslant m + 2$.
Thus $N^2(z^2Pz^1) - N^2(z^1Pz^2) \geqslant 2$. If z^1Pz^2 by G^1's decisiveness, G^1 must have at least three members not in G^2 to ensure majority. Clearly, if $N(G^1) \leqslant m + 2$ we have possibility.

Proof of Theorem 7.3.4
(1) *Necessity* (cf. Batra and Pattanaik (1972) Theroem 1)
By assumption, there exist at least two groups. Let G^i be assigned (x^i, y^i) and G^j be assigned (x^j, y^j). If (x^i, y^i) and (x^j, y^j) are the same pair then, given the groups are disjoint, we can assume the preferences $\forall b \in G^i = x^iP_by^i$ and $\forall b \in G^j = y^jP_bx^j$. Rights implementation will dismiss $y^i(= y^j)$ and $x^j(= x^i)$ from the choice set. Thus the choice set over $\{x^i(= x^j), y^i(= y^j)\}$ will be empty.

If the pairs have *one* element in common, say $x^j = x^i$, then assume that $\forall b \in G^i: x^iP_by^i$, $\forall b \in G^j: y^jP_bx^i$ and $\forall b \in H: y^iP_by^j$. By condition L^{GR1} y^i and x^i will be dismissed from the choice set over $\{y^i, x^i, y^j\}$. By condition P, y^j will be dismissed from this set. Thus the choice set over $\{y^i, x^i, y^j\}$ will be empty.

If all four alternatives $\{x^i, y^i, y^j, x^j\}$ are distinct from each other then assume $\forall b \in G^i: x^iP_by^i$, $\forall b \in G^j: x^jP_by^j$ and $\forall b \in H: \{y^jP_bx^i$ and $y^iP_bx^j\}$. By condition L^{GR1} y^i and y^j will be dismissed from the choice set over these four alternatives. By condition P, x^i and x^j will be dismissed. Thus the choice set over $\{x^i, y^i, x^j, y^j\}$ will be empty.

(2) *Sufficiency*

Let group preference for each group be determined by the following Pareto inclusive group voting rule

$$[\forall x, y \in X \{\forall b \in G^i : xP_b y \leftrightarrow xP^i y\} \text{ and otherwise } yR^i x]$$

This is the Pareto extension rule (see Sen (1970a), p. 74).

Define a social preference relation as

$$xPy \leftrightarrow \{xQ_1 y \text{ or } xQ_2 y\}$$

$$xRy \leftrightarrow \{\text{not } yPx\}$$

where $xQ_1 y \leftrightarrow \{\langle x, y ; G^i\rangle \in \mathscr{R} \text{ and } xP^i y\}$, and $xQ_2 y \leftrightarrow \{\forall b : xP_b y\}$

Define a choice rule as

$$C = [x \mid x \in S \text{ and } (\forall y)[y \in S \rightarrow xRy]]$$

This rule satisfies L^{GR1} and P by construction. Further, the relation R is reflexive, complete and acyclic for all possible sets of individual preferences $\{R_b\}$ and hence it is a choice function $C(S, \{R_b\})$ satisfying the desired properties. Reflexivity and completeness are obvious. To prove the relation is acyclic given $\cap G^i \neq \{\emptyset\}$ assume such a cycle exists, i.e. $x^1 P x^2 P \ldots x^h P x^1$ for some set of alternatives $S = \{x^1, x^2, \ldots x^h\}$. If xPy then whether this is due to $xQ_1 y$ or $xQ_2 y$ one must have $xP_d y$ for individual d who, we can assume, is the individual who is a member of all groups. Thus a cycle would imply intransitive preference for individual d.

The following lemma will be used in the proof of Theorem 7.3.5.

Lemma *Where a group G^i is assigned three or more non-overlapping pairs of social alternatives, and given that group preference for each group is determined by a majoritian inclusive group voting rule, there does not exist a choice function $C(S, \{R_b\})$ satisfying condition P and the condition that G^i's rights are implemented by the standard group rights implementation rule (SGRI), if $N(G^i) = 3$ or $N(G^i) \geqslant 5$.*

Proof: Let (v, s), (x, y) and (z, w) be three non-overlapping pairs over which G^i is decisive. Consider the following preferences for five individuals over the set of six alternatives:

1	2	3	4	5	
w	s	y	y	w	
v	x	z	z	v	
s	y	w	s	s	descending order of
x	z	v	x	x	strict preference
y	w	s	w	y	
z	v	x	v	v	

Consider the group of three individuals $\{1, 2, 3\}$. By the rights of the group, y, s and w will be dismissed from the choice set over the set of six alternatives (a majority of $2:1$ in all cases). By Pareto, v, x and z will be dismissed from the choice set. The choice set over the six alternatives is thus empty.

Consider now the group of five individuals $\{1, 2, 3, 4, 5\}$. Impossibility in an analogous way to the group of three individuals arises. The proof for $N(G^i) = 6$ is clear if we consider the preferences of individuals 1, 2 and 3 and think of them as couples. Hence the majority is $4:2$ for all decisive pairs; thus a seventh person with preferences $wP_b v$, $sP_b x$ and $yP_b z$ will not stop impossibility. Impossibility for eight persons is clear by letting three individuals have the preferences of 1, 2 and 3 above, and the other five have preferences as in $1, 2, 3, 4$ and 5. All numbers greater than eight can be split up into threes, fives, sixes etc., so impossibility is assured for all numbers greater than five.

Proof of Theorem 7.3.5

(1) *Necessity*

(a) For the case of more than two groups, see the proof given by Stevens and Foster (1978, Theorem 1).

(b) We are thus left with the case of *exactly* two groups. From the lemma, $N(G^1) = 1, 2$ or 4 and $N(G^2) = 1, 2$ or 4 if a choice function $C(S, \{R_b\})$ satisfying L^{GR1} and P is to exist for all possible coherent rights assignments taken over any finite subset of X. (Note that the assignment of rights in the lemma is coherent.)

Analogously, from Theorem 7.3.3, either (a) $N(G^1) = m + 1$ where m is odd, or (b) $N(G^1) \leqslant m + 2$ and $G^2 \subseteq G^1$ where m is even, if a choice function $C(S, \{R_b\})$ satisfying L^{GR1} and P is to exist, for all possible coherent rights assignments taken over any finite subset of X.

Case 1 m is odd

To be consistent with the result of Theorem 7.3.3 and the lemma, either (a) $N(G^1) = 2$, $N(G^2) \leqslant 2$, $m = 1$ (a 'two-set'), or (b) $N(G^1) = N(G^2) = 4$, $m = 3$ for a choice function satisfying the stipulated properties to exist.

However, the latter group structure does not avoid impossibility in the following case. Let the preferences of five individuals be:

1	2	3	4	5	
w	w	y	s	s	
v	v	z	x	x	descending order of
s	s	w	y	y	strict preference
x	x	v	z	z	
y	y	s	w	w	
z	z	x	v	v	

Let G^2 have members $\{1, 2, 3, 4\}$ and let it be assigned $\{v, s\}$. Let G^1 have members $\{2, 3, 4, 5\}$ and let it be assigned $\{z, w\}$ and $\{x, y\}$. Note that $m = 3$ and the assignment of rights is 'coherent'. Alternatives v, x and z will be dismissed from the choice set by Pareto, and alternatives s, y and w will be dismissed by the implementation of rights given any majoritian inclusive group voting rule for each group. Hence the choice set is empty over the set of six alternatives. For the case where m is odd, it is thus necessary for the group structure to be a two-set.

Case 2 m is even
To be consistent with the result in Theorem 7.3.3 and the result of the lemma the group structure must be such that $N(G^1) = 4, N(G^2) = 2$ and $G^2 \subseteq G^1$, for a choice function satisfying the stipulated properties to exist. However, this group structure will not prevent impossibility in the following case. Consider again the preferences of the five individuals in case 1. Let G^2 have members $\{2, 3\}$ and let it be assigned $\{v, s\}$. Let G^1 have members $\{2, 3, 4, 5\}$ and let it be assigned $\{z, w\}$ and $\{x, y\}$. Impossibility results in an analogous way to that in case 1.

Thus if possibility is to occur for the case of exactly two groups a general necessary condition is that the group structure is $N(G^1) = 2, N(G^2) \leqslant 2$, and $m = 1$, i.e. the group structure must be two-set; the same group structure that is necessary given *more* than two groups (by Theorem 7.3.2).

(2) *Sufficiency*
Let group preference for each group be determined by the following majoritian inclusive group voting rule

$$[\{N^i(xPy) > N^i(yPx)\} \leftrightarrow xP^iy]$$

and

$$[N^i(yPx) > N^i(xPy)\} \leftrightarrow yP^ix]$$

Define a social preference relation as

$$xPy \leftrightarrow \{xQ_1y \text{ or } xQ_2y\}$$

$$xRy \leftrightarrow \{\text{not } yPx\}$$

where $xQ_1y \leftrightarrow \{\langle x, y; G^i\rangle \in \mathscr{R} \text{ and } xP^iy\}$, and $xQ_2y \leftrightarrow \{\forall b : xP_by\}$.

Define a choice rule as

$$C = [x \mid x \in S \text{ and } (\forall y) [y \in S \rightarrow xRy]]$$

This rule satisfies conditions L^{GR1} and P by construction. The proof that C is in fact a choice function $C(S, \{R_b\})$, given our necessary conditions on group structure, follows by proving that R is complete, reflexive and acyclic for all possible $\{R_b\}$ (see Sen (1970a), Lemma 1*l p. 16).

R is reflexive and complete by observation. It remains to prove that R is acyclic, i.e. cycles of the form $z^1Pz^2Pz^3 \ldots z^hPz^1$ over any set $S = \{z^1, z^2, \ldots, z^h\}$ cannot occur given our necessary conditions on group structure.

Assume such a cycle exists. Consider d, the member common to all groups. If the Pareto component of the strict preference relation P forms a link between z^j and z^{j+1}, then $z^jP_dz^{j+1}$. If the rights of any group forces a link between z^i and z^{j+1} then $z^jR_dz^{j+1}$, by the construction of the two-set. Clearly if the Pareto component of the rule is invoked even once then the preferences of d will be intransitive. However, since assigned pairs are assumed to be assigned coherently, the cycle cannot be caused by group rights alone. Thus social preference cannot be cyclic and the given rule is a choice function satisfying the desired properties.

Proof of Theorems 7.3.6 and 7.3.7

(1) *Necessity*

Define four alternatives as

$$xx = (x_1, x_2, z); \quad yx = (y_1, x_2, z)$$
$$yy = (y_1, y_2, z); \quad xy = (x_1, y_2, z)$$

Where z is a list of feature alternatives $x_3, x_4, \ldots, x_n$, the same for each social alternative. Let G^i be assigned issue 1, and G^j be assigned issue 2. This rights assignment is consistent with both GRS–2 and GRS–1.

(a) Assume $G^i \not\subseteq G^j$ and $G^j \not\subseteq G^i$. Let individuals have the following set of preferences

$G^i - G^j$	$G^j - G^i$	$G^i \cap G^j$
xx	xy	$xxIxyIyxIyy$
yx	xx	
yy	yx	
xy	yy	

Given any majoritian inclusive group voting rule, condition L^{GR1} will dismiss all the alternatives from this set of four alternatives. Thus one group must be a subset of the other.

(b)   Assume $G^j \subseteq G^i$ (without loss of generality). Let individuals have the following set of preferences:

$G^i - G^j$	$G^j(= G^i \cap G^j)$		
	$W1$	$W2$	$W3$
xy	yy	xy	(indifference
yx	xx	yx	between all
xx	yx	xx	pairs of
yy	xy	yy	alternatives)

Where $W1$, $W2$, $W3$ are three subsets of individuals that partition G^j.

If $N(G^j)$ is even, assume that

$$N(W3) = 1$$

$$N(W1) = \frac{N(G^j)}{2}$$

$$N(W2) = \frac{N(G^j)}{2} - 1$$

It follows that if $N(G^i - G^j) > 1$, then impossibility follows by rights implementation.

If $N(G^j)$ is odd, assume that

$$N(W3) = 0$$

$$N(W1) = \frac{N(G^j) + 1}{2}$$

$$N(W2) = \frac{N(G^j) - 1}{2}$$

It follows that if $N(G^i - G^j) > 1$ then impossibility follows by rights implementation.

Thus for any two groups G^i, G^j, $N(G^i) = N(G^j) + 1$ and $G^j \subseteq G^i$ is necessary for possibility.

(c)   Let $N(G^j) \geq 2$. Let preferences of the individuals in the two groups G^i, G^j be:

$G^i - G^j$	G^j		Others (if any)
1	1	2	(indifference
xy	xx	yy	between all
yx	xy	yx	alternatives)
xx	$yy I_1 yx$	$xx I_2 xy$	
yy			

G^i is decisive over $\{xy, yy\}$ and $\{yx, xx\}$. Therefore $yy, xx \notin C(\{xx, yy, yx, xy\}, \{R_b\})$.

G^j is decisive over $\{xx, xy\}$ and $\{yy, yx\}$. Therefore $xy, yx \notin C(\{xx, yy, yx, xy\}, \{R_b\})$.

Thus the choice set over this subset of X is empty. Thus $N(G^j) = 1$. Considering in addition the necessary condition given under (b) above, we can conclude

$$N(G^i) = 2, \ N(G^j) = 1, \ G^i \subseteq G^j \text{ is a necessary condition for possibility}$$

(d)   There cannot exist a third group because the above condition would be violated: if a third group G^t exists it must be a subset or superset of another group, by (a). But if G^t was a subset of G^i it would have to be identical to G^j. If G^t was a superset of G^i then $N(G^t - G^j) > 1$ and impossiblity follows by part (b) of this proof.

(2) *Sufficiency*

Let $N(G^1) = 2, N(G^2) = 1, G^2 \subseteq G^1$. Group 1 can only force an alternative x out of the choice set by revealing a strict preference for some y over x. Given that $N(G^1) = 2$, $yP^1x \rightarrow xR^2x$, i.e. the member of G^1 that is also a member of G^2 cannot oppose if G^1 is to show strict preference in favour of x. G^2 can only, itself, force an alternative x out of the choice set if $\langle y, x ; G^2 \rangle \in \mathcal{R}$ and yP^2x. Further, if the Pareto condition is invoked such that $\forall b : xP_b y$, it must be the case that xP^2y. Thus if all the alternatives are dismissed from the choice set it must be the case that the individual who represents G^2 is exhibiting intransitive preference.

CHAPTER 8

Conclusions

This book began with a brief justification of the role of rights in social choice. A basic mild premise, which justifies the formulation of libertarian conditions in social choice, is that if two states of the world, x and y, differ solely with respect to one person's business alone, then if that one person prefers x to y, then y should not be chosen if x is available. A major objection to this premise is that rights should be considered outside the realm of social choice. Rights should be defined in terms of the personal control an individual has over certain personal affairs, and social choice should only be made over the social options which are left (if any) *after* the individuals have respectively exercised this control. To counter this objection I have made two points.

First, treating rights specifically as some control an individual has over certain states of affairs implicitly denies rights to that individual if he is not mentally or physically able to personally exercise them (e.g. due to some temporary accident which renders him unconscious). Secondly, if rights are to be exercised prior to, and independently of, the social choice process, then one is ruling out the possibility of trading off rights with other socially beneficial factors which might be in contention with the exercising of these rights (e.g. the right of a group of extremists to free speech should be dependent, in part, on the possible and consequential social disruption and violence that can result from it).

How should rights be formally incorporated into a social choice framework? Since it has been argued that a person should have rights over a pair of social alternatives because the alternatives in the pair differ with respect to an issue which is his business alone, one natural way to begin to specify rights is to isolate, and explicitly define this personal issue (and other people's personal issues) by defining a social alternative in terms of component 'feature alternatives', one for each issue in the state of the world. This led, in Chapter 2, to the libertarian condition defined as the combination of the standard rights system (SRS) and the standard rights implementation rule (SRI), i.e. condition L (see p. 7). An individual is given rights to pairs of alternatives which differ solely with respect to the feature alternatives for his personal issue. Unfortunately, condition L cannot be satisfied in social choice for all possible sets of preferences of individuals (the Gibbard paradox).

Given this impossibility result how can it be resolved? Firstly, for some cases, the standard rights system might be considered as inappropriate and could legitimately be weakened. One example of such a weakening is Sen's rights system, SENRS (see p. 10). So long as rights, assigned consistent with SENRS, are assigned 'coherently', then the Gibbard paradox will never arise. However, this does not provide a universal resolution to the problem since we are left with the cases where the standard rights system *is* the appropriate assignment.

Three types of resolution to the Gibbard paradox were discussed in Chapter 2 which involved constructing a libertarian condition which retained SRS but modified the standard rights implementation rule, SRI: first, Gibbard's (1974) condition L^G, which makes an individual's rights to a given pair of alternatives conditional on him exhibiting *unconditional preferences* with respect to his personal feature alternatives throughout his total ordering of all social alternatives; second, my condition L^P which makes an individual's rights to a given pairs of alternatives depend on a subrelation of preferences, which he reveals in addition to his preferences, over the set of available options (cf. Wriglesworth 1985); and third, the justice constrained libertarian conditions which makes an individual's rights to a given pair of alternatives conditional on every individual considering this right 'just', according to some specific justice relation defined in the context of an extended utility framework.

Gibbard's procedure is motivated by the belief that condition L is not a 'reasonable' libertarian condition in the first place because it wrongly and immorally allows an individual rights to a pair of alternatives despite him conditionally ordering his feature alternatives in his preference ordering of social alternatives. In contrast, my motivation behind the formulation of condition L^P stresses the *desirability* of condition L. Given that the standard rights system *is* appropriate, in that the assigned pairs do differ with respect to the individuals' respective personal business, then the standard rights implementation rule *is* desirable. However, condition L cannot be satisfied by a choice function for all configurations of preferences. As such, amendments should achieve 'possibility' in an 'efficient' (but fair) manner, not axing rights of individuals unnecessarily. To this end, condition L^P is attractive in that in *all* cases it allows individuals at least as many rights as condition L^G, and for *some* cases, notably those of conflict, it allows individuals more rights than condition L^G. This extra efficiency is obtained by making use of the extra (non-utility) information in the form of the respective subrelations individuals reveal.

The motivation behind the justice constrained libertarian conditions is again different. Justice is deemed more important than rights, so much so that any individual's rights to a given pair of alternatives will only be implemented if there is unanimous agreement that such a right is just and this according to a specific set of asymmetric and transitive justice relations. In some cases, consideration of justice might imply that a certain individual's rights should be axed, but to specify rights should only be implemented, in all cases if and only if *all* individuals strictly agree that such a right is just, is far too severe. This procedure also demands much utility information. In contrast to obtaining extra 'non-utility' information as used to implement condition L^P, obtaining such extra 'utility' information is exceedingly difficult; it assumes that each individual knows enough of the objective circumstances of every other individual honestly to reveal a set of extended preferences which can compare any alternative 'in the shoes' of any individual b with any other alternative 'in the shoes' of any other individual c.

Given my own assertion that rights should not be axed unnecessarily with amended libertarian conditions, i.e. the rights implementation rule should be 'efficient', the libertarian conditions should be consistent with 'minimal rights', i.e. if a pair assigned to an individual is the *only* pair from which choice is to be made, then that individual should implement his right according to the standard rights implementation rule. Of the three libertarian conditions that are not vulnerable to the Gibbard paradox, only my L^P preserves 'minimal rights'. This comes at the expense of having any choice function which satisifies condition L^P, unable to satisfy the mild 'contraction consistency' rationality condition α. However, any libertarian condition which gives minimal rights to individuals must imply, if it is to be satisfied by a choice function $C(S, \{R_b\})$, that condition α will be violated (see Theorem 2.4.2, p. 28). Given the desirability of rights, specifically minimal rights, this is a price one should have to pay.

In Chapter 3, rights were considered in the context of other social criteria. In addition to conflicts with conditions of justice and rationality in social choice, mild specifications of rights were shown to conflict with the conditions of anonymity, neutrality and Pareto. The conflict of rights with the Pareto condition is the most surprising and the most apparently disturbing. The chapter proceeds to examine this conflict (the Sen paradox) in more detail. The nature of the conflict is brought out by a series of theorems (see Theorems 3.3.1 – 3.3.4, p. 36–41), based on some analogous results in Sen (1976). The 'Paretian epidemic' result (Theorem 3.3.1) shows that giving just *one* person full rights over just *one* pair of social alternatives is sufficient, in the context of a choice function satisfying the Pareto condition, to spread this decisiveness, in a weakened form, to *all* ordered pairs of alternatives. This spread of decisiveness is sufficient to stop any other individual having such rights in social choice. The other theorems show that if, in addition, some other well known conditions are imposed, this spread of decisiveness becomes more exacting. For example, Theorem 3.3.4 shows that, given a choice function satisfying some mild rationality requirement, Pareto, and the condition of 'independence of irrelevant alternatives', then giving one individual a right to a single ordered pair of alternatives, immediately makes him *fully* decisive over *all* pairs, i.e. a dictator. Sen's original theorems were formulated within a 'binary' framework of choice where the choice function is restricted to conform to the condition that the choice set is generated through a relational comparison of pairs of alternatives (an implicit rationality restriction). No such restriction is placed on the choice function $C(S, \{R_b\})$ used in this thesis and my results show how naturally Sen's results can be reformulated within the context of a non-binary framework of choice.

The Sen paradox arises with the mildest of libertarian conditions. All the libertarian conditions defined in Chapter 2 are seen to be inconsistent with the Pareto condition in social choice. How should this conflict be resolved?

In Chapter 4, three types of modifications to the libertarian condition, which enabled rights implementation to be consistent with the Pareto condition, were discussed and evaluated. Firstly, there is Gibbard's (1974) condition L^{GP}, which makes an individual's rights to a given pair of alternatives conditional on the type of preferences revealed by *all* individuals. Secondly, there is Gaertner and Krüger's (1981) condition L^{SSP} which makes an individual's rights to a given pair of alternatives conditional on him satisfying 'self supporting preferences' throughout his own ordering of alternatives. Thirdly, a set of 'justice constrained' libertarian conditions which are consistent with Pareto when individuals 'extend sympathy' in that their extended orderings satisfy the 'axiom of identity'.

Gibbard claims that the rights implementation rule of condition L^{GP} is totally consistent with 'voluntary rights exercising' — rights of an individual are only withheld when it is to *his* overall advantage. This claim is not true; many examples can be constructed that prove that it is not always in an individual's best interest to follow Gibbard's rights implementation rule. Attempts to formulate other 'voluntary exercising' rules are reviewed in Appendix A of Chapter 4. All such attempts fail to conform to voluntary rights exercising. The main reason for this failure is that any rigid rule based only on ordinal preferences of individuals cannot take account of other information that an individual might use in a voluntary judgement about his rights. For example, an individual might examine his preferences, and others' preferences, and agree that it is in his own best interest to waive his right to a certain assigned pair, but, nevertheless, wish on ethical grounds to exercise his right since the benefit he gets from waiving this right might not be morally acceptable to him. Of course, even if a voluntary exercising rule could be constructed there is no guarantee that it will be consistent with the Pareto condition. Gibbard's procedure is thus best assessed independently of the motivation he used to formulate it.

In contrast, Gaertner and Krüger motivate their procedure by arguing that individuals should only have rights if they are not 'meddlesome'. They invoke Blau's 'Golden Rule' that 'persons who do not grossly meddle in the private affairs of others should have their own respected' (Blau (1975), p. 397). According to Gaertner and Krüger, such meddlesomeness manifests itself when individuals fail to exhibit 'self-supporting preferences' (SSP). SSP is a very strong condition and an individual's failure to satisfy it results in *all* his rights being curtailed. This is very severe, especially since such a curtailment of rights for an individual could be due only to the position of *one* alternative in his preference ordering of all alternatives (many pairs of which could well be assigned to him). Moreover, such failure to satisfy SSP need not mean an individual is being 'grossly meddlesome' but justifiably benevolent! Even if an individual was being meddlesome, it is not clear why the appropriate 'punishment' should be to axe all his rights. A pair is assigned to an individual b because it differs with respect to his business *alone*, the business of other individuals in both alternatives remains the same. Meddlesomeness, as revealed by the preferences of an individual b, must be over other pairs of alternatives which differ with respect to *other* people's business. It seems more appropriate to ignore these preferences, rather than preferences over the assigned pairs, if one wishes to penalise meddlesomeness. Condition L^{SSP}, as with Gibbard's condition L^{GP}, is best assessed independently of the original motivation used to construct it.

Taking the view that rights, as implemented by the standard rights implementation rule, are desirable and modifications to this rule should be made for the sole reason of achieving 'possibility' in otherwise 'paradox' cases, then 'efficiency' becomes relevant. Rights should not be axed unnecessarily. Given this criterion, there are some reasons for preferring Gibbard's condition L^{GP} to Gaertner and Krüger's L^{SSP}. Firstly, if individuals' preferences are 'strict' then Gibbard's rights implementation rule is strictly more 'efficient' than Gaertner and Krüger's (see Theorem 4.5.1, p. 73). Secondly, condition L^{GP}, unlike condition L^{SSP}, always grants individuals 'first order rights' in that if an individual is assigned the right to x over y then, at the very least, if y is his sole worst choice his rights will be implemented. Finally, Gibbard's procedure always preserves minimal rights of individuals whereas Gaertner and Krüger's procedure does not. This is because, with Gibbard's procedure, rights are conditional on preferences over the available set whereas Gaertner and Krüger's procedure makes rights conditional on preferences over the universal set X. For the same reason, Gaertner and Krüger's procedure is inconsistent with the condition of independence of irrelevant alternatives.

Turning now to the justice constrained libertarian conditions, I have three main objections. Firstly, the informational requirements are too high. Secondly, justice should not *always* outrank rights and certainly not in such a way as to have rights implemented if and only if all individuals unanimously agree that such a right is just. Thirdly, the resolution to the Sen paradox is only guaranteed if individual preferences satisfy the axiom of identity. I accept that it would be *desirable* if the extended preferences satisfied this axiom but to insist that they do ignores the real possibility that they will not. It is a 'domain restriction' which in effect assumes away types of preference which can result in even the justice constrained libertarian conditions conflicting with Pareto. In this sense, it is not a real resolution to the Sen paradox.

In all of the above approaches, which modify the libertarian condition to make it consistent with the Pareto condition, there is the implicit assumption that Pareto is sacred, or at least more desirable than rights. That Pareto should always outrank rights is questionable, and I will pursue this again a little later in this concluding chapter.

Chapter 5 considered resolutions to the Sen paradox which modified the Pareto condition. Four approaches were discussed. Firstly, there is Sen's (1976) condition *PC* which stipulates that if all individuals prefer an x to y and each respectively 'wishes his preference to count' in social choice, then y should not be chosen if x is available. Secondly, there is Austen-Smith's (1982) condition *RCWP* which stipulates that if all individuals prefer an x to a y and x is not vetoed by an individual's rights, then y should not be chosen if x is available. Thirdly, Hammond's (1980) condition *PP* which stipulates that if all individuals prefer an x to a y according to their respective 'privately oriented strict preference relations', then y should not be chosen if x is available. Lastly, there is the justice constrained Pareto condition PP^J which makes the implementation of the Pareto condition over a pair conditional on all individuals agreeing that such a Pareto judgement is 'just', this formulated in the context of an extended utility framework.

The basis of Sen's approach lies in the belief that the Pareto condition which is based purely on revealed ordinal preferences is not always morally justified. Sen allows individuals morally to evaluate their preferences by allowing them each to select a subrelation which, having taken into account any information they think is relevant, they wish to see count in social choice. Given that there exists at least one individual who 'respects rights' of others via their revealed subrelation, a resolution is guaranteed. The major drawback with Sen's approach is that he does not formally consider how to resolve the potential conflict between rights and the *conditional* Pareto condition, leaving this to some omniscient moral arbitrator.

Austen-Smith's procedure is motivated by his 'important notion of an ethical hierarchy' which stresses that rights have 'a higher order value relative to Paretianism'. Austen-Smith accepts that there is a 'cost' with his procedure in that it does not preserve the Pareto condition when the application of it will not yield a conflict with rights. However he excuses this cost by stating that 'the social decision making process' is not 'critically dependent upon which subset of individuals choose to be liberal' in the way the Sen approach is. In contrast to Austen-Smith I find this feature of the Sen approach attractive in that, given a set of preferences, the outcome (which is sensitive to who is liberal and how they are liberal) can thus also be sensitive to the nature of the case in question *and* the motivations underlying the individual's preferences. Austen-Smith's procedure is altogether too rigid. To axe a Pareto judgement purely because one alternative is vetoed by someone implementing his rights lacks any moral justification and is totally insensitive to the nature of the case in question and individuals' motivations.

Hammond's approach is motivated by the desire 'to establish fairly generally . . . how far the Pareto condition can be followed without violating individual rights'. However, his condition *PP* does *not* achieve this objective. Firstly, over a significantly broad class of subsets of alternatives, independent of the preferences revealed, condition *PP* offers no social judgement over and above that which the libertarian condition does (see Theorem 5.3.1, p. 101) Secondly, in cases of unanimous agreement in the preferences over alternatives (and thus no possible conflict between rights and Pareto) condition *PP* can be seen to axe all Pareto comparisons purely because, for one individual, his privately oriented relation is void, and this without any moral justification. Finally, individuals can only be allocated *one* private issue if one wishes to avoid the possibility of having two (or more) different profiles of privately oriented preferences for one individual.

The justice constrained Pareto condition implements Pareto judgements if and only if *all* individuals consider the judgement to be just according to their respective justice relations. Used in conjunction with the justice constrained libertarian condition, a resolution is guaranteed. That justice should always outrank Pareto and rights in this way is questionable to say the least and the utility informational requirements are very strong. However, there is the advantage of not having to insist that individuals' preference orderings satisfy the axiom of identity – there is no domain restriction involved. If individuals' preferences do satisfy the axiom of identity, then for some justice relations the justice constrained Pareto condition becomes equivalent to the standard Pareto condition and we are back with the procedures used in Chapter 4. If the axiom of identity is *not* satisfied, this approach still has something useful to say, it does not simply ignore the possibility.

All the Pareto modification procedures are inconsistent with either 'independence', 'rationality' or 'minimal Pareto', (see Chapter 5, Section 5.6, p. 109). Dependent on why the Pareto condition is being modified, violation of these conditions could well be justified. If the unanimous preference for x over y is immoral then it might well be immoral independently of other alternatives that might be available – thus violation of minimal Pareto will be justified. Different motivations underlying the same set of preferences over the same set of alternatives might suggest different social outcomes should be chosen for each case — thus violation of independence could well be justified. If, in a conflict case, Pareto is desirable, but less so than rights, then despite, say, x being unanimously preferred to y, y might still be chosen to avoid violation of rights. However, if the available set was only x and y then, given the desirability of Pareto, x should be chosen. This can justify a violation of the rationality condition α.

With all Pareto modification procedures the aim is to modify the Pareto condition such that it is consistent with rights. This is in complete contrast with the rights modification procedures which modify rights in order to make them consistent with Pareto. Different motivational arguments have been brought forward to justify various modifications to one or other of the conditions. The question remains: what motivation *should* a procedure conform to in order that the conflicts between rights and Pareto cannot occur? This was the problem addressed in Chapter 6.

Chapter 6 firstly justifies the incorporation of the 'unrestricted domain' condition into the definition of the choice function $C(S, \{R_b\})$: choice, given any subset of alternatives, must be made for any given logically possible set of individual preferences. It has been suggested that the preference structures that lead to libertarian conflicts will never arise (such preferences 'seem to border on the socially pathological' (Blau 1975, p. 396)). If this is correct, then it would be legitimate to restrict the domain of admissible preferences and not contemplate the paradox cases. However, though the preference structures which lead to these paradox cases are often morally reprehensible, the various examples of such conflicts portrayed in this book justify their plausibility. As such, given that the paradoxes *can* arise, a resolution must be made through modification of the imposed social conditions which are responsible for these conflicts.

There are three different reasons for modifying an imposed condition on our social choice function $C(S, \{R_b\})$:

(a) The social condition, for some cases for which it is constituted, is not, in itself, socially desirable.
(b) The social condition cannot be satisfied by any choice function.
(c) The social condition cannot be satisfied by any choice function, which satisfies *more* desirable social condition(s).

I have argued that reason (a) is *not* an appropriate justification for modifying the libertarian condition. Given that alternatives are assigned to an individual on the basis that they differ with respect to his business alone then there is a positive social value that choice over these alternatives should be based on his preference, irrespective of his motives behind his preference. However (b) and (c) are reasons which would justify modifying a libertarian condition. Firstly, rights of an individual in social choice can conflict with others' rights, and as such, there is a feasibility constraint stopping the full implementation of rights in some cases. In such cases, rights *must* be constrained but in an efficient and fair way. Secondly, rights can conflict with the Pareto condition and for *some* cases (e.g. the oil rig/fence example on p. 115) rights should be made consistent with the Pareto condition.

The Pareto condition is, in contrast to the libertarian condition, not, in itself, always socially desirable to enforce. The desirability of Pareto does depend on the motivations underlying the preferences and the nature of the case in question (see, for example, Sen's interpretation of the *Lady Chatterley's Lover* case, p. 95). In order to modify the Pareto condition, to make it universally desirable, more information is needed, and it should be noted that it is conceivable that the curtailment of the Pareto condition could well be justified in non-conflict cases. Sen's conditional Pareto condition which enforces Pareto judgements only when all individuals wish their respective preferences 'to count in social choice' is a step in the right direction — individuals are given the chance to morally evaluate their preferences and motivations. However, even this conditional Pareto condition can conflict with rights in social choice. As such, in some cases, further modification may be necessary if it is deemed that rights are *more* desirable. Thus reasons (a) and (c) are possible justifications for modifying the Pareto condition.

In conflict cases, how should a resolution be achieved? It is clear from the above discussion that what should be done depends on the nature of the case in question, in particular the motivations underlying individuals' preferences. For some cases rights should be constrained, for other cases the Pareto condition should be constrained. To assess which condition, or conditions, should be modified, and how, more information is needed. The revealed ordinal preferences of individuals is not sufficient information to formulate a 'best' resolution.

Until a framework of social choice can fully incorporate more information on the motivations underlying the preference structure and the nature of social alternatives under consideration, a proper resolution to these liberal paradoxes cannot be formulated via some universally applied inflexible social choice rule.

The above discussion and conclusions are also relevant for cases of group rights, formally analysed in Chapter 7. Giving any two disjoint groups of individuals' rights, then the implementation of these rights, as determined by any Pareto inclusive group voting rules, will conflict with the Pareto condition in social choice in an analogous way to that for individual rights. However, unique to cases of group rights is the possibility that groups are not disjoint from each other. Given that there exists at least one individual who is a member of all decisive groups then there will exist a set of Pareto inclusive group voting rules such that the consequential implementation of group rights *will* be consistent with the Pareto condition (and with themselves); and this is true for any assignment of rights taken over any set of available alternatives (see Theorem 7.3.4, p. 127).

However, given that group voting rules are majoritian inclusive the conditions on group structure become much more heavily restrictive and do depend on the assignment of rights. As such, for many practical cases, the conflicts between group rights and the Pareto principle is a distinct possibility. Resolutions to such conflicts must proceed along analogous lines to those for individual rights, i.e. one or both of the social conditions must be further weakened to secure possibility.

Though many results concerning group rights in social choice can be made through re-examining the analysis of individual rights, it must be stressed that the scope and relevance of the analysis is greatly expanded. Any society which wishes to allow a limited amount of autonomy such that different 'interest' groups of individuals are respectively assigned rights over certain private decisions may well run the risk of obtaining Pareto inferior outcomes. As Batra and Pattanaik (1972) have forcibly argued, a system of group rights in society may constitute a basic precondition for these groups to agree to be part of the same society at all; these groups identifying themselves in terms of 'language, religion, race, colour, economic interest, or any other property'.

References

Arrow, K. J. (1951, 2nd edn 1963). *Social Choice and Individual Values*, New York: Wiley.

Austen-Smith, D. (1979). 'Fair Rights', *Economic Letters*, 4, 29–32.

(1982). 'Restricted Pareto and Rights', *Journal of Economic Theory*, 26, 89–99.

Barnes, J. (1980). 'Freedom, Rationality and Paradox', *Canadian Journal of Philosophy*, 10, 545–65.

Batra, R. N., and Pattanaik, P. K. (1972). 'On Some Suggestions for having Non-Binary Social Choice Functions', *Theory and Decision*, 3, 1–11.

Berlin, I (1958). *Two Concepts of Liberty*, Oxford University Press.

Blau, J. H. (1975). 'Liberal Values and Independence', *Review of Economic Studies*, 42, 395–402.

Breyer, F. (1977). 'The Liberal Paradox, Decisiveness over Issues and Domain Restrictions'. *Zeitschrift Für Nationalokonomie*, 37, 45–60.

Farrell, M. J. (1976). 'Liberalism in the Theory of Social Choice', *Review of Economic Studies*, 43, 3–10.

Fine, B. J. (1975). 'Individual Preferences in a Paretian Society', *Journal of Political Economy*, 83, 1277–81.

Gaertner, W. (1982). 'Envy Free Rights Assignments and Self-Oriented Preferences', *Mathematical Social Sciences*, 2, 199–208.

Gaertner, W., and Krüger, L. (1981). 'Self Supporting Preferences and Individual Rights: The Possibility of a Paretian Liberal', *Economica*, 48, 17–28.

Gibbard, A. (1974). 'A Pareto-Consistent Libertarian Claim', *Journal of Economic Theory*, 7, 388–410.

Hammond, P. (1980). 'Liberalism, Independent Rights and the Pareto Principle'. Paper prepared for the 6th International Congress of Logic, Methodology and Philosophy of Science, August 1979.

Karni, E. (1978). 'Collective Rationality, Unanimity and Liberal Ethics', *Review of Economic Studies*, 45, 571–4.

Kelly, J. S. (1976a). 'The Impossibility of a Just Liberal', *Economica*, 43, 67–75.

(1976b). 'Rights-exercising and a Pareto Consistent Libertarian Claim', *Journal of Economic Theory*, 13, 138–153.

(1978). *Arrow Impossibility Theorems*, New York: Academic Press.

Krüger, L., and Gaertner, W. (1983). 'Alternative Libertarian Claims and Sen's Paradox', *Theory and Decision*, 15, 211–29.

Nozick, R. (1973). 'Distributive Justice', *Philosophy and Public Affairs*, 3, 45–126.

(1974). *Anarchy, State and Utopia*. Oxford: Blackwell.

Sen, A. K. (1970a). *Collective Choice and Social Welfare*, San Francisco:

Holden-Day, and Edinburgh: Oliver and Boyd. Distribution taken over by North Holland.

(1970b). 'The Impossibility of a Paretian Liberal', *Journal of Political Economy*, 78, 152–7.

(1976). 'Liberty, Unanimity and Rights', *Economica*, 43, 217–45.

(1977). 'On Weights and Measures: Informational Constraints in Social Welfare Analysis', *Econometrica*, 45, 1539–72.

(1979). 'Personal Utilities and Public Judgements: or What's Wrong with Welfare Economics', *Economic Journal*, 89, 537–58.

(1983a). 'Liberty and Social Choice', *Journal of Philosophy*, 80, 5–28.

(1983b). 'Social Choice Theory'. In *The Handbook of Mathematical Economics*, vol. III, K. J. Arrow and M. Intriligator, Eds. Amsterdam: North Holland.

Stevens, D. N., and Foster, J. E. (1978). 'The Possibility of Democratic Pluralism', *Economica*, 45, 391–400.

Suzumura, K. (1978). 'On the Consistency of Libertarian Claims, *Review of Economic Studies*, 45, 329–47.

(1980). 'Liberal Paradox and the Voluntary Exchange of Rights-exercising', *Journal of Economic Theory*, 22, 407–22.

(1982). 'Equity, Efficiency and Rights in Social Choice', *Mathematical Social Sciences*, 3, 131–55.

Wriglesworth, J. L. (1982a). 'The Possibility of Democratic Pluralism: A Comment', *Economica*, 49, 43–8.

(1982b). 'Using Justice Principles to Resolve the Impossibility of a Paretian Liberal', *Economic Letters*, 10, 217–21.

(1985). 'Respecting Rights in Social Choice', *Oxford Economic Papers*, 37, 100–17.

Name index

154

Subject index

anonymity (A), 33, 117n
axiom of complete identity (I^C), 50
axiom of identity (I^A), 50, 68, 70

choice function, 6
  for extended utility framework 16
coherent rights system, 10
  for group rights, 127
conditional Pareto condition (PC), 91,
  95–9, 105, 108, 110–12, 121
contraction consistency condition (α),
  28, 38, 76, 110

efficiency
  of modified Pareto conditions, 106–9
  of rights implementation rules, 25–9,
  72–6
expansion consistency condition (δ), 38
extended preference orderings, 16

first group libertarian condition (L^{GR1}),
  124
first order rights, 74
full rights, 36

general possibility theorem (of Arrow),
  36, 40
generalized justice constrained libertarian
  condition (LP^J), 94, 104
generalized justice constrained Pareto
  condition (PP^J), 94, 104, 109, 113
Gibbard paradox, 7, 8
  resolution approaches, 8–19;
  (evaluation), 20–31
group rights system 1 (GRS-1), 124
group rights system 2 (GRS-2), 128
group structure, 123
group voting rules, 124, 131

identity *see* axiom
'inconsistent' libertarian condition (L), 7
  for extended utility framework (L*),
  16
independence of irrelevant alternatives (I),
  40, 77, 110–13
independence of non-optimal alternatives
  (INOA), 39, 77
indirect liberty, 3

justice constrained rights implementation
  rules (and conditions), 18, 70, 71,
  86–90
justice criteria, 16, 17
j-variants, 6

Lady Chatterley's Lover, 35, 63, 95
leximin, 17
liberalism condition (L^S), 10, 34
liberty (in social choice), *see* rights

majoritian inclusive group voting rule, 124
maximin, 17
meddlesomeness, 63–8
'minimal' liberalism condition (ML^S), 35
minimal Pareto (MP), 110
minimal rights (MR), 28, 76
motivation,
  behind resolutions to the Gibbard
  paradox, 20–5
  behind resolutions to the Sen paradox,
  56–70; (Pareto modifications),
  95–105

neutrality (N), 33

ordinal intensity (of preferences), 63

Pareto condition (P and P*), 34
  for extended utility framework (P'), 42
  modified versions, 91–5
'Pareto-consistent' libertarian condition
  (L^{GP}), 49, 55–62, 70, 72, 77
Paretian epidemic, 36
Pareto inclusive group voting rule, 124
potential full rights, 36
potential semi-rights, 36
preferences (defined)
  group, 124
  individual, 6; (extended framework),
  16
  private, 13
  privately oriented, 93
  self-supporting, 49
  unconditional, 12
private Pareto condition (PP), 93, 100–5,
  109, 112
'private preference' libertarian condition
  (L^P), 13, 21–4